Perilous Policing

Policing and police practices have changed dramatically since the 9/11 terrorist attacks and those changes have accelerated since the summer of 2014 and the death of Michael Brown at the hands of then-police officer Darren Wilson in Ferguson, Missouri. Since the November 2016 election of Donald Trump as president, many law enforcement practitioners, policy makers, and those concerned with issues of social justice have had concerns that there would be seismic shifts in policing priorities and practices at the federal, state, county, and local and tribal levels that will have significant implications for constitutional rights and civil liberties protections, particularly for people of color. *Perilous Policing: Criminal Justice in Marginalized Communities* provides a much-needed interrogatory to law enforcement practices and policies as they continue to evolve during this era of uncertainty and anxiety. Key topics include the police and marginalized populations, the use of technology to surveil individuals and groups, the emergence of the Black Lives Matter movement and the erosion of the police narrative, the use of force (particularly deadly force) against people of color, the role of the police in immigration enforcement, the "war on cops," and police militarization.

Thomas Nolan's critique of current practice and his preliminary conclusions as to how to navigate contemporary policing away from the pitfalls of discredited and counterproductive practices will be of interest to advanced undergraduates and graduate students in Policing, Criminology, Justice Studies, and Criminal Justice programs, as well as to researchers, law enforcement professionals, and police policy makers.

Thomas Nolan has been an Associate Professor in Criminal Justice at Boston University, the State University of New York at Plattsburgh, and Merrimack College. He was a Senior Policy Advisor at the Office of Civil Rights and Civil Liberties in the Department of Homeland Security in Washington, D.C., and a 27-year veteran (and former lieutenant) with the Boston Police Department. His doctoral work focused on moral probity among police officers, and his recent publications deal with such topics as civil rights and civil liberties in policing and constitutional issues of surveillance.

A solid academic book tackling some of policing's most important issues—written by a police practitioner/scholar. The topics are timely, and there couldn't be a better time in our field for a policing book of this nature than now.

Peter Kraska, Professor, School of Justice Studies, Eastern Kentucky University, USA

Tom Nolan has produced this scholarly scrutiny that supplements his thirty-plus years of policing experience. It's an important book that should be widely read. Use it in your courses. The "narrative" of U.S. law enforcement's too often violent interaction with the public it serves has rightly given way to a national conversation in the marketplace of ideas.

William Peters, Coordinator for Legal Studies and Associate Professor of Criminal Justice, State University of New York College at Plattsburgh

The human race faces immense challenges: climate collapse, economic inequality, racism and nativism, mass migration, and crises in democratic governance. Cutting across all of these issues are the problems of police and policing. This timely book examines policing's role in upholding the status quo, and the failures of ostensibly free societies to rise to the challenge of adequately policing the police.

Kade Crockford, Director, Technology for Liberty Program American Civil Liberties Union of Massachusetts

Perilous Policing is provocative and well-written. It gives fresh insights into the service practices and patterns of policing. Tom Nolan utilizes his insider perspective to illuminate the modern issues that face police departments today. Unlike many other books on policing, *Perilous Policing* could be used in an upper-level undergraduate course, a graduate-level seminar, or by practitioners in the field.

Alexa D. Sardina Ph.D., Assistant Professor, California State University, Sacramento, Division of Criminal Justice

This book is very timely with its focus on immigration, militarization and Black Lives Matter. While the book is based on American policing, these issues resonate globally and policing has become increasingly contested and perilous (for citizens and for the police themselves).

Monique Marks, Research Professor, Urban Futures Centre, Durban University of Technology, South Africa

Contents

For Chloe Nolan, Rory Nolan, and Martha Gaisford

First published 2019
by Routledge
52 Vanderbilt Avenue, New York, NY 10017

and by Routledge
2 Park Square, Milton Park, Abingdon, Oxon, OX14 4RN

Routledge is an imprint of the Taylor & Francis Group, an informa business

© 2019 Taylor & Francis

Library of Congress Cataloging-in-Publication Data
Names: Nolan, Thomas William, author.
Title: Perilous policing : criminal justice in marginalized communities / Thomas Nolan.
Description: Abingdon, Oxon ; New York, NY : Routledge, 2019. |
Identifiers: LCCN 2018048190 (print) | LCCN 2018051056 (ebook) |
ISBN 9780429398414 (Ebook) | ISBN 9780367026691 (hardback) |
ISBN 9780367026707 (pbk.)
Subjects: LCSH: Police–United States. | Police-community relations–United
States. | Ethnic neighborhoods–United States. | Discrimination in
criminal justice administration–United States. | United States–Ethnic relations.
Classification: LCC HV8139 (ebook) | LCC HV8139 .N65 2019 (print) |
DDC 363.2/30973–dc23
LC record available at https://lccn.loc.gov/2018048190

ISBN: 978-0-367-02669-1 (hbk)
ISBN: 978-0-367-02670-7 (pbk)
ISBN: 978-0-429-39841-4 (ebk)

Typeset in Times New Roman
by Wearset Ltd, Boldon, Tyne and Wear

Perilous Policing

Criminal Justice in Marginalized Communities

Thomas Nolan

Routledge
Taylor & Francis Group

NEW YORK AND LONDON

Introduction

THE first beating that I was exposed to as a rookie police officer in 1978 occurred, ironically, outside of the church where I and my five sisters had been baptized, my parents married, and my grandparents buried. I was an altar boy in that church not ten years earlier; the Catholic school where the Sisters of Charity had reared me during the 1960s was directly across the street. I had never seen so much blood as that which pooled around the man who had been beaten and lay sprawled on the sidewalk. Nor had I ever seen anyone subjected to such a savage thumping at the hands of one very imposing police officer, one of the two officers who I was riding with that night. I was half afraid that the nuns who lived in the convent next door to where the man lay bleeding would peer through the curtains and see me, still one of their charges, standing in the uniform of a Boston police officer, over the unconscious body of the badly mangled man. The man's crime is long forgotten, but I still remember the guffaw of the police officer who administered the beating, welcoming me into the netherworld of policing.

When I began my career in law enforcement over four decades ago, policing was in many ways much more violent, primitive, and dangerous than it is today. Technology was practically non-existent: we had hand-held radios, a novelty in 1970s-era policing, but they rarely functioned and were effectively useless. We were issued vintage six-shot revolvers and 12 rounds of ammunition. In the 1970s the average year saw three times the number of police officers killed in the line of duty than we see in contemporary policing, where the numbers remain fairly consistent at approximately 50 police officers killed feloniously per year. As today, violence was an ever-present component part of the way that policing was enacted on the streets of our cities, and I was a willing and often eager participant in this brand of policing.

I had just turned 22 years old and was six months out of college. Most of my fellow recruits in the January 1978 recruit class in the Boston Police Department (BPD) were Vietnam era war veterans, the war having ended only three years earlier. Owing to an historical anomaly in the BPD dating back to the Boston police strike of 1919, when essentially the entire police force had been fired, the BPD needed to hire almost an entirely new police force every generation. When I joined, the generation of police officers who were hired after World War II were in the twilight of their careers—the average age of a Boston police officer then was 53 years, my father's age at the time.

Physical violence and beatings were routinely administered to those on the street who challenged our police authority, an affront that we saw as a most egregious violation of an unspoken moral code that privileged the rule of law and the unquestioned role of the police in the interpretation and administration of that law, both formal and informal. The informal rules that governed street interactions between the police and those whom they most commonly came into contact with dictated that if you ran from the police you would be beaten, severely. If you did not move quickly enough when commanded to move along, then you risked some "rough handling." And if you ever hit, kicked, or otherwise harmed a police officer, you were almost certain to require a trip to a hospital emergency department.

Although police violence continues to the present day, and particularly in marginalized communities, there exists a level of accountability (such as it is), that was intentionally absent in the earlier decades of policing. The internal investigative apparatus of virtually all police departments during the 1970s through at least the 1990s was ineffective, dysfunctional, impotent, and in many cases non-existent. There were few if any sanctions for violating the constitutional rights and civil liberties of those who were too often unfortunate enough to have interactions with the police. Internal affairs complaints from those who had influence, power, or means, would be investigated, and these were almost without exception white people. There existed no place or reception for complaints against the police from residents of marginalized communities, no matter how grievous the offense or how deadly the outcome.

This book provides the reader with an overview and an insider's perspective on the many issues that continue to confront and confound the police in marginalized communities to the present day. Many of these issues are the unresolved legacy of policing's authoritarian, racist, discriminatory, and violent past. Other issues that are potentially perilous for both the police and residents of these marginalized communities implicate emerging technologies, police militarization, immigration enforcement, and shifting population demographics—issues that have little historical relevance or precedent for police in the United States.

The concept for this book arose out of continuing and strident concerns regarding the escalating disaffection that marginalized communities had toward the police that reached its nadir following the shooting death of Michael Brown by then-police officer Darren Wilson in Ferguson, Missouri in August of 2014. The election of Donald Trump as President of the United States in November of 2016 escalated concerns that police misconduct, violence, and overreach would no longer be subject to federal oversight, evaluation, and regulation. There was a tangible and palpable sense in communities across the United States, particularly in communities of color, that policing would return to the unchecked and unsanctioned violence that had characterized policing early in my law enforcement career. I believe that my 27-year career as a police officer, one that preceded my decades-long career as an academic, lends a unique historical perspective that is grounded in a compelling and timely academic analysis.

This volume will be of value as a course text in upper-division undergraduate college courses as well as graduate courses in policing, criminal justice, criminology, law enforcement ethics, race and the police, the Constitution and civil rights and civil liberties, contemporary issues in criminal justice policy, graduate seminars in criminal justice, communities and crime, corruption, integrity, and accountability, U.S. policing in the twenty-first century, managing organizational culture in policing, crime and cities, crime, and public policy. The book could also be used as a supplemental text in certain law school courses such as human rights law, urban law and policy, constitutional justice, and constitutional law and criminal procedure.

Perilous Policing will also appeal to a much wider audience than college students and I see the work as much more than a course text. I believe that it will have significant appeal as a trade publication as well as having much relevance to law enforcement policy makers, administrators, managers, and other professionals. There is considerable demand for law enforcement professionals seeking enlightened and timely guidance and direction with the rapidly shifting demands of the police practice that have emerged following the 2016 elections. Progressive police policy makers are seeking input from their constituent communities as well as from the academy in forging responses to the complexities of the demands confronting contemporary policing. This text provides a timely, relevant, and unique perspective.

Chapter 1

The Police, the Constitution, and Civil Rights and Civil Liberties

In late April 2016, a journalist telephoned me from the Bay Area in California with a request for comment on yet another recording of the police engaging in what appeared to be an incident involving the use of excessive force (Lawton, 2016). This incident took place in Hayward, California, which has a police department whose chief at the time happened to be a former student of mine. In the aftermath of the police-shooting death of Michael Brown in Ferguson, Missouri in August of 2014, I had been (and continue to be) frequently sought out for commentary following situations where police practices and policies appeared, at least initially, to have violated an individual's civil rights and civil liberties.

In Hayward, police had stopped James Greer, a 46-year-old African American grandfather who weighed close to 380 pounds, when he reportedly drove his pickup truck "erratically" in front of Hayward police lieutenant Jeffrey Lutzinger. Lutzinger and other Hayward police officers who arrived at the scene of the stop began to administer a field sobriety test to Mr. Greer, who they suspected of operating while impaired. The police body-camera video, recorded on a body-camera worn by a Bay Area Rapid Transit police officer who had also responded to the scene, showed that the brief field sobriety test inexplicably concluded when officers decided to take Greer into custody.

One of the officers is seen asking Mr. Greer if he suffered from any medical conditions and Greer can be seen pointing to the area of his stomach and telling the officers that he suffers from a hernia. Greer initially appears to offer minimal resistance to the multiple officers who are by now surrounding him, at least until they violently and decisively slam Greer to the pavement—on his stomach. Six or seven police officers pile on top of Mr. Greer and struggle violently to handcuff him. He is hit multiple times with a Taser weapon, in both drive-stun (direct application of the Taser to the body for "pain compliance") and probe mode (shooting of electrified darts or "probes" into the body for temporary immobilization). Greer is slowly and excruciatingly pummeled into the ground for 19 agonizing minutes until the officers realize that Mr. Greer had become non-responsive, having gone into what doctors refer to as "traumatic asphyxia"—essentially Greer suffocated to death. Policing was indeed perilous for James Greer on that fateful evening.

What surprised and concerned me about the Hayward incident was that it had taken place on May 23, 2014—several months before Michael Brown's death at the hands of then-police officer Darren Wilson in Ferguson, Missouri, an incident that garnered worldwide attention, not least for the highly militarized and arguably heavy-handed police response to the protests that followed Brown's death. Mr. Greer's death had never been publicly reported by law enforcement officials in Hayward or in Alameda County and had only come to the public's attention when documents and records obtained under subpoena by attorneys representing the estate of James Greer were released to the media—in October 2015 (Lawton, 2015), *18 months after Greer's death*.

That the police in the United States, who swear an oath to uphold the Constitution and to protect and honor civil rights and civil liberties, could cause the death of an unarmed African American man following a stop for a traffic violation comes as no surprise to those familiar with the workings of the American criminal justice system. But that an in-custody death at the hands of police could be concealed, hidden, and not reported to the public in the second decade of the twenty-first century should be cause for consternation, if not alarm.

For law enforcement in the United States, the Constitution is often viewed as an obstacle to be overcome rather than a binding legal dictum prescribing the contours and limits to the authority of the police. Few police officers who I know or have met over the decades can enumerate the five freedoms contained in the First Amendment (and I was at times during my career as a police officer certainly guilty of this deficiency). That a police officer could, in a career that spanned decades, be patently unaware of the provisions of the Constitution and the Bill of Rights that relate specifically to the law enforcement function is really quite remarkable if not wholly inimical to the public trust.

Yet despite receiving training at the novice level in constitutional law in the police academy, that training is quickly forgotten and dispensed with once confronted with the vagaries of policing in the street. So, for example, when the bulk of 911 calls that I responded to as a young police officer in the late 1970s were "gathering causing annoyance" reports, there were no deliberations of the provision in the First Amendment regarding freedom of assembly. The "gang" needed to be dispersed and any resistance to this directive on the part of those freely assembled could and would be met with physical violence or arrest (or possibly both). Constitutional rights and civil rights and civil liberties protections had become nothing more than a classroom abstract, quickly dispensed with upon graduation from the police academy.

When Police Run Afoul of the Constitution: The Role of "Commissions"

In considering law enforcement's historical and somewhat tenuous relationship to the Constitution, one that has often been inimical to civil rights and civil liberties protections, it may be instructive to begin in a consideration of the role of the police in the enforcement of the Eighteenth Amendment. Consider this the twentieth century's first foray into an examination of a series of constitutionally questionable policies and practices that persisted with some degree of regularity through the decades that followed the passage of the Eighteenth Amendment in 1919 up until the present day—100 years of police misconduct.

The Eighteenth Amendment, otherwise known as Prohibition, banned the manufacture, sale, or transportation of intoxicating liquors in the United States. It remained the law of the land from 1919 until its repeal 13 years later in 1933. The Volstead Act, the constitutional amendment's enabling statute, detailed the specifics as to how the Eighteenth Amendment was to be enforced.

This is in no way to suggest that corruption in policing began with enforcement activities relating to prohibition circa 1919, to the contrary; policing in the United States since its inception in the mid-nineteenth century had been notoriously corrupt and brutal. But corrupt police practices were so pervasively and thoroughly (and publicly) corrupt in the enforcement of Prohibition that by 1929 President Herbert Hoover found it necessary to establish the National Commission on Law Observance and Enforcement, otherwise known as the Wickersham Commission, to examine issues related to the enforcement of laws relating to Prohibition and to observe relevant police practices being conducted at the state and local levels.

The Wickersham Commission found widespread instances of warrantless searches and seizures being conducted by enforcement agents in violation of the Fourth Amendment. The Commission reported in 1931 that "high-handed methods, shootings and killings, even where justified, alienated thoughtful citizens, believers in law and order." Further, it found:

> Unfortunate public expressions by advocates of the law, approving killings and promiscuous shootings and lawless raids and seizures and deprecating the constitutional guarantees involved, aggravated this effect. Pressure for lawless enforcement, encouragement of bad methods and agencies of obtaining evidence, and crude methods of investigation and seizure on the part of incompetent or badly chosen agents started a current of adverse public opinion in many parts of the land.
> (National Commission on Law Observance and Enforcement, 1931, p. 82)

The Wickersham Commission would be followed in the ensuing decades by many other commissions, panels, committees, and investigatory initiatives that were most often established by elected officials in the aftermath of scandals involving the police and corrupt practices that were violative of the Constitution and the civil liberties and civil rights of individuals and groups.

It was the period beginning in the 1960s through the 1970s that proved to be a watershed for policing in the United States, a time of widespread civil unrest, violence, and crisis. Although there had been rioting in earlier decades in cities in the United States, Chicago in 1919 (Armstrong, 2018), Harlem in 1935 (Robertson, 2016) and 1943 (Lewis, 1990; Leach, 2007), it wasn't until the large-scale civil disorder that occurred in urban areas in the 1960s that actions and policies of the police, specifically as they related to their treatment of African Americans, directly precipitated and were flash points for rioting across the United States.

On August 11, 1965, near the Watts district of Los Angeles, a white California Highway Patrol motorcycle officer arrested a 21-year-old African American male on a drunk driving charge. The arrest drew a crowd that became hostile as more police officers were summoned to the scene; the crowd soon grew to approximately 1000 people according to police and more arrests were made. Chaos, violence, and rioting soon followed as up to 10,000 people, primarily African Americans, took to the streets. After six days, "thirty-four persons were dead, and the wounded and hurt numbered 1032 more. Property damage was about $40,000,000. Arrested for one crime or another were 3952 persons, women as well as men, including over 500 youths under eighteen" (Governor's Commission, 1965).

In the aftermath of the Watts riot, Governor Pat Brown formed what became known as the McCone Commission to investigate the circumstances surrounding the riot. The Commission reported that there had been a long history of tension and animosity between the Los Angeles Police Department (LAPD) and communities of color. The disdain and resentment that African Americans felt toward the LAPD arose from repeated and long-standing incidents of police violence and brutality directed at residents of inner-city communities. "The bitter criticism that we have heard evidences a deep and long-standing schism between a substantial portion of the Negro community and the Police Department. Police 'brutality' has been the recurring charge," detailed the report. LAPD Police Chief Parker (for whom the current LAPD Headquarters building is named), was particularly reviled and despised in the "Negro community" (Governor's Commission, 1965).

Following the riot in Watts in 1965, cities across the United States erupted into what were referred to at the time as "race riots" or "racial disorders," thus squarely affixing the incitement for the disturbances on those aggrieved by the historic and pervasive injustices inflicted upon African Americans by law enforcement.

On July 23, 1965, President Lyndon Johnson established the "President's Commission on Law Enforcement and the Administration of Justice." In February 1967 the Commission issued a report entitled "The Challenge of Crime in a Free Society." Among its many findings, and consistent with McCone, the Commission observed

> that too many policemen do misunderstand and are indifferent to minority-group aspirations, attitudes, and customs, and that incidents involving physical or verbal mistreatment of minority-group citizens do occur and do contribute to the resentment against police that some minority-group members feel.
> (President's Commission on Law Enforcement and Administration of Justice, 1967, p. 100)

On July 28, 1967, President Johnson established the National Advisory Commission on Civil Disorders, otherwise known as the Kerner Commission, to investigate the causes of the unrest. The Commission came to a basic conclusion that "Our nation is moving toward two societies, one black, one white—separate and unequal" (National Advisory Commission on Civil Disorders, 1968). The Commission studied 24 disorders in 23 cities that occurred in 1967, out of a total of 164 reported disorders nationwide. The Commission found that, although the underlying grievances that precipitated the disorders varied somewhat from city to city, the most intense and commonly expressed grievance, and one common in all of the 23 cities studied, were police practices. The report also identified a common underlying issue with policing in affected cities:

> The police are not merely a "spark" factor. To some Negroes police have come to symbolize white power, white racism and white repression. And the fact is that many police do reflect and express these white attitudes. The atmosphere of hostility and cynicism is reinforced by a widespread belief among Negroes in the existence of police brutality and in a "double standard" of justice and protection—one for Negroes and one for whites.
> (National Advisory Commission on Civil Disorders, 1968, ch. 4)

Conspicuous in their absence in the Kerner Commission Report are any references to civil liberties and civil rights; there are but two references to the Constitution in this lengthy report, referring to those individuals who "go beyond constitutionally protected rights." There is no mention in the report of the role of the police as defenders of the Constitution, their responsibility to protect civil rights and to respect civil liberties. There were 83 deaths reported during the civil disorders that occurred in 1967, over 80 percent of them in Newark and Detroit. Ten percent of the dead were public safety personnel—police and firefighters. However, "(t)he overwhelming majority of the persons killed or injured in all the disorders were Negro civilians" (National Advisory Commission on Civil Disorders, 1968, ch. 4).

More commissions would be established in the aftermath of corruption and related scandals involving police departments in the decades following the 1960s. In 1970 then-New York Mayor John Lindsay established the "Commission to Investigate Alleged Police Corruption," otherwise known as the Knapp Commission (Burnham, 1970), following allegations of widespread corruption in the New York City Police Department (NYPD) made by Detective Frank Serpico and others.

In 1992 then-Mayor David Dinkins established the "Commission to Investigate Allegations of Police Corruption and the Anti-Corruption Procedures of the Police Department" otherwise known as the Mollen Commission, to investigate further allegations of entrenched corruption at the NYPD (Commission to Investigate Allegations of Police Corruption and the Anti-Corruption Procedures of the Police Department, 1994).

The Police and the First Amendment: Freedoms Subordinated to "Public Safety"

The summer of 2004 was the beginning of the end of my career as a Boston police officer, and in that year the city of Boston hosted the Democratic National Convention (DNC) at what was then called the "Fleet Center" in the downtown area of the city. John Kerry, then a U.S. senator from Massachusetts, would be confirmed as the party's nominee for president, and the world got its first glimpse of the DNC's keynote speaker and the man who would become the 2007 nominee and later president, Barack Obama. I was a lieutenant in the police department at the time and actively involved in the planning for the DNC, a convention that would bring thousands of the Democratic party faithful, as well as (it was believed) thousands more protesters.

The training in the leadup to the DNC was months long and extensive. As police managers, our leadership role in the tactical and operational components of overseeing the protests and the police response was critical. We were repeatedly shown video and audio recordings of the so-called "Battle of Seattle" that had occurred during World Trade Organization (WTO) summit meeting there on November 30 and December 1, 1999. Approximately 40,000 protesters had descended upon Seattle, and chaos, violence, and widespread destruction of property ensued as the police were outmanned, outmaneuvered, outsmarted, and publicly humiliated. The protesters effectively shut the city down in the several-block area surrounding the WTO summit meeting and the police, despite using tear gas and water cannons, were unable to clear the streets and regain control of the area. It was an embarrassing and shameful experience for police across the country, not just in Seattle. Boston would be no Seattle, we were told, and the DNC would not be our WTO.

We police were aware that there had been a history of protests at Republican and Democratic nominating conventions going back decades, and also that there were those vague and vexing provisions of the First Amendment that provided for freedom of speech, assembly, and the press. Yet the police (and I counted myself as among them), had an unwavering and firmly embraced belief that we had the authority, the right, and the obligation to dictate the terms and to set limits on those constitutionally protected freedoms, under the ever-expanding notion of "public safety."

So, what the police did in Boston was to create a "Demonstration Zone" (DZ) that was several blocks removed from the location of the DNC at the Fleet Center. Thus, those attending the convention, delegates, politicians, and the press, would never see or cross paths with any protesters. The DZ was actually an enclosed "pen" that would contain, stifle, and severely limit the activities of the protesters. The First Circuit Court of Appeals, in *Bl(a)ck Tea Society v. City of Boston* (2004), upheld the order issued by the city of Boston and the Boston Police Department restricting the protests and described the DZ thus:

> It comprised a heavily secured space, approximately 90 feet by 300 feet, located for the most part underneath unused rail tracks. It was surrounded by two rows of jersey barriers topped with eight-foot chainlink fencing; the perimeter was further surrounded by a semi-transparent liquid dispersion mesh fabric; and a widely-woven mesh fabric was hung above the DZ between the rail tracks and the fence. Finally, the City placed coiled razor wire along the edges of the rail tracks in the vicinity of the Fleet Center (including the area above the DZ) in order to inhibit access to the tracks. Although there were three routes of ingress and egress to and from the DZ, the aggregate effect of the security measures was to create an enclosed space that the appellant likens to a pen.
>
> (p. 1)

Very few protesters decided to enter "the pen" to protest and the operation, from the tactical perspective of the police, was a resounding success. The Court found that the City had not, in establishing the DZ, "sought to prevent speech, but, rather, to regulate the place and manner of its expression." The argument weighed heavily on the 2001 terrorist attacks on the World Trade Center towers and the Pentagon, and the possibility of terrorist attacks taking place at the DNC. Having been present at the trainings leading up to the DNC, I can tell you that what was impressed upon most of us there were not the 9/11 attacks—it was Seattle.

What the police did in Boston at the 2004 DNC was to strictly manage, regulate, and to dictate the terms of protesters' expression of constitutionally protected rights in a purported effort to "maintain security" and to diminish the need for police to engage in aggressive and potentially violent confrontations with protesters. The police were no doubt mindful of an earlier generation when the DNC was held in Chicago in 1968 in seeking to avoid situations similar to what occurred there when unrestrained and indiscriminate violence ... was often inflicted upon persons who had broken no law, disobeyed no order, made no threat. These included peaceful demonstrators, onlookers, and large numbers of residents who were simply passing through, or happened to live in, the areas where confrontations were occurring.

(Walker, 1968)

Even so in Boston, police demonstrated a clear and convincing willingness to engage protesters militarily and thus to significantly diminish and to silence free speech and free assembly, even though "reasonable time, place, and manner restrictions" on speech and assembly is a longstanding constitutional doctrine.

In September of 2011, a leaderless protest movement, "Occupy Wall Street" (OWS) began to assemble in Zuccotti Park near Wall Street's financial district in New York City. Those assembled were protesting worldwide economic inequality and OWS spawned similar "Occupy" protests throughout the United States and worldwide. One of the more notorious of the "Occupy" protests was Occupy Oakland. King (2013) observed that the police, during the "Occupy Oakland" protests, mitigated protesters' ability to engage in free speech and free assembly activities through strategies designed to minimize the disruption and inconvenience that such constitutionally protected activities are, by their very undertaking and exercise, intended to accomplish.

According to King (2013), the police in Oakland (and this is a common practice in police departments across the United States) used a two-pronged strategy in controlling, directing, and managing protests and protesters: one was to require those organizing the protest to obtain "permits" from the city to engage in free speech and free assembly activities and to have these activities observed and reported by the press, thus conveying the very public message that the city and its police department somehow have the authority to allow people "permission" to engage in civil rights and civil liberties activities that are protected by the Constitution. The second is for the police to enter into a process of "negotiated management" with leaders of the protests (this would no doubt prove vexing for leaderless protest movements like "Occupy").

Of the permitting process in Oakland, King observed that:

With a permit in place, activities that are legal under the law and constitutionally protected, like sharing food or possessing a blanket, became violations with civil and criminal consequences, even if the suspects never agreed to, or were even aware of, the terms of the permit. The permit served as a tool of repression, criminalizing ordinarily lawful activities for the expressed purpose of legitimating surveillance and physical repression.

(2013, p. 467)

As for the requirement that protesters engage in "negotiated management" with the police, King again sees the rights to assemble and the right of free speech as ultimately being co-opted, diminished, and regulated by the police with the acquiescence of the protesters in what he sees as a "two-sided coin": negotiate and make concessions and agreements to limit your constitutional rights to the police in the interests of "public safety" and "security," or refuse to negotiate (your right), and have the terms of the protest and the inevitable engagement with the police dictated by the police themselves. Protesters in Oakland steadfastly refused to negotiate with the police or, for the most part, to obtain permits and the police violence that ensued was blamed on the protesters refusing to do so.

The outcome was predictable; the police violently engaged protesters with the use of military weapons, arrested hundreds (including journalists), caused several serious injuries (including a serious head injury inflicted on a Marine and Iraq war veteran), as well as sustained allegations that police used black tape to cover their name badges. The protesters, for their part, broke into and vandalized City Hall, set fires, destroyed property, and threw rocks, bottles, incendiary devices, metal pipes and other dangerous objects at police. For King

> there is a dialectical relationship between physical repression and negotiated management, in that the lack of negotiated management usually elicits (and justifies) police violence, while the threat of that police violence elicits acceptance of negotiated management.
>
> (2013, p. 469)

On August 9, 2014, Ferguson, Missouri, police officer Darren Wilson shot and killed Michael Brown, an unarmed African American teenager. In the aftermath of the death of Brown, protesters immediately took to the streets in Ferguson—the spontaneous demonstrations obviated the need for any permits or negotiated management between the police and the protesters. Those who took to the streets of Ferguson in anger, frustration, and outrage at the police engaged in the looting of a variety of stores and businesses as well as sporadic incidents of arson and the discharge of firearms. The protesters were met with a highly militarized response from the variously assembled law enforcement agencies in Ferguson that many observers believed thwarted the First Amendment rights of the protesters and in many cases suspended the provisions of the United States Constitution that guarantee the protections of free speech, free assembly, and a free press. Members of the press were arrested by police and their cameras disabled and vandalized.

The protests instantly went viral and the world saw law enforcement officers engage in a shameless and hysterical display of unrestrained force against a relatively small group of largely peaceful protesters using Long-Range Acoustic Devices (sound cannons designed for use in wars by the military), tear gas, rubber bullets (potentially lethal), smoke bombs and grenades, stun grenades (potentially lethal), wood bullet projectiles, pepper pellet rounds,[1] and bean bag rounds (also potentially lethal).

Law enforcement in Ferguson "deployed" with military vehicles, military aircraft, military weapons, and dressed as soldiers engaging the enemy on the field of battle. Except that this wasn't Fallujah, Anbar Province, or Kandahar: it was a small city in the "Show-Me State." There can be no question that the tactics and strategies employed by law enforcement in Ferguson in August 2014 exacerbated and inflamed tensions (Nye, 2014) among protesters that were already nearing fever pitch, tensions that only began to abate with the assignment of Missouri Highway Patrol Captain Ron Johnson (an African American) as the officer in charge of the police response.

On January 20, 2017, Donald Trump was sworn in as President of the United States. Tens of thousands of people from across the United States traveled to Washington, D.C. to participate in protests against the new administration and they were met, predictably, with thousands of police officers clad in riot gear. The agency with primary responsibility and jurisdiction over most of the areas affected by the protests was the District of Columbia Metropolitan Police Department (MPD).

Although there were sporadic incidents of vandalism that occurred during the protests, the marchers were for the large part peaceful and orderly. But according to a lawsuit filed on June 21, 2017, by the American Civil Liberties Union (ACLU) of the District of Columbia, the MPD unilaterally engaged in acts of violence against demonstrators who had not been identified as or suspected of participating in any activities that were criminal in nature, such as vandalism or destruction of property. The 16-count complaint, *Horse, et al. v. District of Columbia, et al.*, alleges that 170 MPD officers and supervisors arrested hundreds of demonstrators and passersby who had committed no crimes:

> During the chase and then while detaining demonstrators for hours, police fired pepper spray, tear gas, and flash-bang grenades at crowds of demonstrators, journalists, and legal observers, frequently without warning or justification. In the course of the roundup and subsequent processing of demonstrators, police held detainees for hours without food, water, or access to toilets; handcuffed detainees so tightly as to cause injury or loss of feeling; and subjected some detainees to manual rectal probing.
>
> (2017, p. 11)

The ACLU complaint also alleged that the MPD employed a "kettling" strategy to corner and to trap over 200 demonstrators and others who just happened to be in the area of 12th and L Streets NW and, without warning or an order to disperse, repeatedly used "pepper spray, flash-bang grenades, concussion grenades, and stingers … blocking their egress via different routes" (*Horse, et al. v. District of Columbia, et al.*, 2017, p. 2), immobilized and incapacitated those who merely happened to be in the area at an unfortunate time and who were not suspected or believed to have committed any crimes; many weren't even participating in the protest.

The lawsuit claimed violations of the First, Fourth, Fifth, and Fourteenth Amendments to the Constitution in plaintiffs' allegations that the MPD conducted rectal probes, grabbed plaintiffs' testicles, intentionally prolonged their detention, refused access to food, water, and toilets, used zip-tie restraints in ways intended to cause pain and numbness, refused to remove the plastic ties after prolonged periods of time, unlawfully used chemical irritants, and "kettled" (*Horse, et al. v. District of Columbia, et al.*, 2017, p. 11) plaintiffs without warning or without an order to disperse, among other police tactics of dubious constitutional legality or justification.

"Stop and Frisk" — Racial Profiling and Constitutional Implications

As a police sergeant and later lieutenant, it was tacitly understood that a significant component of my managerial responsibilities consisted of keeping subordinate police officers (and even colleagues) out of professional and legal harm's way. This often involved hiding the truth in reports where officers engaged in questionable behavior or outright misconduct. Police officers often made *Terry* stops that were based on little more than "hunches" and that might result in an arrest that could not be justified based on any suspicion that the officers could successfully articulate. It would thus be incumbent upon me as the officer's more experienced purveyor of *Terry* legalese to articulate the basis for the stop for the officer so that the stop and subsequent arrest would pass legal muster. This is common practice in policing and a foundational bedrock of the police subculture. Never allow fellow officers to be exposed in any way: ethically, professionally, legally, or financially. There are of course exceptions to this that will be referenced periodically throughout this text.

In the 1968 U.S. Supreme Court decision, *Terry v. Ohio*, the Court set precedent for allowing the police to engage in the practice that came to be known as "Stop and Frisk." The Court stated that

> where a police officer observes unusual conduct, which leads him reasonably to conclude in light of his experience that criminal activity may be afoot and that the persons with whom he is dealing may be armed … where, in the course of investigating this behavior … he is entitled for the protection of himself and others in the area to conduct a carefully limited search of the outer clothing of such persons in an attempt to discover weapons which might be used to assault him.
>
> (1968, p. 30)

The decision carved out an exception to the protections contained in the Fourth and Fourteenth Amendments that ordinarily constrain intrusive police behavior that is not based on probable cause. In the five decades since the decision was handed down, accusations that police stops have frequently been violative of both the letter and the intent of the limited authority granted to the police in *Terry* have and continue to abound. There have also been frequent, repeated, and long-standing complaints regarding discriminatory practices by the police in conducting the stops, particularly in communities of color. Left open to interpretation and definition were many questions: When is someone armed and what constitutes a weapon? What is a "stop?" What is "suspicious" and "criminal" activity? What is a "limited search" of the "outer clothing?" What is police officer "experience?" How long may a person be stopped? When is one free to leave?

According to *The New York Times*, the NYPD "conducted an astounding 4.4 million stops between January 2004 and June 2012. Of these, only 6 percent resulted in arrests and 6 percent resulted in summonses" (The Editorial Board, 2013), and 83 percent of the stops conducted by the NYPD were of African Americans and Hispanics. Of the individuals stopped who were also frisked for weapons, only 1.5 percent were found to have been armed.

The Center for Constitutional Rights filed lawsuits in the United States District Court in the Southern District of New York against the NYPD in, *Floyd et al. v. City of New York et al.*[2] and a companion case, *Ligon v. City of New York*. On August 12, 2013, Judge Shira Scheindlin found

> that the City had violated the Fourth and Fourteenth Amendments by acting with "deliberate indifference" toward the NYPD's practice of making suspicionless "stops" and "frisks" and by adopting "a policy of indirect racial profiling by targeting racially defined groups" for "stops" and "frisks."
>
> (*Floyd et al. v. City of New York et al.*, p. 2)

In an earlier 2003 case, *Daniels v. City of New York*, also filed in the United States District Court in the Southern District of New York against the NYPD, the court found that the NYPD's "Street Crimes Unit" (SCU) had a "policy, practice and/or custom of stopping and frisking [individuals] based solely on [their] race and/or national origin." A settlement agreement reached with the plaintiffs in the case

> requires the NYPD to maintain a written anti-racial profiling policy that complies with the U.S. and New York State Constitutions and is binding on all NYPD officers. In addition, it requires that the NYPD audit officers who engage in stop-and-frisks, and their supervisors, to determine whether and to what extent the stop-and-frisks are based on reasonable suspicion and whether and to what extent the stop-and-frisks are being documented.
>
> (*Daniels v. City of New York*, 2003, p. 5)

Prior to the *Daniels* case, SCU officers had shot and killed an unarmed African immigrant, Amadou Diallo, on February 4, 1999, firing 41 bullets at Diallo and striking him 19 times. Officers had apparently mistaken Diallo's wallet for a weapon. The four officers who shot and killed Diallo were charged with second-degree murder and reckless endangerment—all four were acquitted at trial. In 2002 the SCU was disbanded.

In addition to the racial discrimination issues implicated in the police conducting *Terry* stops of African American and Hispanic individuals in numbers that far exceed their white counterparts, as evidenced by litigation in cases such as by *Floyd* and *Daniels*, there is the issue of *proportionality* in the use of *Terry* stops as pretexts for invasive and intrusive exploratory detentions, again primarily of residents of communities of color. Since the court in the *Terry* case did not elaborate on its definition of "suspicion" or "criminal activity," the police over the decades since the decision have assumed wide latitude and license as to what constitutes criminal activity and suspicion as any activity that is violative of any statute, ordinance, or by-law, no matter how trivial or insignificant the perceived violation.

David Keenan and Tina Thomas, writing in *The Yale Law Journal* (2014), argued that the police should not have the authority to conduct *Terry* stops for non-criminal offenses or even petty misdemeanor crimes. They ask: "Should officers be able to stop individuals on the basis of *any* suspected offense, no matter how minor?" Massachusetts and Washington courts have already prohibited *Terry* stops for non-criminal offenses, and the law in New York State limits police authority to conduct *Terry* stops to felony and misdemeanor crimes. These authors advocate "a return to *Terry*'s fundamental principle by encouraging courts to explicitly incorporate offense-severity into their analyses of stop-and-frisks" (Keenan & Thomas, 2014). In assessing the reasonableness of a particular stop under *Terry*, courts would adopt an "offense severity" model in determining the proportionality of the suspected criminal offense to the reason for the stop.

So, for example, the Massachusetts Supreme Judicial Court (SJC) in a 2011 case, *Commonwealth v. Benjamin Cruz*, found that police officers who had approached a vehicle that had been parked at a fire hydrant (a civil offense), and from which the officers detected an odor of burning marijuana upon their approach, could not rely upon the odor of marijuana to establish reasonable suspicion under *Terry* and to thus order the occupants from the vehicle. In 2008 Massachusetts had passed a law decriminalizing the possession of under an ounce of marijuana, so the reliance on the odor for an exit order from the vehicle was found insufficient insofar as the marijuana possession, while still against the law, was a civil infraction and not a criminal offense that would satisfy the reasonable suspicion standard necessary for a *Terry* stop. Thus, the SJC in Massachusetts established that the standard necessary for a stop and frisk under *Terry v. Ohio* required reasonable suspicion of a violation of the criminal law and that a civil violation was insufficient to warrant a detention and inquiry by law enforcement.

Likewise, in 2002 the Supreme Court of Washington, in *State v. Duncan*, found that police officers in Seattle lacked sufficient justification to detain Demetrius Duncan at a bus station under *Terry* when Duncan was found to have been in possession of an open container of alcohol, a civil violation of the Seattle Municipal Code. While detaining Duncan in a *Terry* stop for the open container violation, police found him to be in possession of a firearm and charged him with being a felon in possession of a firearm in addition to the open container violation, the original justification for their stop, questioning, and frisk of Mr. Duncan under *Terry*. The court found that

> to stop and detain Duncan, the officers needed a reasonable and articulable suspicion that a crime was about to occur. Possessing or consuming alcohol in public is not a crime and we decline to extend the *Terry* stop exception to include nontraffic civil infractions.
>
> (*State v. Duncan*, 2002, p. 521)

According to Keenan and Thomas then, "the police should not be permitted to use suspicion of minor offenses to engage in fishing expeditions aimed at ferreting out the armed and potentially dangerous" (2014, p. 1625). They propose an "offense-severity" model where, in addition to the disqualification by the court of *Terry* stops that are based on civil infractions or violations, courts would be required to examine stops and frisks based on the severity of criminal offenses where the police intrusion could be deemed inappropriate to the suspected criminal activity. So, for example, an "offense-severity" evaluation of a *Terry* stop and subsequent frisk might determine that non-jailable, petty misdemeanors, (such as trespassing or loitering), may be, standing alone, offenses inadequate to justify an intrusive pat frisk for weapons, in the absence of any specific justification or information that the individual stopped is in fact armed.

The Police and the Fourth Amendment—Warrantless Searches and Consent

When teaching criminal justice students exceptions to the Fourth Amendment warrant requirement for searches, the consent search exception is most often one that students can relate to. Typically, most of the students have not been arrested by the police, nor have they been chased on foot into a building by the police, but many have been asked for consent by the police in one form or another to search a backpack or a vehicle that they may be driving or even a passenger. Most of the students will learn for the first time that the police are not required to inform them that they are free to refuse to give consent to search them, and many feel that if they have nothing to hide that there is no reason not to give consent to search. I will then inform them that it is most often unwise to surrender any of their rights and freedoms guaranteed under the Constitution, and to give the police consent to search them, their belongings, their cars, or their homes is almost always a bad idea that can have unfortunate results.

What follows is something that I have been doing in undergraduate and graduate classes since 2006, a bit of trickery and deception (a well-practised skill from my 27 years as a police officer). Newly aware of their recently discovered constitutional rights, I will give students an example of the police seeking permission for a consent search, something that I have done countless times during my earlier career. I will ask a student if I can have permission to search her backpack, lying on the floor next to her seat. I will then quickly move toward the backpack and lean down toward it saying: "You don't mind if I have a look inside your backpack, do you?" Most of the students will say, "No, go right ahead"; to those who offer a slight bit of resistance (newly aware that they have the right to refuse) I will follow up with: "You don't have anything to hide, do you?" By this point all but one or two have surrendered their rights under the Fourth Amendment and allowed me to search their belongings. To the one or two who may have been stalwart in their reluctance (never outright refusal), I will then threaten to detain them while we wait for the K-9 dog to do a sniff test for contraband or to go to court to obtain a warrant, both of which may take a considerable amount of time. By then all of the students have given consent—not one has ever steadfastly and resolutely refused. Certainly not social science research, admittedly, but what often resonates with students is the coercive nature of the power imbalance in the relationship to the request: professor to student, police officer to citizen. As I will explain to students, to assert your constitutional rights is not anti-law enforcement, disrespectful, impertinent, or unpatriotic; it does not mean that you are supportive of terrorism, against the security of the "homeland," or that you are a "snowflake."

For the Fourth Amendment is yet another area that is fraught with the potential for exploitation and potential manipulation by certain of the police who are inclined to push the often-malleable boundaries of the Constitution. Although the clear majority of the police will most often operate well within the parameters of the Constitution, the ubiquity of the reports of officer misconduct (admittedly amplified through the proliferation of social media and the internet) is concerning.

Although there are numerous exceptions to the warrant requirement, among them "plain view" searches, inventory searches, and searches incident to arrest, the exception most often used and of the most utility to police are "consent searches." Consent searches are also those warrantless searches that most often run afoul of protections contained in the Fourth Amendment whose purpose is to insulate and protect unwary (or just as often wary) citizens from law enforcement misdeeds. By most estimates "over 90% of warrantless police searches are accomplished through the use of the consent exception to the Fourth Amendment" (Simmons, 2005, p. 773), and an examination of the case law governing consent searches as exceptions to the warrant requirement is thus indicated. The Fourth Amendment warrant requirement for searches to be deemed "reasonable" is predicated on the belief that searches are themselves inherently unreasonable. U.S. Supreme Court and appellate court case law have created exceptions to the warrant requirement and the "consent search" exception, being the most widely utilized by law enforcement, is fraught with the most potential for abuse.

In order for a consent search to be considered valid, there are two requirements that must be met: the consent must be given "voluntarily," that is, absent any form of coercion or duress, and the person giving the consent must have the authority, actual as well as apparent, to give consent to the search. In an early consent to search case, *Amos v. United States*, the Court found that property seized after a wife gave consent to have her husband's property searched under clear and admitted coercion by agents of the government was not properly admitted at trial. Revenue agents searching for untaxed whiskey had appeared at the Amos home demanding to be admitted to conduct a search of the premises. The defendant Amos was not at home, but his wife acceded to the agents' demands and the contraband whiskey was discovered and seized. The "consent" search was found not to have met the "voluntariness" standard necessary for the consent to be lawful.

A 1948 decision rendered in the Ninth Circuit Court of Appeals, *Johnson v. United States*, again addressed the issue of coercive consent obtained through the police demand for entry into living quarters to conduct a warrantless search for drugs. Detective Lieutenant Ballard of the Seattle Police Department received information from a drug-user informant that unknown persons were smoking opium at the Europe Hotel. Accompanied by federal narcotics agents, Ballard went to the hotel and detected an odor of burning opium emanating from one of the hotel rooms. Ballard knocked on the door of the room in question and announced his office and when the female hotel guest opened the door Ballard and the agents entered the room, told the woman that she was under arrest and that they were going to search the room. The Ninth Circuit ruled that the officers only developed probable cause to arrest the defendant once they had made the warrantless entry into her private living quarters. The court stated that "the Government is obliged to justify the arrest by the search and at the same time to justify the search by the arrest. This will not do" (*Johnson v. United States*, 1948, p. 333). While the officers had probable cause to obtain a search warrant to search the room, they failed to do so and argued that the defendant "stepped back acquiescently and admitted us," thus consenting to the search. The Court ruled otherwise and reversed the conviction.

In a 1973 decision of the Ninth Circuit Court of Appeals regarding consent searches, *Schneckloth v. Bustamonte*, the court ruled that the test for whether or not consent to search was given voluntarily would be determined by an examination of the "reasonableness" in light of the "totality of the circumstances," and that the police are under no affirmative obligation to inform the individual from whom they are seeking consent to search that he or she has a right to refuse to provide that consent. The Court held that "while knowledge of a right to refuse consent is a factor to be taken into account, the State need not prove that the one giving permission to search knew that he had a right to withhold his consent" (1973, p. 223).

A 1996 U.S. Supreme Court case, *Ohio v. Robinette*, addressed the issue of voluntariness in yet another consent search. Robinette had been stopped for speeding by an Ohio deputy sheriff and had been given a warning and, as he was about to leave the scene of the traffic stop, was asked by the deputy if he was carrying any contraband in his vehicle. Robinette replied that he was not and gave the deputy consent to search his vehicle, whereupon the officer found a small amount of marijuana and an MDMA (ecstasy) pill. Robinette argued that he should have been advised that he was "free to go" at the conclusion of the traffic stop, and that his continued detention (the "seizure") was unlawful and as a result the consent given was not voluntary. Again, citing the "reasonableness" standard and the "totality of the circumstances" perspective, the court ruled that it would be thoroughly impractical to impose on the normal consent search the detailed requirements of an effective warning, so too would it would be unrealistic to require police officers to always inform detainees that they are free to go before a consent to search may be deemed voluntary.

(pp. 5–6)

In *Florida v. Jimeno*, the Court refused to restrict the extent of a permissible search once consent has been given, absent any objection from the defendant or any attempt to restrict the scope of the consent search. Mr. Jimeno had given consent to Officer Trujillo to search his vehicle; Trujillo had been following Mr. Jimeno after overhearing him appear to engage in a drug transaction. In a search of Mr. Jimeno's vehicle Trujillo found cocaine in a folded paper bag that was on the floor of the vehicle. The Court held that "there is no basis for adding to the Fourth Amendment's basic test of objective reasonableness a requirement that, if police wish to search closed containers within a car, they must separately request permission to search each container" (pp. 250–252).

Consent to search that has been granted after police claim to have a search warrant to search the premises, when in fact no warrant is produced, nor is it relied upon at trial, is not a knowing and valid consent to search, according to the U.S. Supreme Court's 1968 decision in *Bumper v. North Carolina*. When four white law enforcement officers went to the rural home of Mr. Bumper's elderly African American grandmother, with whom he lived, and told the woman, Mrs. Hattie Leath, that they had a warrant and were there to search her home, she told them to "go ahead" and went about her work. The officers recovered a rifle that they presented as evidence at Bumper's trial for rape, then a capital offense in North Carolina. Authorities claim that they obtained the rifle in a consent search of Mrs. Leath's home and Bumper was convicted of the rape and sentenced to life in prison. The Court found "that Mrs. Leath did not consent to the search, and that it was constitutional error to admit the rifle in evidence against the petitioner" and "that there can be no 'consent' given when the official conducting the search has asserted that he possessed a warrant" (p. 391). Thus, the police cannot lie about the possession of a search warrant in order to obtain what they later claim is "consent."

Having established the "reasonableness" and "totality of the circumstances" standards for the "voluntariness" of a consent search, case law also articulates the basis upon which the authority to authorize consent resides, and in particular third-party consent (i.e., when a person who is not the target of the criminal investigation provides consent to search the suspect's property).

In the *United States v. Matlock*, the U.S. Supreme Court ruled that third-party consent is freely given when one member of a couple who share a part of a home provides consent to search. And that

proof of voluntary consent, is not limited to proof that consent was given by the defendant but may show that permission to search was obtained from a third party who possessed common authority over or other sufficient relationship to the premises effects sought.

(1974, pp. 169–172)

That the defendant Matlock was present during the search (he was arrested in the front yard of the home), and did not object to the search, further established the legitimacy of the consent claim, as the Court has previously held, in *Georgia v. Randolph*, that when "one occupant consents to a search of shared premises, but a physically present co-occupant expressly objects to the search, the search is unreasonable" (pp. 18–19).

That the couple was not married and that their names did not appear on a lease was insufficient in the eyes of the Court to render the search violative of Fourth Amendment protections, since the officers reasonably believed, beyond a preponderance of evidence (or more likely than not), that Mrs. Graff, who gave officers permission to search the bedroom that she shared with Mr. Matlock, had joint control over the bedroom and the apparent authority to provide consent to the officers to search.

In another U.S. Supreme Court case, *Chapman v. United States*, the Court ruled that a landlord, who had entered Mr. Chapman's locked home after detecting an odor of whiskey mash, and who had then summoned authorities and allowed them to enter the premises and to conduct a search, did not have the legal authority to provide consent for the officers to search. That the landlord breached the lock in a secure home and only then uncovered evidence of criminal activity did not obviate the officers' need to secure a search warrant and to uphold such an entry, search and seizure "without a warrant would reduce the [Fourth] Amendment to a nullity and leave [tenants'] homes secure only in the discretion of [landlords]" (1961, p. 365).

Likewise, in *Stoner v. California*, the U.S. Supreme Court ruled that a hotel clerk did not have the authority to give officers consent to search the room of a hotel guest who was not in his room at the time of the search. In investigating a robbery in Monrovia, California, officers were led to a hotel where they believed the suspect was staying and, after obtaining permission from the hotel clerk, the officers searched Mr. Stoner's room and found incriminating evidence that led to his arrest and conviction. In reversing the conviction, the Court ruled that

a hotel guest is entitled to the constitutional protection against unreasonable searches and seizures. The hotel clerk had no authority to permit the room search, and the police had no basis to believe that petitioner had authorized the clerk to permit the search.

(1964, pp. 488–490)

In *Frazier v. Cupp* (1969) the Supreme Court ruled that a co-defendant in a homicide case, Mr. Rawls, did have the authority, however, to provide consent to police officers to search a duffel bag that the defendants had shared and that contained clothing that was used to incriminate both Mr. Rawls and the petitioner Mr. Frazier at trial.

In another third-party consent case, *Illinois v. Rodriguez*, the Court was asked to consider

whether a warrantless entry is valid when based upon the consent of a third party whom the police, at the time of the entry, reasonably believe to possess common authority over the premises, but who in fact does not do so.

(1990, p. 179)

Officers, believing that Gail Fischer lived in a shared apartment with Mr. Rodriguez in Chicago (she referred to it as "our" apartment and said that she had clothing and furniture there), went to the apartment with Ms. Fischer and were let into the locked apartment with her key where they conducted a search of the apartment with her consent, finding evidence criminally implicating Mr. Rodriguez. Again, using the "reasonableness" standard, the Court determined that the consent search was not violative of the Fourth Amendment, since the officers had a reasonable belief that Ms. Fischer did in fact share the apartment with Mr. Rodriguez (she did not).

Conclusion

Policing as undertaken and enacted since at least the beginning of the twentieth century up to the present has had an often tenuous and discordant relationship with the Constitution and with accompanying civil rights and civil liberties protections and guarantees. The guidance and requirements provided through U.S. Supreme Court and appellate court case law have articulated the parameters and limitations of lawful police conduct, yet there continue to be reported and documented instances where the police exceed the bounds of their legitimate and lawful authority. Incidents such as the death of James Greer in Hayward, California, described at the beginning of this chapter, continue to challenge the confidence and trust that are essential for the police and their constituent communities to coexist in environments that are safe, just, and respectful, for the police as well as for those entrusted to their care.

NOTES

1 These weapons are of the type that Boston police used when officers killed 21-year-old Emerson College student Victoria Snelgrove on October 21, 2004, during a street celebration that followed the Red Sox victory in the American League Championship Series.
2 The Scheindlin decision was stayed on appeal; the New York City administration never pursued the potential legal consequences of the appellate court's correction. But Scheindlin was judicially admonished and removed from further involvement in the matter due to irresponsible public commentary of her "personal views."

REFERENCES

Amos v. United States, 255 U.S. 313, 1921.

Armstrong, K. (2018). The 1919 race riots. *Chicago Tribune*. Retrieved from: www.chicagotribune.com/news/nation world/politics/chi-chicagodays-raceriots-story-story.html.

Bl(a)ck Tea Society v. City of Boston, 378 F.3d 8, 13, 1st Cir. 2004.

Bumper v. North Carolina, 391 U.S. 543, p. 391, 1968.

Burnham, D. (1970, May 22). Lindsey appoints corruption unit. *The New York Times*. Retrieved from: https://times machine.nytimes.com/timesmachine/1970/05/22/80028472.html?pageNumber=44.

Chapman v. United States, 365 U.S. 610, 365 U.S. 617, 1961.

Commission to Investigate Allegations of Police Corruption and the Anti-Corruption Procedures of the Police Department. (1994). *Commission to combat police corruption report*. Retrieved from: www.scribd.com/document/248581606/1994-07-07-Mollen-Commission-NYPD-Report.

Commonwealth v. Benjamin Cruz, 459 Mass. 459, 2011.

Daniels v. City of New York, 99 civ. 1695 (SAS), September 24, 2003.

Florida v. Jimeno, 500 U.S. 248, pp. 500 U.S. 250–252, 1991.

Floyd, et al. v. City of New York, et al. 959 F.Supp. 2d 540, 562 (S.D.N.Y.), 2013.

Frazier v. Cupp, 394 U.S. 731, 1969.

Georgia v. Randolph, 547 U.S. 103, 2006.

Governor's Commission. (1965, December 2). *A report by the Governor's Commission on the Los Angeles Riots.* Retrieved from: https://ia801602.us.archive.org/34/items/ViolenceInCity/violence%20in%20city.pdf.

Horse, et al. v. District of Columbia, et al., Case 1:17-cv-01216-ABJ, 2017.

Illinois v. Rodriguez, 497 U.S. 177, 1990.

Johnson v. United States, 333 U.S. 10, p. 333, U.S. 17, 1948.

Keenan, D. & Thomas, T. (2014). An offense-severity model for stop-and-frisks. *The Yale Law Journal,* 123 (5).

King, M. (2013). Disruption is not permitted: The policing and social control of Occupy Oakland. *Critical Criminology,* 21 (4), pp. 463–475.

Lawton, D. (2015, October 17). Hayward: Officer-involved death prompts lawsuit by family, questions about handling of case. *San Jose Mercury News.* Retrieved from: www.mercurynews.com/2015/10/17/hayward-officer-involved-death-prompts-lawsuit-by-family-questions-about-handling-of-case/.

Lawton, D. (2016, May 16). Hayward police body cameras detail how man died after traffic stop. *East Bay Times.* Retrieved from: www.eastbaytimes.com/2016/05/16/hayward-police-body-cameras-detail-how-man-died-after-traffic-stop/.

Leach, L. (2007). Margie polite, the riot Starter: Harlem, 1943. *Studies in the Literary Imagination,* 40.

Lewis. H. (1990). Harlem riot of 1943 reports. *Schomburg Center for Research in Black Culture, Manuscripts, Archives and Rare Books Division.* Retrieved from: http://archives.nypl.org/scm/20584.

Ligon v. City of New York, 925 F. Supp. 2d 478—Dist. Court, SD New York, 2013.

National Advisory Commission on Civil Disorders. (1968). *Report of the National Advisory Commission on Civil Disorders.* Retrieved from: www.eisenhowerfoundation.org/docs/kerner.pdf.

National Commission on Law Observance and Enforcement. (1931, January 7). *National Commission on Law Observance and Enforcement, report on the Enforcement of the Prohibition Laws of the United States.* Washington D.C.: United States Government Printing Office, p. 82.

Nye, J. (2014, August 14). A decade of racial profiling: how tensions between Ferguson's police and black community boiled over after years of ill-treatment. *Daily Mail.* Retrieved from: www.dailymail.co.uk/news/article-2724515/A-decade-racial-profiling-How-tensions-Fergusons-police-black-community-boiled-years-ill-treatment.html.

Ohio v. Robinette, 519 U.S. 33, pp. 5–6, 1996.

President's Commission on Law Enforcement and Administration of Justice. (1967, February). *The Challenge of Crime in a Free Society: A Report by the President's Commission on Law Enforcement and Administration of Justice.* Washington D.C.: United States Government Printing Office.

Robertson, S. (2016, October 28). Toward a spatial narrative of the 1935 Harlem riot. *Dr Stephen Robertson.* Retrieved from: http://drstephenrobertson.com/presentation/toward-a-spatial-narrative-of-the-1935-harlem-riot/.

Schneckloth v. Bustamonte, 412 U.S. 218, pp. 412 U.S. 223–249, 1973.

Simmons, R. (2005). Not "voluntary" but still reasonable: a new paradigm for understanding the consent searches doctrine. *Indiana Law Journal,* 80, p. 773. Retrieved from: http://ilj.law.indiana.edu/articles/80/80_3_Simmons.pdf.

State v. Duncan, 43 p. 3d 513—Wash: Supreme Court, 2002.

Stoner v. California, 376 U.S. 483, 376 U.S., pp. 488–490, 1964.

Terry v. Ohio 392, U.S. 1, 1968.

The Editorial Board. (2013, August 13). Racial discrimination in stop and frisk. *The New York Times*. Retrieved from: www.nytimes.com/2013/08/13/opinion/racial-discrimination-in-stop-and-frisk.html.

United States v. Matlock, 415 U.S. 164, pp. 415 U.S. 169–172, 1974.

Walker, D. (1968). "Rights in conflict: the violent confrontation of demonstrators and police in the parks and streets of Chicago during the week of the Democratic National Convention of 1968" in *Summary Report to the National Commission on the Causes and Prevention of Violence*. Retrieved from: http://chicago68.com/ricsumm.html.

Chapter 2

Technology and Privacy in the Era of Homeland Security

At the beginning of my career in law enforcement in the late 1970s, the technology that was available to the police was of extremely limited utility and even less sophistication. Having a hand-held two-way radio to take out of the vehicle with you when responding to 911 calls was still a novelty and could often prove useful, although the radios frequently malfunctioned and were largely unreliable. Aside from radio communications capability, there were few technological innovations available to police until the 1990s and the advent of the internet and computers.

In the second decade of the twenty-first century, the array of devices, weapons, and technologies that are available to law enforcement is considerable and consequential, and their acquisition and deployment have raised constitutional issues as well as privacy and civil rights and civil liberties concerns. The ability and inclination of law enforcement at the local, county, and state level to leverage technology in order to engage in the pervasive and ubiquitous surveillance of individuals and groups, in public spaces as well as private, is without precedent, and the legal issues implicated have been outpaced by the ever-increasing development of more intrusive and advanced technologies.

Drones

In the spring of 2018, the City of Chicago championed legislation that would allow the police to use drone technology to conduct warrantless surveillance of groups who were engaging in constitutionally protected activity. The state of Illinois had passed ground-breaking legislation just three years before that required the police to obtain a judicial warrant in that state authorizing the use of drones for surveillance. The Chicago legislation, passed on May 2, 2018 (Lukitsch, 2018), would "allow drones to be used to make video, audio and still recordings of crowds, and worse, to be equipped with facial recognition technology" (American Civil Liberties Union, 2018, May 2).

The City of Chicago and its police department claimed that the drone use would ensure public safety at large public gatherings such as parades and sporting events, but civil rights and civil liberties advocates feared that the police use of the drones for surveillance at protest events, particularly those equipped with facial recognition technology, would have chilling consequences for individuals and groups engaging in activities that are protected under the First Amendment to the Constitution, specifically the rights of free speech, assembly, and petitioning the government for redress of grievances, all while being reported by a free press.

And in Boston, the American Civil Liberties Union (ACLU) of Massachusetts raised concerns when the Boston Police Department, without any public disclosure, input, or approval, purchased drones and began flying them over a public housing project in that city, one almost exclusively populated by people of color (Crockford, 2017). Police departments across the United States are beginning to acquire and to deploy drones, from the New York State Police (Shueh, 2018), to the Las Vegas Metropolitan Police (Raz, 2017), to the Colorado State University Police (Niedringhaus, 2018).

While there are without doubt legitimate and even lifesaving (Friedersdorf, 2018) instances where drone technology will prove an invaluable tool for operational use by law enforcement, as in locating lost children or elderly persons, or in searching for individuals who have committed crimes of violence, such surveillance technology, particularly in the hands of county sheriffs and local and special jurisdiction police such as campus police, needs necessarily to be prudently and very publicly considered in a methodically deliberative process that includes all who may be affected by drone use, particularly by those residents of communities of color who have seen decades of often heavy-handed police tactics and policies that have had demonstrably discriminatory and oppressive results.

Of concern regarding law enforcement use of drones is the speed with which the technology is developing, and the relatively sluggish pace that regulatory and case laws that regulate the technology are established by comparison. For example, it took the U.S. Supreme Court until 2018, in *Carpenter v. United States*, to issue a ruling that required law enforcement to obtain a search warrant prior to accessing historical cell phone location data, and cell phones have been in use since the early 1990s. The accelerated pace with which drone technology is evolving will render regulatory oversight ineffective and almost immediately obsolete. According to the ACLU's Crockford,

> these technologies will enable forms of surveillance that are not discernable to the human eye, making our current legal frameworks for surreptitious surveillance obsolete. Why bother with a warrant if cops can use a tiny drone to record a conversation in someone's home, and then use parallel construction to find evidence in another manner?
>
> (2018)

Surveillance drones, or "Unmanned Aerial Systems," are licensed and regulated by the Federal Aviation Administration, and according to the Electronic Frontier Foundation (EFF), a San-Francisco-based international digital rights group,

> drones are capable of highly advanced surveillance, and drones already in use by law enforcement can carry various types of equipment including live-feed video cameras, infrared

cameras, heat sensors, and radar. Some military versions can stay in the air for hours or days at a time, and their high-tech cameras can scan entire cities, or alternatively, zoom in and read a milk carton from 60,000 feet. They can also carry wi-fi crackers and fake cell phone towers that can determine your location or intercept your texts and phone calls. Drone manufacturers even admit they are made to carry "less lethal" weapons such as tasers or rubber bullets.

(2018b)

Andrew Talai, writing on the police use of drones in the *California Law Review*, argues that, rather than focusing solely on concerns related to privacy in police drone use, the more salient issue is one of a broader consideration: the "abuse of government discretion" (2014, p. 734). Talai sees three primary areas of concern that present troubling Fourth Amendment considerations. One is that "drone surveillance is an excessively powerful tool, entrusted to executive discretion devoid of constitutional safeguards" (2014, p. 751), and that, at minimum, a warrant should be required to authorize drone use. The second is "that the Supreme Court's current privacy-centric Fourth Amendment search framework leaves us without a path to follow. Moreover, it largely fails to check police discretion over aerial surveillance" (2014, p. 751), and that considerations of privacy issues alone are "underinclusive" to an adequate Fourth Amendment assessment of other relevant drone-related issues such as police overreach, personal liberty, and the abuse of discretion. Talai's third and final concern is that drone technology can actually be used to control "locomotion" (our freedom of movement) in at least three ways:

First, the ever-present and pervasive surveillance of a Predator drone equipped with ARGUS (the most powerful drone technology available as of this writing) could induce self-policing of movement. Second, drones working in conjunction with actual officers make policing discretionary stops all the more efficient. Third, drones may eventually have the ability to physically seize a person.

(2014, p. 777)

For Talai, "there is at least a simple initial solution for this serious problem—an ex ante warrant requirement" (2014, p. 778).

Automated License Plate Readers

The city of Boston Police Department announced in the spring of 2018 that it would resume its use of so-called "automated license plate readers" (ALPRs), after a significant data breach had caused the release of thousands of records that it had collected using the technology in 2013 (Musgrave, 2018). Privacy and civil liberties advocates have raised concerns about the use of such devices by law enforcement, since they are used to capture information on motorists who are not suspected of involvement in any criminal activity and without their awareness or consent. The ACLU has voiced concern that "enormous databases of innocent motorists' location information are growing rapidly. This information is often retained for years or even indefinitely, with few or no restrictions to protect privacy rights" (American Civil Liberties Union, 2013).

According to the EFF,

> automated license plate readers (ALPRs) are high-speed, computer-controlled camera systems that are typically mounted on street poles, streetlights, highway overpasses, mobile trailers, or attached to police squad cars. ALPRs automatically capture all license plate numbers that come into view, along with the location, date, and time. The data, which includes photographs of the vehicle and sometimes its driver and passengers, is then uploaded to a central server.
>
> (2018a)

Randy Dryer and Shane Stroud (2015) have identified several concerns with the use of ALPRs that have emerged since their deployment has become widespread by law enforcement across the United States. First, they cite the proliferation of the devices themselves as cause for concern. While the devices have been available for some time, their use by the police has increased exponentially over the last decade. Their second concern is owing to "the data collected ... being aggregated in massive regional databases, raising the specter of location tracking." Location tracking allows the police to determine travel routes, destinations, arrival times, and travel patterns, many of which may involve travel in or to constitutionally protected activities such as to a place of worship, to a demonstration, to visit an associate, or a government official. Location tracking also implicates privacy issues in the case of someone traveling to a doctor's office, a pharmacy, a safe house for victims of domestic violence, a union hall, or a case worker or advocate for victims of sexual assault. Dryer and Stroud's third concern with ALPRs is the "lack of uniform standards governing retention and use of ALPR data collected or accessed by government." For example, the Boston Police Department, in reactivating the use of ALPRs has adjusted its policy to retain the data that it collects for 30 days, erasing it thereafter.

Other police departments keep the data indefinitely. Some departments use the data to collect fines for unpaid parking tickets, and others use it in the course of criminal investigations, in so-called crime "hot spots" to deter criminal activity, or for child-abduction "Amber Alerts." Dryer and Stroud (2015) go on to cite the unregulated use of ALPRs by private companies, an area often beyond constitutional scrutiny:

> Finally, there is a growing public awareness of the potential privacy dangers arising from geolocation tracking in light of the U.S. Supreme Court's decision in *United States v. Jones*, which held that the warrantless installation of a GPS tracking device on a suspect's vehicle implicated Fourth Amendment protections.
>
> (p. 225)

Constitutional and privacy issues aside, M. Murat Ozer (2016), in a study of the Cincinnati, Ohio, Police Department, found the use of ALPR technology was a cost-effective means by which the police could make more arrests and solve more crimes using fewer officers. Studying ALPR devices that were attached to police vehicles (as opposed to fixed locations such as bridges or traffic lights), Murat Ozer found that "ALPR mobile units effectively do the same job (produce follow-up arrests) with fewer officers compared with traditional policing" (p. 130). Additionally, he discovered that "ALPR mobile units have high detection capability for stolen vehicles and identification of delinquents who did not pay their legal financial obligations (i.e., traffic tickets, insurance)" (p. 130).

In 2012, the ACLU and the EFF filed a lawsuit against the Los Angeles Police Department (LAPD) and the Los Angeles County Sheriff's Department (LASD) after both departments refused to disclose information regarding data that they had collected and stored using ALPRs following a public records request. According to *The Washington Post*, reporting on *ACLU of So. Cal. v. Superior Court*, the California Supreme Court found that the LAPD and the LASD would be precluded from handing over the ALPR data to the ACLU and the EFF, not out of concerns that information regarding criminal investigations would be compromised, or that the public's right to know the information contained in the databases outweighed the need for the security of the information, but owing to the privacy concerns of the personal information contained in the databases (Volokh, 2017). The court ruled that,

> although we acknowledge that revealing raw ALPR data would be helpful in determining the extent to which ALPR technology threatens privacy, the act of revealing the data would itself jeopardize the privacy of everyone associated with a scanned plate. Given that real parties each conduct more than one million scans per week, this threat to privacy is significant.
>
> (Volokh, 2017)

The Washington Post also reported on the sheer volume of records that the agencies collected using ALPRs and the length of time that it retains the data:

> The Los Angeles Police Department (LAPD) estimates that it records data from 1.2 million cars per week. It retains license plate scan data for five years. The Los Angeles Sheriff's Department (LASD) estimates that it records between 1.7 and 1.8 million license plates per week. It retains scan data for two years.
>
> (Volokh, 2017)

Cell Phone Site Simulators

On June 25, 2014 the U.S. Supreme Court, in the combined cases of *Riley v. California* and *United States v. Wurie*, decided unanimously that Fourth Amendment protections applied to the police conducting a warrantless search of a cell phone, and that police needed a search warrant based on probable cause in order to be able to conduct such searches. The questions left unanswered in this decision pertained to the police use of technology that is capable of intercepting cell phone devices and monitoring, capturing, collecting, and storing information contained in the phones. The devices, known as cell phone site simulators, mimic actual cell phone towers, "tricking" all cell phones in a particular vicinity into connecting to the simulator.

The 2018 U.S. Supreme Court decision in *Carpenter v. United States* has relevant applications to the use of stingray devices in the collection of historical location data. The Fourth Amendment requirement that law enforcement obtain a search warrant in order to listen in on telephone calls or, in the aftermath of *Carpenter*, to obtain cell site location information from a cellular provider, may be seen as unnecessary by law enforcement in their use of stingray devices. According to the ACLU's Crockford,

> Stingrays enable law enforcement agencies to wiretap without involvement from phone companies. Because the cops can wiretap without involvement from other parties, there's a real risk they are violating wiretap law and using parallel construction to hide these violations from the public and defendants.
>
> (2018)

The cell site simulators, often called "stingrays" or "dirtboxes," are in widespread use by police departments across the United States. Designed for military use and for use by the Federal Bureau of Investigation (FBI) and the National Security Agency (NSA), these "spy tools" are used to monitor transmissions from cell phones, such as voice calls, text messages, location data, and other personally identifiable information, not only on specific individuals, but on any other person in the general vicinity of the cell site simulator (usually about 650 feet). George Joseph, writing for *CityLab* (2017), sent public records requests to 50 of the country's largest police departments and found that 76 percent of the departments were using cell phone interception or extraction devices. According to Joseph,

> at least nineteen police departments acquired cellphone extraction devices, which allow police to crack open locked devices and collect vast amounts of phone data, such as call logs, emails, social media messages, time-stamped past location data, and even deleted texts and photos—without any assistance from cellphone companies.
>
> (2017)

Even cloud user data and personal information from social media sites such as Facebook and Instagram are not immune from police surveillance with some of the more advanced devices available to police. Joseph discovered that

> the Baltimore, Seattle, Oklahoma City, Jacksonville, Kansas City, Louisville, Tucson, and Miami police departments' Cellebrite "Pro Series" purchases all appear to include the firm's Cloud Analyzer tool, which extracts "private-user cloud data" by "utilizing login information extracted from the mobile device." According to Cellebrite (an Israeli technology firm), in some cases cloud data does not only include communications on platforms like Facebook and Instagram, but also individuals' "timestamped movements minute by minute," based on private Google Location History collected from Google cloud servers.
>
> (2017)

Jeremy Scahill and Margot Williams, writing in *The Intercept* (2015), obtained a secret, internal, U.S. government catalogue of devices that had historically been available only to the military and federal law enforcement agencies, such as the CIA, FBI, and NSA, but that are now widely available for acquisition and use in domestic law enforcement operations, including local police departments. The catalogue can be found online (*The Intercept*, 2015). In describing the devices, Scahill and Williams observed that

> a few of the devices can house a "target list" of as many as 10,000 unique phone identifiers. Most can be used to geolocate people, but the documents indicate that some have more advanced capabilities, like eavesdropping on calls and spying on SMS messages.
>
> (2015)

The catalogue contained descriptions for devices seized by law enforcement "as having the ability to extract media files, address books, and notes, and one can retrieve deleted text messages" (Scahill & Williams, 2015).

And while federal law enforcement guidance from the Department of Justice and the Department of Homeland Security has generally required that federal law enforcement officers obtain search warrants prior to utilizing cell site simulators in federal investigations, local law enforcement officers have generally avoided obtaining search warrants and have sidestepped Fourth Amendment requirements by claiming that they are collecting "metadata" that is transmitted to a third-party vendor (the cell phone provider), that thus evades the "particularity" clause of the Fourth Amendment.

Recent appellate court decisions in Maryland and in Washington, D.C., however, have ruled that information contained on cell phones, such as text messages, phone calls, and location information are protected under the Fourth Amendment and that police using cell site simulators are required to obtain search warrants prior to using the devices. In the Maryland case, *Maryland v. Andrews*, the Court of Special Appeals of Maryland found that

> people have a reasonable expectation that their cell phones will not be used as real-time tracking devices by law enforcement, and—recognizing that the Fourth Amendment protects people and not simply areas—that people have an objectively reasonable expectation of privacy in real-time cell phone location information. Thus, we hold that the use of a cell site simulator requires a valid search warrant, or an order satisfying the constitutional requisites of a warrant, unless an established exception to the warrant requirement applies.
>
> (2015/2016)

In the D.C. case, *Prince Jones, Apellant, v. United States*, the District of Columbia Court of Appeals found that

> the government's use of the cell-site simulator to locate Mr. Jones was a search. The government did not obtain a warrant and has not argued that the search "f[ell] within a specific exception to the warrant requirement," and therefore the search was unlawful under the Fourth Amendment.
>
> (2017)

Of note: state, county, and local police departments that sought to acquire the cell site simulator devices have been required to enter into non-disclosure agreements (NDAs) with the FBI that kept the acquisition of the devices a secret, even from defense attorneys and judges. The Boston Police Department entered into just such an NDA, one that required the department to notify the FBI if it received any public information request such as a federal Freedom of Information Act request or any similar state "sunshine law" request. The agreement can be found online (United States Department of Justice, and Federal Bureau of Investigation, 2013). The NDA also required the Boston Police Department to keep the acquisition of the device as well as its capabilities a secret. Of alarming concern is a requirement contained in the NDA that

> the Boston Police Department will, at the request of the FBI, seek dismissal of the case in lieu of using or providing, or allowing others to use or provide, any information concerning Harris Corporation (the manufacturer of the devices) wireless equipment/technology … if using or providing such information would potentially or actually compromise the equipment/technology.
>
> (United States Department of Justice & Federal Bureau of Investigation, 2013)

Police Monitoring Social Media

Bolton, Massachusetts, a town 25 miles outside of Boston and home to fewer than 5000 residents, was once also home to a company called "Geofeedia," one that provided services to law enforcement as well as military and intelligence agencies in monitoring and mining social media activities and postings and associating real-time geo-locations with the postings. Their software allowed police to conduct warrantless surveillance of the public postings that individuals and groups made to social media platforms such as Twitter, Instagram, and Facebook, in real time, and with the location information of the poster. The law enforcement agencies could customize their surveillance through the use of keywords such as #blacklivesmatter, #muslimlivesmatter, and #pussyhatproject. Following an October 2016 report by the ACLU of Northern California (Cagle, 2016), the social media platforms Facebook, Twitter, and Instagram suspended Geofeedia's access to users' public postings. Geofeedia was out, but other social media monitoring and surveillance technology was and is still widely (and publicly) available.

The ACLU made public records requests of 63 law enforcement agencies in California in preparing its report and discovered that Geofeedia claimed to have agreements and arrangements with Instagram, Twitter, and Facebook that would allow it enhanced access to public user data posted on the various social media platforms. In its sales pitch to law enforcement agencies, the company claimed to have "covered Ferguson/Mike Brown nationally with great success" (Geofeedia.com, 2015).

In Boston, the police dropped plans for a $1.4 million contract to purchase social media monitoring software from another company (it had used the now-defunct Geofeedia in 2014 and 2015), following backlash from the ACLU of Massachusetts (ACLUM) and other groups. According to a report published in February of 2018 by the ACLUM,

> In a trial of Geofeedia in November 2014, the Boston Police Department used the service to monitor online speech associated with the Black Lives Matter movement in Boston,

tracking terms like "protest" and "#blacklivesmatter." Later, after contracting with the company in 2015, the BPD used Geofeedia primarily to target so-called "Islamic Extremist Terminology," including both commonly used terms like "ISIS" and a list of Arabic words used regularly by ordinary members of Muslim communities.

(American Civil Liberties Union, 2018)

The ACLU report found that the Boston Police Department's use of social media monitoring software prevented no acts of terrorism and solved no crimes nor prevented any violence. Instead, the BPD used the Geofeedia software "for discriminatory purposes: to track online racial justice activism in the wake of the events in Ferguson and to conduct broad surveillance of ordinary Muslims in Boston" (American Civil Liberties Union, 2018, February 7). Kade Crockford, the Director of the Technology for Liberty Program at the ACLU of Massachusetts (2018), said that

police officers are charged with protecting not only public safety but also individual rights … Social media monitoring that turns Muslims, politically active residents, and others into "persons of interest" without demonstrated utility in solving crimes accomplishes neither of these aims.

According to *Forbes*, Geofeedia was by no means the only player in the arena of police surveillance of social media content, and its demise is no sign that the use of the technology had abated or even stalled: "The use of social media monitoring, including for real-time protest response and profiling of individuals, is fully entrenched in the modern surveillance state" (Leetaru, 2016). And the Geofeedias of the police-surveillance state hardly operated in secret; they openly touted their services and advertised extensively in the law enforcement and intelligence communities. Following the ACLU report in California (Cagle, 2016), both Twitter and Facebook "issued public statements claiming to be completely and utterly unaware of what one of their licensees had been doing with their data over a period of several years." Yet, as the *Forbes* article observed: "It is difficult to imagine that neither Facebook nor Twitter had any idea of any kind that one of their licensees was using their data to provide surveillance capabilities to law enforcement" (Leetaru, 2016). Thus, it is difficult to argue that at least two of the largest social media platforms in the world are unaware of their complicity in facilitating law enforcement's surveillance of their user base.

Even campus law enforcement agencies are using surveillance tools to monitor social media use by students. According to the magazine *Campus Safety* (Rock, 2018), the University of Virginia Police Department began monitoring social media in the fall of 2017; the school pays $18,500 per year to a company called "Social Sentinel" to notify the campus police when they detect the use of keywords from their "library of harm" such as "bomb" or "kill"; "The program also allows users, such as UVA police officer and crime analyst Beth Davis, to add tailored keywords for specific events such as concerts and sporting events" (Rock, 2018).

And it is here where privacy and civil rights and civil liberties advocates see one of many causes for concern, as campus police officers are in no way considered intelligence or crime analysts in any conventional concept of the term as used in the law enforcement profession. Adding "tailored" keywords such as "protest" or "demonstration" or even "gathering" risk running grievously afoul of constitutionally protected activity, specifically First Amendment protected activities. William Farrar of the ACLU in Virginia responded to news of the campus police social media surveillance operation with: "This really isn't the way to find the bad guys, because they're texting and emailing and using private groups" (Rock, 2018). "This is used to monitor everyday people" commented Rock (2018).

Ryne Weiss, writing in *FIRE*, (the Foundation for Individual Rights in Education), identifies a major issue in having campus police monitor social media: context and an ability to actually understand the message or the posting that an algorithm has flagged as a concern or threatening.

> The "whole context" of a post is almost never available to someone as far removed from the post as an officer or school administrator reading it. Innocuous or inside jokes, and a whole host of other protected speech, will often be completely lost on them and could appear threatening without that crucial context.
>
> (Weiss, 2018)

The Police and Body Cameras

In 2014 the Department of Justice Office of Community Oriented Policing Services (COPS) issued a report entitled "Implementing a Body-Worn Camera Program" (Police Executive Research Forum, 2014), wherein it issued guidance and recommendations for police departments considering the implementation of programs to equip officers with body-worn cameras (BWCs) in order to record their interactions with the public. Calls to equip officers with body cameras have become more strident following the deaths of unarmed African American men and boys, such as Michael Brown, Freddie Gray, and Akai Gurley, where video recordings of the incidents did not exist.

The COPS report was based on research conducted in 2013 by the Police Executive Research Forum (PERF). The PERF study described several benefits to police departments that had implemented or were considering implementing body-camera programs: "body-worn cameras have made (police) operations more transparent to the public and have helped resolve questions following an encounter between officers and members of the public" (Police Executive Research Forum, 2014, p. 5). Also, the police executives interviewed by PERF in the study "overwhelmingly report that their agencies experienced a noticeable drop in complaints against officers after deploying body-worn cameras" (p. 6), as well as "by helping agencies identify and correct problems within the department" and that "body-worn cameras have significantly improved how officers capture evidence for investigations and court proceedings" (p. 9).

Concerns raised in PERF's research emphasized privacy issues and specifically policies that departments would establish regarding the circumstances and situations in which officers would activate the recording devices. The PERF report offered a 33-point guidance for law enforcement agencies in establishing policies governing the use of body cameras and advocated for a certain amount of discretion in officers' recording of incidents that they respond to and interactions that they have with the public: "There are certain situations, such as interviews with crime victims and witnesses and informal, non-law enforcement interactions with members of the community, that call for affording officers some measure of discretion in determining whether to activate their cameras" (p. 12). This is of particular concern when interacting with victims of sexual assault, intimate partner abuse, people who are in their homes, or people who may be in a state of undress or some other potentially embarrassing situation.

In 2018, the ACLU issued an updated version of its policy recommendations for police department policies regarding the use of BWCs (American Civil Liberties Union, 2018, June) and the ACLU has also issued a revised version of its model legislation recommendation (Marlow and Stanley, 2017). The ACLU's BWC policy (and their accompanying model legislation) advocated for the following:

1 For privacy reasons, the majority of body-camera video should not be subject to public release. The exception is where there is a strong public interest in that video that outweighs privacy concerns: where there is a use of force, or a complaint against an officer.

2 Police departments cannot use "investigative privilege" as a basis for withholding footage where the suspect is a police officer.

3 Videos that capture police use of force or that are the subject of a police complaint must be released to the public, irrespective of any contrary provisions in state open records laws.

4 Videos in which a subject is killed, shot by a firearm, or grievously injured need to be released within five days of a public request because of the urgent public interest in access to such footage.

5 Requests for footage must provide some degree of specificity as to the video being sought, so disruptive requests for "all body camera videos" can be rejected.

6 Explicit rules for the use of redaction technology to protect privacy are now included.

7 The rules for body-camera video also apply to any audio collected by such devices: sometimes a camera will fall off an officer or otherwise fail to capture useful images, for example, but the authorities must still release whatever audio might have been captured.

8 The question of who has the right to inspect (without receiving a copy) a body-camera video is clarified.

9 The new policy includes language ensuring that videos cannot be voluntarily released by police without first securing the video subject's approval (so the police and public have same rights).

10 The new policy clarifies that the prohibition against officers viewing video footage in advance of filling out reports applies only to videos depicting a use of force.

11 The new policy clarifies rules and warrant requirements for using facial recognition technology or other video analytics on policy body-camera videos.

(American Civil Liberties Union, 2018, June)

One of the first studies to examine the use of BWCs was conducted in 2013 in Rialto, California, by Barak Ariel, William Farrar, and Alex Sutherland for the Police Foundation (Ariel et al., 2015). Rialto is a community of approximately 100,000 residents that is policed by a department of 115 sworn officers. In this mid-sized department, the "use-of-force is a relatively rare event, with approximately 65 incidents per year, or 1.46 incidents for every 1,000 police-public contacts. Similarly, complaints lodged by citizens against police-officers are infrequent, with 28 grievances filed against officers in 2011" (2013, p. 7). The findings of this study suggest a 50 percent reduction in the total number of use-of-force incidents during the treatment period (during which BWCs were utilized) as opposed to the control period (before BWCs were used). Also reported were nearly ten times more citizens' complaints in the 12-months prior to the experiment, or an over 90 percent reduction in the number of citizen complaints following the implementation of the BWC program (2013, p. 9).

A 2016 study by William Sousa, James Caldren, Denise Rodriguez, and Anthony Braga examined BWC use in the Las Vegas Metropolitan Police Department (LVMPD) and focused on the technological, political, and administrative challenges that the implementation of a BWC program pose for law enforcement agencies and their administrators, rank-and-file officers, union officials, as well as for political leaders (Sousa et al., 2016, p. 363). The LVMPD is a force of approximately 2500 sworn officers, of which 1100 are uniformed patrol officers. It was from these 1100 uniformed officers that the researchers would draw a sample of 400 officers for a randomized controlled trial (RCT). The researchers ran into several difficulties in conducting an RCT study while the LVMPD was simultaneously launching its BWC program, and this complicated the results of the study.

Nonetheless, the study serves as a cautionary to other police departments and researchers who might consider such a two-pronged strategy. The research did report on the complexities in maintaining separate control and treatment groups within the same police command, as well as on the technical limitations of BWCs themselves as well as the ancillary charging and storage equipment necessary to maintain the cameras. The LVMPD was also "faced with community pressure to begin implementation, but concerned that union challenges would delay the program, LVMPD made the decision to make BWCs voluntary for current officers" (Sousa et al., 2016, p. 370), another complication for the researchers. This study highlighted the inherent difficulties and challenges not only in implementing a BWC program, but in conducting research on these programs and drawing even tentative conclusions about the efficacy of BWC programs.

A 2017 study conducted in Washington, D.C. involving the District of Columbia Metropolitan Police Department (MPD) caused concern to many observers and advocates for the mandatory use of police body cameras. David Yokum, Anita Ravishankar, and Alexander Coppock conducted a RCT of 2224 MPD officers who were randomly assigned to two groups: one wearing the cameras and the other not equipped with body cameras. The goal of the study was to determine what effect, if any, the use of BWCs would have on the numbers of citizen complaints made against the police. The study found "that BWCs have no effect on police use of force, citizen complaints, policing activity, or judicial outcomes" (Yokum et al., 2017, p. 18). This research suggests that BWCs are not a panacea for issues involving the police use of force and citizen complaints against the police, and that departments considering the implementation of BWC programs should temper their expectations. The D.C. researchers conclude that

law enforcement agencies (particularly in contexts similar to Washington, D.C.) that are considering adopting BWCs should not expect dramatic reductions in use of force or complaints, or other large-scale shifts in police behavior, solely from the deployment of this technology.

(p. 22)

Researchers at Stanford University (Voigt et al., 2017) conducted a study that examined police body-camera footage using computational linguistic techniques from 981 vehicle stops conducted by Oakland, California, police during April 2014, viewing 183 hours of footage and examining 36,738 utterances made by the officers and directed toward the motorists. The study attempted to determine if the officers treated black and white motorists more or less respectfully during the vehicle stops. The Stanford researchers found "strong evidence that utterances spoken to white community members are consistently more respectful, even after controlling for contextual factors such as the severity of the offense or the outcome of the stop" (Voigt et al., 2017, p. 6522), and "that police officers' interactions with blacks tend to be more fraught, not only in terms of disproportionate outcomes (as previous work has shown) but also interpersonally, even when no arrest is made and no use of force occurs" (p. 6524).

Barak Ariel, one of the authors of the 2013 study conducted in Rialto, California, wanted to examine the use of BWCs in a larger department to see if the results would be similar to those reported in Rialto. His 2016 study, published in *The Journal of Criminal Law and Criminology*, examined the use of BWCs in a large urban police department: Denver, Colorado (2016). The Denver study found that

> overall, the comparisons (between treatment groups of officers who wore body cameras and control groups of officers who did not wear the cameras) show no discernable effect of BWCs in Denver on the likelihood of reporting of use of force.
>
> (p. 751)

And, unlike the earlier study conducted in Rialto, California, the Denver study found that the "overall number of complaints (against both misconduct and use of force) increased by 38%—or 1105 at pre-treatment compared to 1524 post-treatment," i.e., after the officers were equipped with BWCs. However, "when looking at the specific subcategory of complaints filed against the police for use of force, we find that the odds of a complaint in control districts was 35% higher compared to the treatment district." The study also found that misconduct complaints against the police who did not wear body cameras increased by 14 percent over complaints of misconduct against police who were equipped with BWCs. Further, as relates to the number of arrests that officers made, the study found that "the odds of an arrest were overall about 18% higher in control conditions (no BWC) compared to treatment area (with BWC)." So, the study found that, while officers equipped with BWCs had fewer complaints of misconduct or excessive force and made fewer arrests, the overall number of complaints against the police once the body-camera program was implemented increased significantly, by 38 percent. This is in direct contrast with the study conducted in Rialto, which saw an overall decrease of 90 percent in the number of complaints filed against the police once the BWC program was implemented (Ariel, 2016, pp. 751–752).

A qualitative component of the Denver study found that officers, when asked about the BWC program, expressed four common reservations and concerns about BWCs: one was the sentiment that "BWCs are perceived as mechanisms of control over officers," and one that would severely restrict their discretion and hamper their ability to perform their duties effectively. Officers also expressed concerns regarding mistrust and that the BWC program was a manifestation of the public's lack of trust in the police. Also, "officers also expressed doubt about how footage would be viewed by the public or line managers," fearing that their actions in the field may be misjudged or misinterpreted (Ariel, 2016, p. 753).

Lily Hay Newman, writing for *Wired* (2018), described the extent to which police body-camera footage can be hacked and altered, compromising "the integrity of that footage so it can be trusted as a record of events." She interviewed Josh Mitchell, a security consultant at Nuix, who tested five of the body cameras most commonly used by law enforcement. Mitchell discovered that four of the five cameras tested had

> vulnerabilities (that) would allow an attacker to download footage off a camera, edit things out or potentially make more intricate modifications, and then re-upload it, leaving no indication of the change. Or an attacker could simply delete footage they don't want law enforcement to have.
>
> (Newman, 2018)

Newman also reported that "the bodycams don't have a cryptographic mechanism to confirm the validity of the video files they record either," an additional security lapse.

BWC footage has been used during criminal trials to establish that the police were being untruthful in testimony before the court. According to *The Boston Globe*, "at least three criminal cases, all involving illegal guns, were dismissed based on body camera footage from the pilot program, which began in September 2016, according to records compiled by the American Civil Liberties Union of Massachusetts" (Valencia, 2018). But the cameras have also been useful in supporting police actions and in resolving disputed claims made by defendants at trial. The police themselves have even been supportive of the use of the cameras and see the value in their recording the interactions that they have with civilians, "particularly after an internal affairs investigation was dismissed due to body camera footage that justified the officer's actions" (Valencia, 2018).

In Baltimore, a BWC showed a police officer fabricating evidence in a drug case. The officer, Richard Pinheiro, was suspended from the Baltimore Police Department and indicted by a grand jury on criminal charges relating to the planted evidence; a man had been arrested on drug charges as a result of the officer planting the drugs in a can that was in an alley. According to *The New York Times*, following the discovery of Pinheiro's doctored camera footage, "two more videos showing questionable activity by a member of the Baltimore Police Department" (Fortin, 2018) surfaced, the state's attorney's office said in a statement: "Together, the three videos led prosecutors to review hundreds of criminal cases. Those that relied heavily on the testimonies of officers under investigation were dropped by the dozens."

Panoptic "Predictive Policing"

The use of actuarial formulas and calculations by the police in an attempt to identify individuals who may be prone to recidivate is not a new undertaking for law enforcement in the United States. Harcourt (2005) raised concerns and objections to law enforcement's use of "the new actuarial paradigm" and suggests three reasons why we should be skeptical of the use of datasets and checklists to administer criminal justice resources in identifying future criminal activities and targeting those suspected of future criminal involvement for law enforcement intervention.

Harcourt's first reason for skepticism in the use of predictive models lies in "the reliance on predictions of future offending may be counterproductive to the primary goal of law enforcement, namely fighting crime" (p. 3). Specifically, those targeted for law enforcement contact may be *"less* responsive" to being singled out by the police and act out in criminogenic ways as a means of objecting to the police targeting them. Second, "it creates a dissymmetry between the distribution of actual offenders and of persons who have contact with the criminal justice system through arrest, conviction, incarceration, or other forms of supervision and punishment," and "this, in turn, compounds the difficulty of many members of targeted groups to obtain employment, pursue educational opportunities, or lead normal family lives" (p. 3).

In other words, this "new actuarial paradigm" creates a class of potential offenders, who are usually members of a particular race or ethnic origin group, and who may have had contact with the criminal justice system, for systematic and targeted re-contact with that same system based on little other than the prior contact itself, and in so doing foreclosing opportunities for the productive participation in society that was ostensibly the goal of the initial involvement with the criminal justice system. Finally, according to Harcourt, such actuarial schemes serve "to dictate the path of justice" through "render(ing) more natural theories of selective incapacitation and sentencing enhancements for citizens who are at greater risk of future dangerousness" (pp. 3–4). In embracing the belief that prediction models and formulas actually work, absent empirical support to sustain these beliefs, the actors in the criminal justice system engage in confirmation bias in selectively targeting and administering enhanced punishments to those whom law enforcement confirm as conforming to the predictive model.

Much has occurred in the years since Harcourt's observations on the "new actuarial paradigm" that has acted as a technological "force multiplier" in the capacity of law enforcement to significantly broaden its panoptic reach. George Joseph, writing in *The Appeal* (2018) reported that the LAPD employs a software program produced by a company called "Palantir" to enhance its predictive policing model in using a "probable offender" formula. Palantir's software programs, which use sophisticated multi-source data analysis and integration tools, are called "Gotham" and "Foundry,"[1] and were initially developed for use by the military, the CIA, and the Department of Homeland Security; they are now widely marketed for use in domestic law enforcement surveillance and intelligence analysis. The "Gotham" program is the platform used by law enforcement.

According to *The Appeal* (Joseph, 2018), a community-based alliance group called the "Stop LAPD Spying Coalition" called the LAPD's "Chronic Offender" program "a 'racist feedback loop' in which police surveil a set number of people based on data that's generated by their own racially biased policing, creating more monitoring and thereby more arrests." The community group says that African Americans are grossly overrepresented in those designated as "probable offenders" using the LAPD/Palantir matrix. These "pre-crime investigations" conducted by LAPD analysts use a point system to establish "their predictive risk scores, which are based on factors, such as whether they are on parole and their number of police contacts in the last two years." *The Appeal* also reported that analysts are assigned a quota of 12 "Chronic Offender Bulletins" as well as five backup bulletins. Those identified in the bulletins are then targeted for police "engagement," which refers to a street stop. The bulletins do not establish reasonable suspicion for a stop by police as is required under *Terry v. Ohio*, and every police officer in the United States is (or should be) well versed in the requirements for a stop to be authorized under *Terry*. In an attempt to do a somewhat clumsy end run around the *Terry* requirement, the LAPD states on its bulletins that the individuals named thereon are "not suspects but persons of interest" and that the purpose of the distribution is "for informational purposes only and for officer safety."

Peter Waldman, Lizette Chapman, and Jordan Robertson (2018), writing for *Bloomberg*, also reported on law enforcement's use of Palantir, "named after the omniscient crystal balls in J. R. R. Tolkien's Lord of the Rings trilogy," and the fact that police and sheriff's departments in Chicago, New York, and New Orleans used the software (in addition to the LAPD), "frequently ensnaring in the digital dragnet people who aren't suspected of committing any crime." According to the article in *Bloomberg*

> people and objects pop up on the Palantir screen inside boxes connected to other boxes by radiating lines labeled with the relationship: "Colleague of," "Lives with," "Operator of [cell number]," "Owner of [vehicle]," "Sibling of," even "Lover of." If the authorities have a picture, the rest is easy. Tapping databases of driver's license and ID photos, law enforcement agencies can now identify more than half the population of U.S. adults.
>
> (Waldman et al., 2018)

Mark Harris, reporting for *Wired* (2017), has also recounted the widespread use of the Palantir technology by domestic law enforcement agencies, including the Cook County Sheriff's Department, the DCMPD, the Virginia State Police, as well as many departments in California, where over 90 percent of Palantir's sales originate. According to *Wired*, Palantir is the likely link between the Cook County Sheriff's Department and Immigration and Customs Enforcement, where information contained in a purported gang database led to the detention of two immigrants who were erroneously included in the database. This led to two federal lawsuits in Chicago. Palantir

> provided an "intelligence management solution" for the Cook County Sheriff's Office to integrate information from at least 14 different databases, including gang lists compiled by state and local police departments, according to county records. Palantir also has a $41 million data mining contract with ICE to build the agency's "investigative case management" system.
>
> (Harris, 2017)

Facial Recognition Technology

According to *The Washington Post*, Amazon has begun providing facial recognition technology to law enforcement agencies in Oregon and Orlando, Florida, at no cost in an effort to achieve an eventual buy-in from the larger law enforcement technology community. The technology, called "Rekognition," utilizes Amazon Web Services and houses data in Amazon's cloud storage system. The ACLU raised concerns regarding Rekognition in a letter to Jeffrey Bezos, Amazon's founder and Chief Executive Officer, stating that

> people should be free to walk down the street without being watched by the government. Facial recognition in American communities threatens this freedom. In overpoliced communities of color, it could effectively eliminate it. The federal government could use this facial recognition technology to continuously track immigrants as they embark on new lives. Local police could use it to identify political protesters captured by officer body cameras.
>
> (American Civil Liberties Union, 2018, May 22)

The Washington Post reported that the use of the technology has raised alarm with privacy and civil liberties advocates, since "facial recognition can allow strangers to identify people who don't wish to be identified, such as shoppers in stores, individuals in a crowd, or people who appear in photos that get posted on social media" (Dwoskin, 2018). According to the article, "the technology works through pattern recognition. Customers put known images … into a database. The more images that are fed into the system, the more accurate the software becomes."

According to *The New York Times*, "domestic law enforcement agencies are increasingly using the technology at home for more routine forms of policing" (Wingfield, 2018), and additionally, the Center on Privacy & Technology at Georgetown Law School reported that "more than 130 million American adults are in facial recognition databases that can be searched in criminal investigations." It would appear that it is not just individuals who have criminal records whose images may be stored in such databases.

According to the ACLU's Crockford,

> One particularly pernicious aspect of face surveillance is that, like stingrays, it is technology completely in the hands of the police. They don't need any external agency or entity to help them facilitate this surveillance. That's part of the reason why the ACLU has called for a moratorium on the use of this technology by police.
>
> (2018)

Conclusion

Given that there are currently over 18,000 state, county, local, tribal, and special jurisdiction law enforcement agencies operating in the United States and given that half of these agencies employ fewer than ten police officers (only 7 percent of police agencies employ more than 100 officers), there is ample cause for concern in the ubiquity of highly advanced technologies in the hands of local law enforcement agencies. Technologies that have been developed for use by the military and federal law enforcement agencies undertaking complex criminal investigations with national and international implications are now widely available and marketed to police departments investigating mundane and routine criminal activities.

That these police agencies could (and often do) use these technologies in ways that run afoul of the Constitution in surveilling and spying on individuals and groups who are not suspected of or associated with criminal activity is alarming. Local police have the capability and the inclination to observe, to collect, to store, to analyze, and to disseminate information on us without our awareness or permission as we travel, work, pray, access medical treatment, communicate, drive, associate with others, and use the internet (among myriad other daily activities). This is done in the interest of "public safety" or justified and rationalized as part of the "War on Terror" or whatever the expediency of the day dictates. As well intentioned as these initiatives may be on the part of law enforcement, we are equally well intentioned in interrogating the propriety, the necessity, and the legality of the widespread adoption of advanced technology by police in the United States.

NOTE

1 For more details, visit: www.palantir.com/products.

REFERENCES

American Civil Liberties Union. (2013). You are being tracked: How license plate readers are being used to record Americans' movements. *ACLU*. Retrieved from: www.aclu.org/issues/privacy-technology/location-tracking/you-are-being-tracked.

American Civil Liberties Union. (2018, February 7). New report: Social media monitoring in Boston targets protected speech. *ACLU Massachusetts*. Retrieved from: www.aclum.org/en/press-releases/new-report-social-media-monitoring-boston-targets-protected-speech.

American Civil Liberties Union. (2018, May 2). New legislation threatens to roll back drone surveillance rules for protestors. *ACLU Illinois*. Retrieved from: www.aclu-il.org/en/press-releases/new-legislation-threatens-roll-back-drone-surveillance-rules-protestors.

American Civil Liberties Union. (2018, May 22). Letter to Jeffrey P. Bezos, Founder and Chief Executive Officer, Amazon.com, Inc., Seattle, WA. *ACLU Northern California*. Retrieved from: www.aclunc.org/docs/20180522_AR_Coalition_Letter.pdf.

American Civil Liberties Union. (2018, June). A model act for regulating the use of wearable body cameras by law enforcement. *ACLU*. Retrieved from: www.aclu.org/other/model-act-regulating-use-wearable-body-cameras-law-enforcement.

Ariel, B. (2016). Police body cameras in large police departments. *Journal of Criminal Law & Criminology*, 106 (4), pp. 729–768.

Ariel, B., Farrar, W., & Sutherland, A. (2015). The effect of police body-worn cameras on use of force and citizens' complaints against the police: A randomized controlled trial. *Journal of Quantitative Criminology*, 31 (3), p. 509.

Cagle, M. (2016, October 11). Facebook, Instagram, and Twitter provided data access for a surveillance product marketed to target activists of color. *ACLU Northern California*. Retrieved from: www.aclunc.org/blog/facebook-instagram-and-twitter-provided-data-access-surveillance-product-marketed-target.

Carpenter v. United States, 585 U.S. ___, 2018.

Crockford, K. (2017, September 27). Boston police bought three drones but didn't tell anyone. We need accountability for surveillance now. *ACLU*. Retrieved from: www.aclu.org/blog/privacy-technology/surveillance-technologies/boston-police-bought-three-drones-didnt-tell.

Crockford, K. (2018, September 6). Personal communication.

Dryer, R. L., & Stroud, S. S. (2015). Automatic license plate readers: An effective law enforcement tool or big brother's latest instrument of mass surveillance? *Jurimetrics: The Journal of Law, Science & Technology*, 55 (2), pp. 225–274.

Dwoskin, E. (2018, May 22). Amazon is selling facial recognition to law enforcement—For a fistful of dollars. *The Washington Post*. Retrieved from: www.washingtonpost.com/news/the-switch/wp/2018/05/22/amazon-is-selling-facial-recognition-to-law-enforcement-for-a-fistful-of-dollars/?utm_term=.015b5fb447b9.

Electronic Frontier Foundation. (2018a). Street-level surveillance: Automated license plate readers (ALPRs). *EFF*. Retrieved from: www.eff.org/pages/automated-license-plate-readers-alpr.

Electronic Frontier Foundation. (2018b). Surveillance drones. *EFF*. Retrieved from: www.eff.org/issues/surveillance-drones.

Fortin, J. (2018, January 24). Baltimore police officer charged with fabricating evidence in drug case. *The New York Times*. Retrieved from: www.nytimes.com/2018/01/24/us/baltimore-officer-video-drugs.html.

Friedersdorf, C. (2018, February 16). How two police drones saved a woman's life. *The Atlantic*. www.theatlantic.com/politics/archive/2018/02/police-drones/553406/.

Geofeedia.com. (2015, October 20). Who is your biggest competitor? Why Geofeedia over them? (Unknown author, private communication). *ACLU Northern California*. Retrieved from: www.aclunc.org/docs/20161011_geofeedia_twitter_instagram_riverside_pd.pdf.

Harcourt, B. (2005) Against prediction: Sentencing, policing, and punishing in an actuarial age. *University of Chicago Public Law & Legal Theory Working Paper*, 94.

Harris, M. (2017, August 9). How Peter Thiel's secretive data company pushed into policing. *Wired*. Retrieved from: www.wired.com/story/how-peter-thiels-secretive-data-company-pushed-into-policing/.

Joseph, G. (2017, February 8). Cellphone spy tools have flooded local police departments. *Citylab*. Retrieved from: www.citylab.com/equity/2017/02/cellphone-spy-tools-have-flooded-local-police-departments/512543/.

Joseph, G. (2018). The LAPD has a new surveillance formula, powered by Palantir. *The Appeal*. Retrieved from: https://theappeal.org/the-lapd-has-a-new-surveillance-formula-powered-by-palantir-1e277a95762a/.

Leetaru, K. (2016, October 12). Geofeedia is just the tip of the iceberg: The era of social surveillance. *Forbes*. Retrieved from: www.forbes.com/sites/kalevleetaru/2016/10/12/geofeedia-is-just-the-tip-of-the-iceberg-the-era-of-social-surveillence/#4b284b5f5b90.

Lukitsch, B. (2018, May 2). Illinois Senate approves plan that would allow police to monitor large crowds with drones. *Chicago Tribune*. Retrieved from: http://cc.bingj.com/cache.aspx?q=illinois+senate+approves+plan+that+would+allow+police+to+monitor+large+crowds+with+drones&d=4585377615840651&mkt=en-GB&setlang=en-US&w=COHjiSLNQGEIMD9BtjXZQMb4s1mh1ZOw.

Marlow, C., & Stanley, J. (2017). We're updating our police body camera recommendations for even better accountability and civil liberties protections. *ACLU*. Retrieved from: www.aclu.org/blog/privacy-technology/surveillance-technologies/were-updating-our-police-body-camera.

Maryland v. Andrews, Court of Special Appeals of Maryland, No. 1496, September Term, 2015, Decided: March 30, 2016.

Murat Ozer, M. (2016). Automatic license plate reader (ALPR) technology. *Police Journal*, 89 (2), pp. 117–132.

Musgrave, S. (2018, May 6). Boston police resume using license plate readers after accidental release of data. *The Boston Globe*. Retrieved from: www.bostonglobe.com/metro/2018/05/06/boston-police-resume-using-license-plate-readers-after-accidental-release-data/gZrC8ozxad9GxcymIxtLfO/story.html.

Newman, L. H. (2018, August 11). Police body cameras can be hacked to doctor footage. *Wired*. Retrieved from: www.wired.com/story/police-body-camera-vulnerabilities/?mbid=social_twitter_onsiteshare.

Niedringhaus, C. (2018, January 20). Fort Collins police using drones in crash investigations. *The Denver Post*. Retrieved from: www.denverpost.com/2018/01/20/fort-collins-police-drones-crash-investigations/.

Police Executive Research Forum. (2014). *Implementing a Body-Worn Camera Program: Recommendations and Lessons Learned*. Retrieved from: www.justice.gov/iso/opa/resources/472014912134715246869.pdf.

Prince Jones, Appellant, v. United States, Appellee. No. 15-CF-322, Decided: September 21, 2017.

Raz, N. (2017, December 27). Las Vegas police drones will monitor New Year's Eve crowds. *Las Vegas Review-Journal*. Retrieved from: www.reviewjournal.com/entertainment/new-years-eve-in-vegas/las-vegas-police-drones-will-monitor-new-years-eve-crowds/.

Riley v. California, 134 S. Ct. 2473—Supreme Court, 2014.

Rock, A. (2018, March 12). Social media monitoring: Beneficial or big brother? *Campus Safety*. Retrieved from: www.campussafetymagazine.com/university/social-media-monitoring/.

Scahill, J., & Williams, M. (2015, December 17). Stingrays: A secret catalogue of government gear for spying on your cellphone. *The Intercept*. Retrieved from: https://theintercept.com/2015/12/17/a-secret-catalogue-of-government-gear-for-spying-on-your-cellphone/.

Shueh, J. (2018, January 19). New York's first police drone program takes flight. *Statescoop*. Retrieved from: https://statescoop.com/new-york-deploys-first-drone-program-for-state-police.

Sousa, W. H., Coldren, J. J., Rodriquez, D., & Braga, A. A. (2016). Research on body worn cameras: Meeting the challenges of police operations, program implementation, and randomized controlled trial designs. *Police Quarterly*, 3, pp. 363–384.

Talai, A. (2014). Drones and Jones: The Fourth Amendment and police discretion in the digital age. *California Law Review*, 102 (3), pp. 728–780.

Terry v. Ohio, 392 U.S. 1, 1968.

The Intercept (2015, December 17). Government cellphone surveillance catalogue. Retrieved from: https://theintercept.com/document/2015/12/17/government-cellphone-surveillance-catalogue/.

United States v. Wurie, 728 F.3d 1, United States Court of Appeals, First Circuit, 2013.

United States Department of Justice, & Federal Bureau of Investigation. (2013, April 5). *Acquisition of Wireless Collection Equipment/Technology and Non-Disclosure Obligations*. Retrieved from: https://assets.documentcloud.org/documents/2516046/boston-pd-fbi-nda-5apr2013.pdf.

Valencia, M. (2018, March 26). As body camera footage gets used in court, both sides agree on its usefulness. *The Boston Globe*. Retrieved from: www.bostonglobe.com/metro/2018/03/26/body-camera-footage-gets-used-court-both-sides-agree-its-usefulness/JlDHoT4TdASK9Bt74QWqHP/story.html.

Voigt, R., Camp, N., Prabhakaran, V., Hamilton, W., Hetey, R., Griffiths, C., Jurgens, D., Jurafsky, D., & Eberhardt, J. (2017). Language from police body camera footage shows racial disparities in officer respect. *Proceedings of the National Academy of Sciences*. Retrieved from: www.pnas.org/content/pnas/114/25/6521.full.pdf.

Volokh, E. (2017, August 31). L.A. police must release automated license plate reader data, though in anonymized form. *The Washington Post*. Retrieved from: www.washingtonpost.com/news/volokh-conspiracy/wp/2017/08/31/l-a-police-must-release-automated-license-plate-reader-data-though-in-anonymized-form/?utm_term=.1b3f658c7a23.

Waldman, P., Chapman, L., & Robertson, J. (2018, April 19). Palantir knows everything about you. *Bloomberg*. Retrieved from: www.bloomberg.com/features/2018-palantir-peter-thiel/.

Weiss, R. (2018, March 16). University police surveil student social media in attempt to make campus safer. *FIRE*. Retrieved from: www.thefire.org/university-police-surveil-student-social-media-in-attempt-to-make-campus-safer/.

Wingfield, N. (2018, May 22). Amazon pushes facial recognition to police. Critics see surveillance risk. *The New York Times*. Retrieved from: www.nytimes.com/2018/05/22/technology/amazon-facial-recognition.html.

Yokum, D., Ravishankar, A., & Coppock, A. (2017). Evaluating the effects of police body-worn cameras: a randomized controlled trial. *The Lab @ DC, Working Paper*. Retrieved from: https://bwc.thelab.dc.gov/TheLabDC_MPD_BWC_Working_Paper_10.20.17.pdf.

Chapter 3

Deadly Force

Compliance, Confrontation, and Consequences for African Americans

---

Police Deadly Force Incidents

How many people are killed by police in the United States in a given year? How many are African American? Native American? Hispanic? Women? Children? The answer is plainly: We don't know. While we certainly know how many police officers are killed in the line of duty in every year going back to at least the 1960s, both feloniously and by accident, there exist no repositories of such information relating to the number and circumstances of deadly force incidents involving civilians killed by the police. The Federal Bureau of Investigation (FBI), through the Bureau of Justice Statistics, keeps meticulous records of police officer deaths but has not been successful in maintaining a similar database of those whose encounters with the police turn deadly, despite federal legislation established specifically to collect such information.

In 2013 the 113th Congress passed the "Death in Custody Reporting Act" (DCRA), "to *encourage* States to report to the Attorney General certain information regarding the deaths of individuals in the custody of law enforcement agencies, and for other purposes" (author italics). According to *The Guardian* however, "only 224 of 18,000 law enforcement agencies reported fatal shootings in 2014" (Swaine & Laughland, 2015), largely owing to the reporting being, for the large part, voluntary. For example, the widely publicized deaths of Tamir Rice and Eric Garner were not reported to the FBI. The DCRA contains a provision whereby the Attorney General *may* withhold up to 10 percent of federal grant funding for states that fail to report "in custody" deaths. Since the vast majority of the over 18,000 law enforcement agencies in the United States are local and county agencies, the possible withholding of a small fraction of federal grant monies to states will have little financial incentive for local and county police agencies to volunteer to report deaths of civilians that occur at the hands of their officers. Further, the term "in custody" is, whether intended or not, vague enough to potentially eliminate for the reporting request many of the individuals who are killed by police. The 12-year-old Tamir Rice was not "in custody" when a Cleveland police officer shot him dead, nor was

Michael Brown, Philando Castile, or Samuel DuBose. And as far as can be determined as of this writing, no federal grant funds have been withheld from any law enforcement agency for a failure to comply with House of Representatives 1147 of 2013 (H.R. 1447), the "Death in Custody Reporting Act."

Perhaps ironically, the most reliable and authoritative data sets regarding deadly force incidents involving the police in the United States are maintained by two news media organizations. *The Washington Post* maintains a "Fatal Force" database and keeps a running tally of deadly force incidents involving police (*The Washington Post*, 2018). *The Guardian* maintains a similar running tally of those killed by police called "The Counted" (*The Guardian*, 2016). In the several years that these news organizations have been tracking police killings of civilians, an average of over 1000 people have been reported to have been killed by police nationally. For example, in 2016, according to *The Guardian*, 1093 people were killed by police in the United States: 62 were female (24 of whom were unarmed); 1031 were male (146 of whom were unarmed); 253 were black; 181 were Hispanic or Latino; 532 were white; 19 were Native American; and 24 were Asian or Pacific Islander.

According to *The Washington Post* "Fatal Force" database, there were 978 people fatally shot by police in 2017. Of those killed, 457 were white, 223 were black, and 179 were Hispanic. Males accounted for 940 of the deaths and females 45 (two were not identified by gender). Of those shot and killed by the police, 579 had a firearm, 156 had a knife, 68 were unarmed, and 26 had a toy weapon. As of this writing in summer 2018, 679 people have been shot and killed by police: 261 were white, 121 were black, and 94 were Hispanic. Of those killed by police, 644 were male and 32 female (three were "unknown"). *The Washington Post* also reported that "there have been 25 more fatal shootings this year (2018) than at the same time last year" (*The Washington Post*, 2018).

My first exposure to the very real potential for danger and terror inherent in interactions between the police and young black men (and boys) in July of 1980 when a 14-year-old African American boy, Levi Hart, was shot and killed by Boston police officer Richard Bourque. I had been a Boston police officer for a little over two years when Bourque scuffled with Hart following the pursuit of a stolen car that Hart was allegedly riding in with two others. According to the police version of the event, Hart had attempted to grab Officer Bourque's gun during the scuffle and Bourque, fearing for his life, shot and killed Hart. Witness accounts differed sharply from the police version of the incident, and a number of people who saw the confrontation came forward to report that there was no scuffle and that Bourque struck Hart on the head with the butt of his firearm before shooting him. In the days before DNA analysis, investigators were able to determine that hair matching Hart's had been found on the handle of Bourque's weapon. An autopsy also revealed the Hart had suffered a fractured skull in addition to the fatal gunshot wound.

A judicial inquest was held in the weeks following Hart's death and the judge, Richard L. Banks, a highly respected African American jurist, found "ample cause to believe that the death of Levi Hart was the result of an unlawful act or acts on the part of Richard W. Bourque [the police officer] and that further judicial inquiry is warranted" (Overbea, 1980). Nonetheless the grand jury hearing evidence in the case failed to return an indictment and Bourque was never charged criminally in the death of the 14-year-old. Protesters took to the streets of Boston that summer and there was grave concern that the demonstrations would turn violent. Bourque and his family were provided 24-hour police protection out of fear for their safety.

As a young police officer (I was not yet 25), I was being socialized into the police world view, one that is never critical of the actions of a fellow officer, one that never passes judgment ("You weren't there"). I never wavered in my belief that Bourque had to be justified in his use of deadly force; surely Hart had attacked Bourque and tried to steal his weapon in order to kill him and Bourque's response was entirely appropriate, expected. We police never questioned the skull fracture, the eyewitness accounts that sharply differed from the police rendition of the incident, or why the 14-year-old Hart, who was 5'8" and weighed 125 pounds, would physically confront and engage Bourque, who was 6'1" and weighed 210 pounds (Levinson, 2015). Bourque never worked the streets again as a police officer; he was assigned to headquarters and worked as a dispatcher. Officer Bourque died in 1992 of a heart attack suffered while he was dispatching—he was 41 years old.

African American Victims of Police Violence

At the time I had no realization that I was witnessing the continuation of a troubling trend in police excessive force and violence being directed at African American men, women, boys, and girls, a disturbing and frightfully lethal history that unfortunately continues to the present. The practice persists; the recounting of events is ongoing, showing no signs of abating.

Contemporary reports of eerily similar deadly confrontations between the police and African Americans have a hauntingly familiar refrain. On July 5, 2016, Alton Sterling, a 37-year-old African American man known for selling CDs outside of a convenience store, was shot and killed by police in Baton Rouge, Louisiana (Fausset et al., 2016). The following day, on July 6, a police officer in Falcon Heights, Minnesota, shot and killed Philando Castile, a 32-year-old African American motorist who had been stopped by police while driving with his girlfriend and her four-year-old daughter (Smith, 2017). In the aftermath of these shootings on July 7, a gunman in Dallas, Texas, Micah Johnson, shot and killed five Dallas police officers and wounded nine others (Fausset et al., 2016). Ten days later, a gunman in Baton Rouge, Louisiana, Gavin Long, opened fire on Baton Rouge police officers, killing three officers and wounding three others (Swaine, 2016). Many law enforcement officers decried a so-called "war on cops." Calls for the escalation of the militarization of the police re-emerged in the public discourse.

Earlier events that began in 2014 in Ferguson, Missouri; Staten Island, New York; North Charleston, South Carolina; Baltimore, Maryland; Washington, DC, Cleveland and Cincinnati, Ohio; Chicago, Illinois; Waller County, Texas; and Sacramento, California have brought the lethal disconnect between domestic law enforcement practitioners and the communities that they police into a worrisome and troubling focus. That grand juries hearing evidence in both Staten Island (Goodman and Baker, 2014), and St. Louis County (United States Department of Justice, 2015), have failed to bring indictments against police officers who killed unarmed African American men, Eric Garner and Michael Brown—both black men initially confronted by police officers after being suspected of minor misconduct—is cause for grave concern regarding the ability of our criminal justice system to ensure equal protection under the law as well as compliance with the provisions of the Constitution that guarantee civil rights and civil liberties to all. Grand juries that fail to return indictments against police accused of wrongdoing, which too often results in the deaths of men, women, and children of color as a matter of common practice, conveys unspoken yet unequivocal support for police practices that are routinely violative of the First, Fourth, and Fourteenth Amendments to the Constitution.

In December of 2015 a grand jury declined to return an indictment against a white Cleveland police officer, Timothy Loehmann, who had shot and killed Tamir Rice, a 12-year-old boy who had been playing with a toy gun in a neighborhood playground (Williams & Smith, 2015). Also, in December 2015, a grand jury in Waller County Texas failed to return any indictments in the death of Sandra Bland, a 28-year-old African American woman who died under questionable circumstances while in police custody. Bland had been stopped by a Texas state trooper, Brian Encinia, for a lane change violation and was subsequently arrested by Encinia when she refused to extinguish her cigarette (Smith, 2015).

And further, we have seen instances where police officers have actually been indicted or charged criminally in the deaths of African American men, women, and children only to see acquittal at trial, or extremely rarely, a plea to reduced charges. In May 2017, Betty Shelby, a white Tulsa, Oklahoma, police officer was found not guilty in the shooting death of an unarmed African American man, Terrence Crutcher (Krehbiel-Burton, 2017).[1] In June of 2017, Officer Jeronimo Yanez was found not guilty by a jury in Minnesota in the shooting death of Philando Castile, despite damning video and audio evidence from both the officer's dashboard mounted camera as well as recordings made in real time by Castile's fiancé from within the vehicle when Castile was shot (Smith, 2017, June 16).

On July 19, 2015, Samuel DuBose, a 43-year-old African American resident of Cincinnati, Ohio, was shot to death by white University of Cincinnati police officer Ray Tensing. Tensing initially reported that DuBose had dragged him with his car and that he feared for his life before shooting him in the head. That version of the events leading to the death of DuBose at the hands of then-officer Tensing would no doubt have been believed without question, and the usual "investigation" would have followed to substantiate Tensing's narrative—until video obtained from Tensing's own body camera showed Tensing shooting DuBose in the head without provocation or any apparent precipitating actions on the part of Mr. DuBose. According to CNN, "after two mistrials for Ray Tensing, the prosecutor in the case said Tuesday (July 18, 2017) he is moving to dismiss the murder indictment against the University of Cincinnati police officer" (McLaughlin, 2017). In 2018, Tensing received a settlement from the University of Cincinnati worth almost $350,000.00 after having been fired by the university police department; as part of the settlement, he agreed to resign from the department (Murphy & Curnutte, 2018).

In October of 2014 Chicago police officer Jason Van Dyke shot and killed 17-year-old Laquan McDonald after a confrontation following a report that McDonald had a knife and was breaking into cars. Van Dyke fired 16 rounds at McDonald from a distance of at least ten feet and nine of the shots fired by Van Dyke struck McDonald in the back. The initial police reports from at least five officers in addition to Van Dyke followed a familiar pattern in describing McDonald lunging at officers and attempting to stab them repeatedly with the knife in an "aggressive, exaggerated manner." Officers additionally made the preposterous and incredible claim in their reports "that even after McDonald had been shot by Van Dyke, the teen tried to lift himself off the ground with the knife pointed toward the officers, and though he had been mortally wounded, still presented a threat" (Laquan McDonald police reports, 2015).

Inexplicably, the Chicago Police Department (CPD) refused to release the police reports and the result of their investigation until December of 2015, 14 months after McDonald's death at the hands of Officer Van Dyke. (In December 2014 the CPD had ruled the shooting a "justifiable homicide"). With the 2015 release of investigatory documents, officials also released a dash cam video of the shooting incident that showed McDonald trying to get away from the officers and being shot repeatedly by Van Dyke while making what appeared to be a half-hearted attempt to elude the officers. The video also shows Van Dyke standing over the teenager after having shot him repeatedly and continuing to fire rounds into McDonald's obviously lifeless body. However, an animated re-enactment of the shooting—from Van Dyke's viewpoint and angle—presented by defense attorneys during Van Dyke's trial, purports to show a very different picture. The knife that McDonald had been carrying lay next to him in death; it contained a three-inch blade. The public outcry and condemnation were swift and strident. Protestors took to the streets of Chicago and elsewhere, demanding that action be taken against Officer Van Dyke and his colleagues who had obviously lied in their rendition of events in an attempt to cover up the questionable circumstances that led to the death of yet another African American teenage boy at the hands of police.

Following the release of the investigatory reports and the video, Van Dyke was indicted on multiple charges, including first-degree murder in the death of McDonald. The trial is scheduled to begin in September 2018. Then-Illinois Attorney General Lisa Madigan requested that the Department of Justice (DOJ) initiate an investigation into the shooting death as well as into wider issues implicated in practices and policies of the CPD (Madigan, 2015).

On January 13, 2017, the DOJ released the results of its investigation into the CPD (United States Department of Justice, 2017). The report "found reasonable cause to believe that CPD has engaged in a pattern or practice of unreasonable force in violation of the Fourth Amendment," and that "officers use unnecessary and unreasonable force in violation of the Constitution with frequency, and that unconstitutional force has been historically tolerated by CPD" (United States Department of Justice, 2017, pp. 22–24). The DOJ also reported that the CPD's use of deadly force as well as less-lethal force was consistently violative of both the Fourth Amendment and CPD policy; that video evidence examined indicated "a broader pattern or practice of unconstitutional force, and that internal investigative processes and disciplinary procedures did little to discourage or impede the use of unnecessary and unconstitutional force."

The DOJ also found that the CPD had a longstanding practice of engaging in unnecessary foot pursuits without any basis for believing that the person running from police had actually committed a crime and that these foot pursuits, often for no other reason than the person ran when he or she saw police, frequently triggered gunfire from CPD officers that too often proved fatal for the person running from police. CPD officers also had a practice of dangerously shooting at moving vehicles, again often with fatal results. Further, the DOJ investigation revealed that

> CPD's pattern or practice of unreasonable force and systemic deficiencies falls heaviest on the predominantly black and Latino neighborhoods on the South and West Sides of Chicago, which are also experiencing higher crime. The impact of these widespread

constitutional violations, combined with unaddressed abusive and racially discriminatory conduct, have undermined the legitimacy of CPD and police-community trust in these communities.

(United States Department of Justice, 2017, p. 144)

On October 3, 2013, federal law enforcement officers in Washington, D.C. fatally shot a 34-year-old African American woman after she led officers on a vehicular pursuit through streets near the U.S. Capitol and the White House. The woman, Miriam Carey, a dental hygienist with a history of mental illness, was traveling with her young daughter in the back seat of the vehicle when police opened fire on the vehicle. An autopsy report following Ms. Carey's death found no traces of drugs or alcohol in her blood and that she had been shot five times—from behind (Almasy, 2014). Police departments nationwide generally discourage the discharge of firearms at moving vehicles and many departments prohibit such discharges as a matter of policy. No criminal charges were filed against the officers who fatally wounded Ms. Carey, and the DOJ investigation concluded that the officers involved in the shooting death of Ms. Carey were justified in their use of deadly force (United States Attorney's Office, 2014). Nonetheless, questions regarding the necessity and justification for the use of deadly force in this instance remain for many experts.

Consider the February 16, 2014, shooting death of an unarmed 47-year-old African American woman, Yvette Smith, by police in Bastrop County, Texas. Smith had called police and was apparently acting as a peacemaker between two men who had been involved in an altercation that had involved a gun. Published reports on the killing of Ms. Smith indicated that she was shot within three seconds of opening her door for police and that the police deputy who shot Ms. Smith "was using his personal AR-15 semi-automatic rifle" (Dart, 2016). The officer, Daniel Willis, was found not guilty of criminal charges stemming from the shooting death of Ms. Smith. Following the death of Ms. Smith, the sheriff's department in Bastrop County issued a press release wrongly claiming that

after the subjects disregarded all commands to come out, a woman came to the doorway of the residence displaying a firearm. The woman disregarded the deputy's commands, which resulted in shots being fired by the Bastrop County Deputy and the woman being shot.

(Dart, 2016)

This was an obvious attempt to cover up a deadly force incident involving a white police officer killing an unarmed African American woman; no firearm was ever discovered and the officer, who had been with the department for less than a year, was subsequently fired. The deception and the lying on the part of the sheriff's department in Bastrop County would prove to be a formulaic response on the part of law enforcement agencies nationwide when faced with deadly force incidents involving African American men and women as well as boys and girls that occur under questionable circumstances and without justification.

On November 20, 2014, a 28-year-old African American man, Akai Gurley, was shot and killed by New York City police officer Peter Liang in the stairwell of a Brooklyn housing project. Liang, who had only recently graduated from the police academy, and his partner were patrolling the building's stairwell when Liang's weapon accidently discharged, striking and killing Gurley, who was walking in the stairwell with his girlfriend. In February 2016 Liang was convicted of second-degree manslaughter and official misconduct in a jury trial in the State Supreme Court in Brooklyn (Nir, 2016). Liang was sentenced to five years' probation and 800 hours of community service following the verdict (Pearce & Hansen, 2016). He was subsequently fired from the police department.

Gurley's death followed the July 17, 2014, death of Eric Garner, also at the hands of New York City police officers. Garner, a 43-year-old African American man, was approached by plainclothes police officers on Bay Street in Staten Island, who suspected him of selling untaxed, loose cigarettes ("loosies"), and when confronted by officers told them to back off and to leave him alone. The officers, Daniel Pantaleo and Justin Damico, decided to take Mr. Garner, who stood 6' 2" tall and weighed 395 pounds, into custody and wrestled him to the ground. In so doing, one of the officers applied a so-called "choke hold" to Garner's neck, cutting off his ability to breathe. Mr. Garner pleaded with the officers, repeatedly telling them "I can't breathe." Those words would prove to be Mr. Garner's last, as Garner died following the application of the choke hold and accompanying chest compression (Baker et al., 2015). Garner, who was morbidly obese with a history of serious medical conditions, died of a cardiac arrest 15–25 minutes after use of the chokehold while in transport by an ambulance. A grand jury failed to indict the police officers who had applied the choke hold to Mr. Garner that preceded his death, setting off widespread protests by Black Lives Matter and other social activist groups. The use of so-called "choke holds" by police officers is prohibited by the New York City Police Department.

On August 9, 2014, Michael Brown, an 18-year-old African American man, was shot and killed by a white police officer, Darren Wilson, in Ferguson, Missouri. Brown, an unarmed teenager, had crossed the street in front of Wilson in a "manner of walking" offense that violated one of the many ordinances that the city of Ferguson had established for the sole purpose of generating revenue from the fines and fees levied against violators, mostly the city's African American residents. Wilson alleged that Brown had grabbed for the officer's firearm when confronted and he shot and killed Brown "in fear for his life."

The shooting death of Brown triggered a wave of protests that lasted for several months and brought worldwide attention to the startling level of tension and animosity between law enforcement agencies in the United States and communities of color. It also brought the glare of the public spotlight onto the militarization of America's police: Police in Ferguson used tear gas, sound cannons, rubber and wooden bullets, military vehicles, weapons, aircraft, and ordnance in confronting the largely peaceful protesters, all while dressed in military "Battle Dress Uniforms," as if soldiers on the field of battle. The protesters, who never numbered more than a couple of hundred, were met by a police and military response (the National Guard was activated), that numbered in the thousands (Buchanan et al., 2015).

A grand jury empanelled in St. Louis County to hear evidence in the case of Brown's death returned a "no bill," meaning that no criminal culpability was found in then-officer Wilson's role in the death of Michael Brown. Wilson subsequently resigned from the Ferguson Police Department. The District Attorney who presented the evidence to the grand jury, Robert McCulloch, was defeated in his re-election bid in 2018.

In Los Angeles, two days after the death of Michael Brown, police shot and killed 25-year-old Ezell Ford on August 11. Ford, an unarmed African American man, had a history of mental illness, and allegedly grabbed for an officer's weapon when confronted by police on a sidewalk in Florence. According to the Los Angeles Police Department, two veteran gang-unit officers "were conducting an investigative stop," and "that Ford whirled around and basically attacked the lead officer" (Mather et al., 2014). According to Ford's mother, the younger Ford had long struggled with "depression, bipolar disorder, and schizophrenia," and this was well known to police and residents in Florence.

In June 2015 "the Los Angeles Police Commission went against the recommendations of Los Angeles police officials, finding that one of the two officers who shot 25-year-old Ezell Earl Ford in 2014 was unjustified in drawing and firing his weapon" (*Los Angeles Times* staff, 2015). Nonetheless, the officers, Sharlton Wempler and Antonio Villegas, faced no criminal charges in the shooting death of Ford.

On February 3, 2015, Natasha McKenna, a 37-year-old African American woman who had long struggled with mental health issues,[2] died at the hands of sheriff's deputies in the Fairfax County, Virginia, jail. McKenna had resisted officers' attempts to restrain her while being transported to another facility, and a six-man "special emergency response team" wrestled Ms. McKenna to the ground and shot her four times with an electronic control device in an attempt to subdue her. After being moved to a holding cell following the administration of the electric shocks, Ms. McKenna was found unresponsive and subsequently died on February 8. Her death was ruled "an accident linked to the use of the stun gun and being restrained" and attributed to a controversial condition called "excited delirium" (Jouvenal, 2016). During the 19-minute encounter with the deputies, Ms. McKenna can be heard saying: "You promised you wouldn't kill me. I didn't do anything" (Jouvenal, 2015). No criminal charges were filed against any of the sheriff's deputies who were involved in the altercation that led to Natasha McKenna's death.

On April 4, 2015, Walter Scott, an unarmed 50-year-old African American man, attacked North Charleston, South Carolina, police officer Michael Slager and attempted to steal the officer's Taser weapon, causing the officer to fear for his life and necessitating officer Slager to fire eight times at Scott, killing him (at least according to the initial police reporting of the incident). That all too familiar narrative was accepted as factual and truthful, at least until the video surfaced—the video showing officer Slager shooting Scott in the back as he ran away from the officer, and then planting the Taser weapon on Scott's lifeless body. Scott had been stopped in his vehicle by Slager for driving with a broken taillight. Slager had faced a retrial on first degree murder charges of Scott's death in a South Carolina court after a first trial ended in a mistrial, but in May 2017, the former North Charleston, South Carolina, police officer pled guilty to reduced federal charges relating to civil rights violations in the shooting death of Scott and is serving a 20-year prison sentence (Blinder, 2017). He would not be retried in state court.

On April 12, 2015, a 25-year-old Baltimore man, Freddie Gray, was arrested and charged with weapons-related offenses after Baltimore police officers on bicycles observed Gray eyeing them "suspiciously." While being taken to the police station in a prisoner transport van Gray sustained injuries to his spinal cord that proved fatal—he died on April 19. Following Gray's death, widespread protests occurred in Baltimore as thousands of Black Lives Matter and other activists and community residents took to the streets. Six police officers were suspended and subsequently charged with crimes related to Gray's death, including murder and manslaughter. All of the officers were subsequently cleared of the criminal charges, and federal prosecutors declined to charge the officers with crimes under federal law (Ruiz, 2017). All six of the officers charged have since returned to duty with the Baltimore Police Department, although several had been charged with administrative rule and policy violations by the department.

On May 5, 2015, police in Los Angeles shot and killed an unarmed 29-year-old African American man, Brendon Glenn. Investigators found that Officer Clifford Proctor, who is also African American, shot Glenn, a homeless man, twice in the back as he lay on the ground trying to drag himself into an upward position. In a notable departure from past practice, the LAPD Police Chief, Charlie Beck, recommended that criminal charges be filed against Proctor and that he be prosecuted in Glenn's death (Mather, 2016). Proctor had reported, falsely, that he had seen Glenn trying to reach for his and his partner's gun and fired in response to Glenn's trying to arm himself. Video surveillance footage obtained from a nearby video camera showed Glenn nowhere near the officers' weapons, and it was reported that "Proctor's partner told investigators he did not know why the officer opened fire."

As noted earlier, Sandra Bland, a 28-year-old African American woman, was found hanging in a jail cell in Waller County, Texas, on July 13, 2015. Ms. Bland had been taken to the jail on July 10, following her arrest by Texas state trooper Brian Encinia after a traffic stop. The reasons for the arrest remain unclear, but dashboard camera video taken from Encinia's police vehicle clearly show Encinia initiating an altercation with Ms. Bland after she questioned his order to extinguish her cigarette. Ms. Bland's death was officially ruled a suicide, but Bland's family members and friends have long been skeptical of this finding.[3]

Bland's death in law enforcement custody was the subject of a lawsuit filed by her family that was settled in 2016 for $1.9 million as well as an agreement for significant procedural and policy changes in the jail in Waller County where Bland died (Hassan et al., 2016). The traffic stop and subsequent arrest of Ms. Bland have also been sharply questioned and criticized as lacking a sufficient legal foundation (Rebecca Lai et al., 2015), and my sense is that Bland was arrested and thrown to the ground on that highway in Waller County for failing to show obsequious deference to then-Trooper Encinia in refusing to put out her cigarette. (Encinia was subsequently fired from the Texas Highway Patrol and indicted on a perjury charge in an unrelated incident.)

Further, on August 8, 2015, police in Arlington, Texas, shot and killed an unarmed 19-year-old man, Christian Taylor, an African American student and football player at Angelo State University. Police had been called to an auto dealership on a report of a possible burglary when they encountered Taylor; according to police a "confrontation" ensued that led officer Brad Miller, a 49-year-old white police officer, to fatally shoot Taylor. Miller was fired as a result of the shooting death, but a grand jury refused to return an indictment that would have led to the criminal prosecution of Miller (McGee & Fernandez, 2015).

On February 25, 2016, a 58-year-olf African American man, a grocer, was shot and killed by a white police officer outside his Montgomery, Alabama home. Gregory Gunn, who had been returning from a late-night card game, was unarmed and lived with his 87-year-old mother:

> According to Montgomery Police Chief Ernest Finley, who is black, the officer thought Gunn looked "suspicious" when he spotted him walking along McElvy Street in Mobile Heights (an historically African American neighborhood in Montgomery) at about 3:20 a.m. Thursday morning.
>
> (Miller, 2016)

The police alleged that Gunn was carrying an object that the officer who killed Gunn, A. C. Smith, an officer with less than four years' experience, believed was a weapon. The object turned out to be something that the police later described as a "retractable painting stick." Days following the shooting death of Gunn, the 23-year-old officer was arrested and charged with murder (Blinder, 2016). He is scheduled to stand trial in August 2018.

In May of 2017 a white police officer in the Balch Springs (Texas) Police Department, Roy D. Oliver II, was arrested and charged with murder in the shooting death of an unarmed African American teenager, Jordan Edwards. Oliver shot the 15-year-old in the head with his rifle as the car in which the teenager was a passenger drove away from a house party that police had been called to. Body cameras worn by the officers showed that the officers' initial recounting of the incident, that the car containing the teenagers had driven toward them, was untruthful and that in fact the teenager had been shot by Officer Oliver as the car was driving away from the scene (Fernandez & Haag, 2017). Oliver was found guilty of murder in a Texas court in August 2018 and was sentenced to 15 years in prison.

On March 18, 2018, police in Sacramento, California shot and killed 22-year-old Stephon Clark, an unarmed African American man, in his grandmother's back yard after responding to a 911 call reporting that someone was breaking car windows. Officers believed that Clark, who was holding his cell phone, was armed when they shot at him 20 times, striking him eight times, including six shots in his back. The police reported that Clark had lunged at them and that they feared for their lives. Of the police reporting of the shooting death of Clark, Tanya Faison, founder of the Sacramento chapter of Black Lives Matter, told *Vox*

> They put one story out that he may have been armed. They put out another that he had a "tool bar," whatever that is. Then they put out that he had a wrench, and then they put out that he just had a cellphone. They need to get it together.

> (Lockhart, 2018)

And the list of women killed by police demands mention: Kendra James, killed by police in Portland, Oregon; Latanya Haggerty in Chicago; Margaret Laverne Mitchell in Los Angeles; Michelle Shirley in Torrance, California; Renee Davis in Auburn, Washington; Korryn Gaines in Randallstown, Maryland; Melissa Venture in Yuma, Arizona; Jessica Williams in San Francisco; Laronda Sweatt in Gallatin, Tennessee; Loreal Tsingine in Winslow, Arizona; Sherissa Homer in Phoenix, Arizona; Sahlah Ridgeway in Syracuse, New York; Jacqueline Salyers in Tacoma, Washington; Janet Wilson in Dearborn, Michigan.

The Police and the Evasion of Criminal Responsibility

So why do law enforcement officers seem so consistently to evade criminal culpability and administrative sanction in the shooting and in-custody deaths of those with whom they come into contact? Why are the police so rarely indicted by grand juries in the deaths that they cause? Why do prosecutors so seldom charge the police with murder, manslaughter, or even criminal negligence? How do the police who kill unarmed African American men and women as well as boys and girls remain employed as police officers (yes, girls—consider the May 16, 2010, shooting death of Aiyana Jones, a seven-year-old African American girl shot and killed in a raid by Detroit police officers) (Crimesider staff, 2015).

The standards of criminal liability to which police officers are held, specifically in use of deadly force incidents, is often misunderstood. While virtually all law enforcement agencies operate under rules, policies, and procedures that govern the use of force generally and deadly force specifically, the standards are ultimately guided and determined by case law. From 1973 through 1989, under *Johnson v. Glick*, "most courts analyzed excessive force claims under a substantive due process standard governed by the Fourteenth Amendment" (O'Connell, 1990, p. 741). Those charged with assessing the justifiability or propriety of a law enforcement officer's use of force would be charged with determining whether the officer conduct in question "shocked the conscience" in applying a four-factor analysis. The finder of fact would determine:

> 1) the need for the officer's application of force, 2) the relationship between the amount of force needed and the amount that was used, 3) the severity of the plaintiff's injuries, and 4) whether force was applied in good faith.
>
> (O'Connell, 1990, p. 742)

Beginning in 1989 however, the U.S. Supreme Court set a new standard for the finder of fact in deciding the justifiability of the use of force by police, one that was less restrictive than the *Glick* standard and more favorable to the law enforcement position in determining the propriety of the use of force. The new standard was set in *Graham v. Connor*. *Graham* did away with the Fourteenth Amendment standard set in *Glick* and replaced it with the Fourth Amendment's "objective reasonableness" standard. Thus, the "objective reasonableness" of an officer's use of force

> should be judged by the perspective of an officer on the scene and should take into account factors such as the severity of the crime, the threat posed by the suspect, and any attempts by the suspect to resist or evade arrest.
>
> (1989, p. 490)

Graham states that reasonable force does not equate with the least amount of force possible. On the contrary, even if it appears later that the level of force applied was excessive:

> [T]he appropriate inquiry is whether the officers acted reasonably, *not whether they had less intrusive alternatives available.* Officers must not avail themselves of the least intrusive means of responding to an exigent situation; they need only act within the range of conduct we identify as reasonable.
>
> (1989, p. 490)

Graham only prohibits unreasonable force considering the *totality of circumstances* confronted by the officer in an exigent situation, as judged by a hypothetical police officer put in a similar situation (and not some other non-police observer).

It is the application of the *Graham* standard that frequently causes consternation, misunderstanding and arguably justifiable outrage when it appears as though police officers are not being held criminally responsible for deaths that occur when they use deadly force in confrontations and encounters where unarmed African American men and women are killed at the hands of white police officers.

The Double Standard and "Loyalty"

Tacit messages conveyed to me during my 27 years as a Boston police officer and lieutenant were these: That the provisions of the Constitution pertaining to freedom of speech, freedom of assembly, freedom of the press, search and seizure, probable cause, due process and equal protection (and other constitutional protections), could be disregarded and dispensed with as obstacles to "street justice." Criminal justice system failures and injustices, such as what is arguably the failure of the grand jury process in both Missouri and New York and elsewhere, do little to counter the widespread perception, held most closely by the police themselves, that law enforcement officers are held to a much different standard of legal culpability than ordinary citizens.

Grand juries are typically populated with people who have had little if any exposure to the vagaries of the experiential world of the police or the police subculture and may glean what understanding they do have from the popular culture and the media. They may believe that the day-to-day experiences of law enforcement officers are fraught with ever-present danger, peril, and violence. That the police themselves do little if anything to dispel this commonly understood yet wholly inaccurate myth may contribute to the emergence of this criminal justice double standard. The double standard exists where an unarmed African American teenager can be shot and killed with impunity by police, or where the police can choke an African American man leading to his death for the crime of selling untaxed cigarettes. Yet how can it be that officers, who are sworn to uphold the law and the Constitution, will not speak out about (or even acknowledge) the institutional and structural discrimination, oppression, and racialized violence that characterize the American criminal justice system?

Consider the following: A bedrock tenet of the police subculture, and one taught to me very early in my career in law enforcement, is that another officer's judgment, particularly as it pertains to his or her use of force, is never to be questioned or second guessed. The use of force is never even to be discussed with those who are not "on the job," i.e., fellow police officers. Police officers will occasionally discuss among themselves what is known as a "bad shoot" in referring to what has all too obviously been a careless, unwarranted, or unjustified use of deadly force, but will unwaveringly, even reflexively, preface any such muted, in-house assessment with the qualifier: "I wasn't there, but…" Thus, it is unheard of for a police officer to provide any type of formal testimony that would call into question the judgment of a fellow officer in deciding the propriety of a use of force incident, especially a deadly force incident that resulted in a serious injury or death. But why won't officers speak out about the many "bad shoots?"[4]

Kleinig refers to this type of "faux" loyalty that the police so steadfastly embrace as the "uneasy virtue" and the "last refuge of scoundrels" (1996, pp. 71–73). Police officers are socialized early in their careers that absolute loyalty to their fellow officers is something that is both expected of them and provided in return, insofar as they can be "trusted" to engage in individual and collective misrepresentation of the truth when called upon to do so. And this is especially paramount in instances where officers use force and the more brutal, excessive, and deadly the force used, the more compelling the need to "get your stories straight."

As an example: Twenty-one Boston police officers falsified reports that they submitted following the January 1995 beating of plainclothes Boston police officer Michael Cox by his fellow officers who mistook him for a fleeing suspect (see Chapter 8). Not one officer suffered any adverse consequences for this "conspiracy of silence." And in the aftermath of the shooting death of Laquan McDonald by then-Chicago police officer Jason Van Dyke, three Chicago police officers were charged criminally with felony conspiracy, official misconduct, and obstruction of justice after they collaborated in the filing of false reports that backed up Van Dyke's false reporting of having been attacked by McDonald, an assertion proven demonstrably untrue by the dash cam video of the encounter. The "uneasy virtue" that these officers embraced will no doubt prove to have serious consequences, possibly including a prison term.

Conclusion

The due process and equal protection clauses of the Fourteenth Amendment to the Constitution are unequivocal in requiring that no state or state actor shall "deprive any person of life, liberty, or property, without due process of law; nor deny to any person within its jurisdiction the equal protection of the law." Yet those engaged in domestic law enforcement operations, particularly in communities of color, too often believe that the "process" that plays out in the streets of our communities supersedes the mandates of the Constitution. The exoneration and vindication that prosecutors and juries unfailingly grant to the police when they kill unarmed African American men confirms this constitutional and criminal justice system duality: The police may occasionally make costly mistakes, but if the cost is the life of a black man at the hands of a white police officer, the cost is one that the criminal justice system is prepared to bear. In the eyes of many, that is exactly what has caused the justice system to become criminal.

NOTES

1   *The Washington Post* reported in August of 2018 that Shelby, who resigned from the Tulsa force following her acquittal, was appointed as a police officer in a neighboring county, and was teaching a course entitled "The Ferguson Effect" that deals how to "survive" an event such as the one in which she shot and killed Crutcher "when a police officer is victimized by anti-police groups and tried in the court of public opinion" (Stanley-Becker, 2018).

2   It should be noted that in a number of the deadly force incidents discussed in this section the decedents had suffered from long-term significant mental health issues that undoubtedly contribute to a consideration of the "totality of circumstances" issue when evaluating the propriety of the use of deadly force.

3   Bland had previously attempted to take her own life and was medicated for a disorder of the nervous system. She self-reported upon her jail intake form that she had considered ending her own life within the past year, and that she was currently feeling very depressed.

4 A "bad shoot" is police subcultural jargon and refers to a questionable shooting that is discussed among police officers themselves and never with outsiders—it is a commonly understood code term for an unjustifiable shooting.

REFERENCES

Almasy, S. (2014, April 10). Woman killed during D.C. chase was shot five times from behind, autopsy shows. *CNN*. Retrieved from: www.cnn.com/2014/04/08/us/miriam-carey-autopsy/index.html.

Baker, A., Goodman, J. D., & Mueller, B. (2015, June 13). Beyond the chokehold: The path to Eric Garner's death. *The New York Times*. Retrieved from: www.nytimes.com/2015/06/14/nyregion/eric-garner-police-chokehold-staten-island.html.

Blinder, A. (2016, March 2). White officer is arrested in killing of black man. *The New York Times*. Retrieved from: www.nytimes.com/2016/03/03/us/white-officer-in-alabama-is-arrested-in-killing-of-black-man.html.

Blinder, A. (2017, May 2). Ex-officer who shot Walter Scott pleads guilty in Charleston. *The New York Times*. Retrieved from: www.nytimes.com/2017/05/02/us/michael-slager-walter-scott-north-charleston-shooting.html.

Buchanan, L., Fessenden, F., Rebecca Lai, K. K., Park, H., Parlapiano, A., Wallace T., Watkins D., & Yourish. K. (2015, August 10). What happened in Ferguson? *The New York Times*. Retrieved from: www.nytimes.com/interactive/2014/08/13/us/ferguson-missouri-town-under-siege-after-police-shooting.html.

Crimesider staff. (2015, January 30). Final charge dropped against Detroit cop in fatal raid. *CBS News*. Retrieved from: www.cbsnews.com/news/aiyana-stanley-jones-case-final-charge-dropped-against-detroit-cop-in-fatal-raid/.

Dart, T. (2016, April 8). Former Texas officer who fatally shot unarmed woman found not guilty. *The Guardian*. Retrieved from: www.theguardian.com/us-news/2016/apr/07/fdaniel-willis-not-guilty-fatal-police-shooting-yvette-smith-texas.

Fatal force. (2018). *The Washington Post*. Retrieved from: www.washingtonpost.com/graphics/national/police-shootings-2017/.

Fausset, R., Fernandez, M., & Blinder, A. (2016, July 9). Micah Johnson, gunman in Dallas, honed military skills to a deadly conclusion. *The New York Times*. Retrieved from: www.nytimes.com/2016/07/10/us/dallas-quiet-after-police-shooting-but-protests-flare-elsewhere.html.

Fausset, R., Perez-Pena, R., & Robertson, C. (2016, July 6). Alton Sterling shooting in Baton Rouge prompts Justice Dept. investigation. *The New York Times*. Retrieved from: www.nytimes.com/2016/07/06/us/alton-sterling-baton-rouge-shooting.html.

Fernandez, M., & Haag, M. (2017, May 5). Police officer who fatally shot 15-year-old Texas boy is charged with murder. *The New York Times*. Retrieved from: www.nytimes.com/2017/05/05/us/roy-oliver-charged-murder-dallas-police-shooting-jordan-edwards.html.

Goodman, J., & Baker, A. (2014, December 3). Wave of protests after grand jury doesn't indict officer in Eric Garner chokehold case. *The New York Times*. Retrieved from: www.nytimes.com/2014/12/04/nyregion/grand-jury-said-to-bring-no-charges-in-staten-island-chokehold-death-of-eric-garner.html.

Graham v. Connor, 490 U.S. 386, 1989.

Hassan, C., Yan, H., & Blau, M. (2016, September 15). Sandra Bland's family settles for $1.9M in wrongful death suit. *CNN*. Retrieved from: www.cnn.com/2016/09/15/us/sandra-bland-wrongful-death-settlement/index.html.

Johnson v. Glick, 481 F.2d 1028, 2d Cir., 1973.

Jouvenal, J. (2015, September 10). Inmate who died after jail encounter with Fairfax deputies: "You promised you wouldn't kill me." *The Washington Post*. Retrieved from: www.washingtonpost.com/local/crime/video-of-encounter-that-preceded-inmates-death-at-fairfax-jail-is-released/2015/09/10/0e7b6104-57e1-11e5-8bb1-b488d231bba2_story.html?utm_term=.935b1b918887.

Jouvenal, J. (2016, June 3). $15.3 million lawsuit filed in inmate's death at Fairfax County jail. *The Washington Post.* Retrieved from: www.washingtonpost.com/local/public-safety/15-million-lawsuit-filed-in-inmates-death-at-fairfax-county-jail/2016/06/03/f162dd32-28ea-11e6-a3c4-0724e8e24f3f_story.html?utm_term=.79c7e64f1866.

Kleinig, J. (1996). *The Ethics of Policing.* Cambridge: Cambridge University Press.

Krehbiel-Burton, L. (2017, May 17). White Tulsa police officer acquitted over fatal shooting of unarmed black. *Reuters.* Retrieved from: www.reuters.com/article/us-oklahoma-police-verdict-idUSKCN18E09X.

Laquan McDonald police reports differ dramatically from video. (2015, December 5). *Chicago Tribune.* Retrieved from: www.chicagotribune.com/news/ct-laquan-mcdonald-chicago-police-reports-met-20151204-story.html.

Levinson, E. (2015, June 23). Boston's history of police shootings of unarmed teens. *The Boston Globe.* Retrieved from: www.boston.com/news/local-news/2015/06/23/bostons-history-of-police-shootings-of-unarmed-teens.

Lockhart, P. R. (2018, March 30). Police shot and killed an unarmed black man in his own backyard. All he was holding was a cellphone. *Vox.* Retrieved from: www.vox.com/identities/2018/3/21/17149092/stephon-clark-police-shooting-sacramento.

Los Angeles Times staff. (2015, June 11). L.A. Police Commission faults 2 officers in Ezell Ford shooting death. *Los Angeles Times.* Retrieved from: http://homicide.latimes.com/post/lapd-chief-finds-officers-justified-fatal-shooting-mentally-ill-man-sources-say/.

Madigan, L. (2015). Madigan letter to United States Attorney General Lynch calls for outside, independent investigation into CPD. *Illinois Attorney General.* Retrieved from: www.illinoisattorneygeneral.gov/pressroom/2015_12/20151201.html.

Mather, K. (2016, January 11). L.A. Police Chief Beck backs charges against officer who fatally shot Venice homeless man. *Los Angeles Times.* Retrieved from: www.latimes.com/local/crime/la-me-venice-shooting-20160112-story.html.

Mather, K., Winton, R., & Vives, R. (2014, August 11). The homicide report. *Los Angeles Times.* Retrieved from: http://homicide.latimes.com/post/ezell-ford/.

McGee, P., & Fernandez, M. (2015, August 11). Arlington, Tex., officer is fired in fatal shooting of Christian Taylor. *The New York Times.* Retrieved from: www.nytimes.com/2015/08/12/us/arlington-tex-officer-is-fired-in-fatal-shooting-of-christian-taylor.html.

McLaughlin, E. (2017, July 18). Ex-police officer Ray Tensing will not be tried again in fatal shooting. *CNN.* Retrieved from: www.cnn.com/2017/07/18/us/ray-tensing-will-not-be-tried-again/index.html.

Miller, M. (2016, March 1). "They stood over him and watched him die": Outrage in Alabama after white officer kills black man. *The Washington Post.* Retrieved from: www.washingtonpost.com/news/morning-mix/wp/2016/03/01/they-stood-over-him-and-watched-him-die-outrage-in-alabama-after-white-cop-kills-unarmed-black-man/?utm_term=.9e26402573d5.

Murphy, K., & Curnutte, M. (2018, March 22). University of Cincinnati pays $250k to ex-cop who killed Sam DuBose. *Cincinnati Enquirer.* Retrieved from: www.cincinnati.com/story/news/2018/03/22/university-cincinnati-pays-cop-who-killed-sam-dubose/450587002/.

Nir, S. M. (2016, February 11). Officer Peter Liang convicted in fatal shooting of Akai Gurley in Brooklyn. *The New York Times.* Retrieved from: www.nytimes.com/2016/02/12/nyregion/officer-peter-liang-convicted-in-fatal-shooting-of-akai-gurley-in-brooklyn.html.

O'Connell, D. (1990). Excessive force claims: Is significant bodily injury the sine qua non to proving a Fourth Amendment violation? *Fordham Law Review, 58* (4). Retrieved from: https://ir.lawnet.fordham.edu/cgi/viewcontent.cgi?referer=&httpsredir=1&article=2873&context=flr.

Overbea, L. (1980, August 20). Black, white leaders try to keep racial peace in newly tense Boston. *The Christian Science Monitor*. Retrieved from: www.csmonitor.com/1980/0820/082043.html.

Pearce, M., & Hansen, M. (2016, April 19). No prison time for ex-NYPD Officer Peter Liang in fatal shooting of Akai Gurley. *Los Angeles Times*. Retrieved from: www.latimes.com/nation/la-na-liang-sentencing-20160419-story.html.

Rebecca Lai, K. K., Park, H., Buchanan, L., & Andrews, W. (2015, July 22). Assessing the legality of Sandra Bland's arrest. *The New York Times*. Retrieved from: www.nytimes.com/interactive/2015/07/20/us/sandra-bland-arrest-death-videos-maps.html.

Ruiz, R. (2017, September 12). Baltimore officers will face no federal charges in death of Freddie Gray. *The New York Times*. Retrieved from: www.nytimes.com/2017/09/12/us/freddie-gray-baltimore-police-federal-charges.html.

Smith, M. (2015, December 21). Grand jury declines to indict anyone in death of Sandra Bland. *The New York Times*. Retrieved from: www.nytimes.com/2015/12/22/us/grand-jury-finds-no-felony-committed-by-jailers-in-death-of-sandra-bland.html?_r=0.

Smith, M. (2017, June 16). Minnesota officer acquitted in killing of Philando Castile. *The New York Times*. Retrieved from: www.nytimes.com/2017/06/16/us/police-shooting-trial-philando-castile.html.

Smith, M. (2017, June 20). Video of police killing of Philando Castile is publicly released. *The New York Times*. Retrieved from: www.nytimes.com/2017/06/20/us/police-shooting-castile-trial-video.html.

Stanley-Becker, I. (2018, August 28). She fatally shot an unarmed black man. Now she's teaching other police officers how to "survive" such incidents. *The Washington Post*. Retrieved from: www.washingtonpost.com/news/morning-mix/wp/2018/08/28/she-fatally-shot-an-unarmed-black-man-now-shes-teaching-other-cops-how-to-survive-such-incidents/?utm_term=.f898d4a1fd29.

Swaine, J. (2016, July 18). Baton Rouge suspect Gavin Long was marine with alias Cosmo Setepenra. *The Guardian*. Retrieved from: www.theguardian.com/us-news/2016/jul/17/baton-rouge-gunman-gavin-e-long-cosmo-setepenra-marines.

Swaine, J., & Laughland, O. (2015, October 15). Eric Garner and Tamir Rice among those missing from FBI record of police killings. *The Guardian*. Retrieved from: www.theguardian.com/us-news/2015/oct/15/fbi-record-police-killings-tamir-rice-eric-garner.

The counted. (2016). *The Guardian*. Retrieved from: www.theguardian.com/us-news/ng-interactive/2015/jun/01/the-counted-police-killings-us-database.

Williams, T., & Smith, M. (2015, December 28). Cleveland officer will not face charges in Tamir Rice shooting death. *The New York Times*. Retrieved from: www.nytimes.com/2015/12/29/us/tamir-rice-police-shootiing-cleveland.html.

United States Attorney's Office. (2014). *U.S. Attorney's Office Concludes Investigation into the Death of Miriam Carey (sic) No Charges to Be Filed in Shooting Near U.S. Capitol*. Retrieved from: www.justice.gov/usao-dc/pr/us-attorney-s-office-concludes-investigation-death-miriam-careyno-charges-be-filed.

United States Congress. (2013). *Death in Custody Reporting Act of 2013*. Retrieved from: www.congress.gov/bill/113th-congress/house-bill/1447/text.

United States Department of Justice. (2015). *Report Regarding the Criminal Investigation into the Shooting Death of Michael Brown by Ferguson, Missouri Police Officer Darren Wilson*. Retrieved from: www.justice.gov/sites/default/files/opa/press-releases/attachments/2015/03/04/doj_report_on_shooting_of_michael_brown_1.pdf.

United States Department of Justice. (2017). *Investigation of the Chicago Police Department*. Retrieved from: www.justice.gov/opa/file/925846/download.

Chapter 4

Black Lives Matter

Interrogating and Challenging the Law Enforcement Narrative

The Narrative

As a young police officer in the late 1970s and through the 1980s, I was inducted very early on into the default "narrative" in the realm of the police use of force. Later in my career as a police sergeant and then lieutenant, it became a prominent part of my role as a supervisor and manager of novice and even experienced officers to frame the narrative of the police use of force for those officers who followed me, handing down and perpetuating that same narrative legacy for future generations of police officers as had been done for me as an initiate.

And although the narrative may vary somewhat depending on the specific details of a particular use of force incident, the language and the words used to frame the narrative remain consistent: "resist," "overcome," "vigorous," "violent," "subdue," "fear," "attack," "safety," "suspect," "custody," "serious bodily injury," "refuse," "lawful," "restraint," "comply," "self-defense," and of course "danger." As for example:

> In attempting to place the suspect under arrest and to take him into custody, the suspect violently attacked me and vigorously resisted my attempts to subdue him and refused to comply with my directives. In fear of serious bodily injury, and for my safety and for the safety of innocent bystanders and aware of the danger to myself and others, and in self-defense, I struck (or applied, or discharged) the suspect in order to subdue him and to ensure compliance with my lawful commands to cease resistance.
>
> (Cop-speak: the "narrative")

This stilted, imprecise "legalese" is the commonly used verbiage found in the police lexicon and forms the base of the narrative that police use throughout the United States. The purpose of the narrative is ultimately to exculpate the police from any blame or allegation that the use of force being described was unnecessary, inappropriate, excessive, or unlawful. It also serves to

...dent from any meaningful examination, review, or criticism from
...ne and irksome outsiders such as members of the media, the defense
...nities of color who might express skepticism, question, challenge,
...ce version of incidents when officers use force.

...he ubiquitous and widely available smart phone and other devices
...ce in their interactions with members of the public as well as the
...eo recording cameras and recorders mounted in places both public
...ve remained largely unchallenged and untrammeled, at least by the
...who have historically remained unaffected and largely untouched
...... The ranks of the 800,000 police officers who staff the 18,000 law
enforcement agencies in the United States are largely drawn from this population of middle-
class and working-class white men who have historically been supportive of the police and who
have rarely questioned or challenged the "narrative," and the tone, style, substance, and the
superfluous circumlocution provide the brief narrative arc necessary for the story to remain
intact, unchallenged, and inviolable.

In a study of the differing narratives employed by the police and citizens in describing and
accounting for police use of force incidents, Jeff Rojek, Geoffrey Alpert, and Hayden Smith
(2012) suggest that "accounts, stories, or narratives provide an excellent opportunity for social
scientists to describe and understand the ways in which we experience and identify our views,
the views of others, and the social world in which the actions occur" (p. 306). They use Marvin
Scott and Stanford Lyman's (1968) definition of an "account" as "a linguistic device employed
whenever an action is subjected to valuation inquiry" (p. 46). These authors discovered (to no
one's surprise) that the police and the citizens upon whom the police use force have starkly
divergent accounts for and narratives of incidents and instances where the police decide to
employ force.

Rojek, Alpert, and Smith found that "all the officers presented their actions during the force
encounters as reasonable behavior, and each of the citizens claimed the officer's actions were
improper, if not excessive" (2012, p. 310), and this was no doubt the expected result. Their
study found that the police officers who were the subjects of their research commonly employed
three elements to their narrative justifications for the use of force. One such justification was a
subject's disregarding an officer's command and attempts to dictate the terms of the encounter
by refusing to comply with the officer's orders or escalating the situation. Common to this narrative justifying the use of force are descriptions such as:

> The officer states that she or he only used force when multiple verbal instructions were inef-
> fective. This account clearly attempts to connect the officer's maintenance of authority by
> means of a legal and reasonable response to the suspect's aggressive combative behavior.
>
> (Rojek et al., 2012, p. 312)

This is particularly true when the officer believes that there is the possibility that the individual
may be armed or capable of arming himself.

A second common component of the police narrative contained an account of the individual
being under the influence of some intoxicating substance in justifying the need to use force, as
in one officer's account that "in past experiences, I have seen where people under the influence

of drugs and alcohol were not affected by pressure points or a TASER" (Rojek et al., 2012, p. 312). Finally, officers in the same study provided accounts that described their fear of losing a weapon as justification for the use of force:

> Because of close quarters and being in the bushes, I decided to use the TASER to avoid injury to myself and the suspect. If I used a takedown, he could have made a grab for my gun. It was the right thing to use.
>
> (p. 312)

In contrast, Rojek, Alpert, and Smith also found that "a unanimous theme of injustice was observed across the citizens' accounts," and that "citizen vocabularies of injustice extended along a continuum of culpability and included complete denial of culpability, an acceptance of partial fault, and the accusation of improper police procedures" (2012, p. 313). The most commonly heard component of the citizen narrative was the complaint that, when the police did use force, the *amount* of force that they used was *excessive*.

The study found that the police are most likely to share their accounts of the use of force with other, likeminded police officers and as a result receive the necessary affirmation that their narratives and accounts are indeed accurate, and the force justified. Likewise, those who see themselves as the "victims" of the police use of force are likely to seek affirmation of their "victimhood" from those who share their perspective about the police.

> A consequence of these entrenched accounts is that social actors repeat their biased perceptions to receptive audiences, and such perceptions resonate throughout social net-works, thus encouraging a disconnect in police–community relations. This, at least, offers a partial explanation for some community members' lost trust and confidence in the police.
>
> (Rojek et al., 2012, p. 324)

On July 19, 2015, at about 8:30 p.m. a University of Cincinnati campus police officer, Ray Tensing, stopped a motor vehicle on Thill and Vine Streets being operated by Sam DuBose, a 43-year-old African American man who was unarmed. Tensing stopped DuBose's Honda Accord allegedly owing to the vehicle missing a front license plate. Thill and Vine Streets is not on or near the campus of the University of Cincinnati, but it had apparently been the practice for campus police officers to make vehicle stops in parts of the city of Cincinnati that were outside of campus grounds. According to the report written by University of Cincinnati campus police officer Eric Weibel "Officer Tensing stated that he was attempting a traffic stop (No front license plate) when, at some point, he began to be dragged by a male black driver who was operating a 1998 Green Honda Accord." The report continues:

> Officer Tensing stated that he almost was run over by the driver of the Honda Accord and was forced to shoot the driver with his duty weapon (Sig Sauer P320). Officer Tensing stated that he fired a single shot. Officer Tensing repeated that he was being dragged by the vehicle and had to fire his weapon. The vehicle came to a final stop at the corner of Rice Street and Valencia Street. From outside the vehicle, I could see a Male Black slumped over motionless with a gunshot wound to his head. Officer Kidd was on scene with OIT (Officer

in Training) Lindenschmidt. Officer Kidd told me that he witnessed the Honda Accord drag Officer Tensing, and that he witnessed Officer Tensing fire a single shot. It is unclear how much of this incident OIT Lindenschmidt witnessed.

(University of Cincinnati, 2015)

Officer Tensing was equipped with a body-worn camera, which recorded the stop and the shooting. When subsequently viewed by authorities, the video did not show any movement of DuBose's vehicle until after he had been shot in the head by Tensing.[1] Tensing had not been dragged by the vehicle and Kidd had not "witnessed the Honda Accord drag Officer Tensing" (2015). In the official police report documenting the shooting death of Sam DuBose, the officers employed the narrative that provided generations of police officers caught in similar circumstances the cover necessary to justify an unjustifiable shooting: They lied. Notice the stilted legal-sounding jargon in the police narrative; Tensing "began to be dragged," "was almost run over," "repeated that he was being dragged," and "had to fire his weapon" because he was in fear for his life (University of Cincinnati, 2015).

The police report describes the officer as the victim, not Sam DuBose, the man just fatally shot in the head. The officer had no choice, confronting the fictive and contrived threat to his life, he "had to fire his weapon." And his fellow officer, Phillip Kidd, gave cover to the lie and repeated it himself, stating for the record the he too had seen the Honda drag Tensing. In keeping with the police subcultural norm, the trainee, David Lindenschmidt, is conspicuously left out of the narrative, the lie, the coverup, and merits only a passing reference, "unclear how much he witnessed" (University of Cincinnati, 2015). A textbook police narrative of a deadly force incident, that would no doubt have remained unchallenged, believed, supported, perhaps even rewarded, but for the video.

On April 4, 2015, at about 9:30 a.m., in North Charleston, South Carolina, police officer Michael Slager stopped a motorist driving a 1991 Mercedes Benz in the parking lot of an auto parts store. The vehicle was being operated by an unarmed 50-year-old African American man, Walter Scott (Dwyer, 2017). After providing his driver's license and registration to Officer Slager, Mr. Scott inexplicably exited his stopped vehicle and ran away on foot. Officer Slager began pursuing Mr. Scott on foot, and the dash mounted camera in Officer Slager's police vehicle, that had recorded the stop up until this time, does not record the foot pursuit. According to Officer Slager, he was forced to "deploy" his Taser weapon in an effort to subdue Mr. Scott, but the Taser failed to slow Mr. Scott down, and instead he turned on Officer Slager and a violent confrontation ensued during which, according to Officer Slager, Mr. Scott took Officer Slager's Taser weapon from him and pointed it at him as if to "tase" him with the weapon. Fearing for his life, Officer Slager shot Mr. Scott with his pistol, killing him.

There was much more to the story that was not, at least initially, contained in the police narrative, for within days of Scott's death, a video of the encounter between the police officer and Mr. Scott surfaced. According to *The New York Times*,

A video shot by a barber on his way to work shows a brief tussle between the two men. Mr. Scott broke free and ran. Instead of giving chase, Mr. Slager fired his service weapon eight times as Mr. Scott staggered and collapsed to his death in a grassy field behind a pawnshop just a mile from the officer's home. The video shows Mr. Slager dropping something beside

Mr. Scott's body. Most civil rights activists who watched the video believe the object was a Taser that the officer said Mr. Scott had grabbed.

(Robles et al., 2015)

Following the release of the video, Slager was immediately removed from the North Charleston Police Department. He was also arrested and charged with murder in the killing of Mr. Scott. At trial, then-Officer Slager testified "that he had been afraid of Scott. He contended, as he has previously, that Scott had taken his Taser stun gun," according to *National Public Radio*.

Slager said he chased Scott because he "must have been running for a certain reason." He testified that as he tried to handcuff Scott, Scott grabbed his Taser. Slager's voice cracked as he said he had been "in total fear." "I saw that Taser coming at me," he said. "I fired until the threat was stopped, like I'm trained to do."

(Hersher, 2016)

Again, the police framing of the narrative portrays the officer as the victim, not the man who he shot multiple times in the back. In the police rendition, it is the dead man who is armed and on the attack against the police officer who is "in total fear for his life." In the police telling of the confrontation, it is the 50-year-old Scott overpowering the much younger 33-year-old police officer.

According to *The Post and Courier*, the initial account of the shooting death of Mr. Scott was reported by the North Charleston Police Department in the perfunctory manner of the initial stage of the time-worn police narrative, the "statement":

A statement released by North Charleston police spokesman Spencer Pryor said a man ran on foot from the traffic stop and an officer deployed his department-issued Taser in an attempt to stop him. That did not work, police said, and an altercation ensued as the men struggled over the device. Police allege that during the struggle the man gained control of the Taser and attempted to use it against the officer. The officer then resorted to his service weapon and shot him, police alleged.

(Elmore & MacDougall, 2015)

Think Progress observed that "the story clearly came from Slager but he was able to use the authoritative voice of the police department to bolster his narrative" (Legum, 2015). The narrative, thus given the initial imprimatur of the larger organization, simply echoes the all-too-common delivery of the performance that follows the deaths of unarmed men and women (and boys and girls) of color at the hands of the police.

The officer, simply trying to stop someone who was no doubt a criminal (and doing his job to catch said criminal), uses his Taser weapon. Failing in that, an "altercation ensued," (criminal in unprovoked attack on police officer), and "the men struggled" (officer is overpowered). "The man gained control of the Taser and attempted to use it against the officer" (officer in fear for his life), who "then resorted to his service weapon and shot him" (left no choice, he did what had to be done). Thus, the narrative is re-enacted to the general satisfaction as far as all who matter are concerned (at least and in the eyes of the police and their supporters).

The Interrogation and Interruption of the Narrative

Following the 2013 acquittal of George Zimmerman in the Florida shooting death of 17-year-old Treyvon Martin, an unarmed African American high school student, three African American women activists: Alicia Garza, Opal Tometi, and Patrisse Khan-Cullors founded the social and political movement "Black Lives Matter" (BLM) (Hunt, 2016). The organization initially used the social media hashtag #BlackLivesMatter on platforms such as Twitter and Facebook "as a call to action for Black people" in "response to the anti-Black racism that permeates our society and also, unfortunately, our movements" (Garza, 2014). Garza's posting on social media led to Khan-Cullors coining the hashtag #BlackLivesMatter. What Garza wrote following Zimmerman's acquittal was a "love letter to black people":

> The sad part is, there's a section of America who is cheering and celebrating right now. and that makes me sick to my stomach. We GOTTA get it together y'all. stop saying we are not surprised. That's a damn shame in itself. I continue to be surprised at how little Black lives matter. And I will continue that. stop giving up on black life. Black people. I love you. I love us. Our lives matter.
>
> (Lowery, 2017)

The activist group quickly gained a substantial and formidable foothold on social media and rapidly became a street movement following the August 2014 killing of 18-year-old Michael Brown in Ferguson, Missouri, at the hands of then-police officer Darren Wilson. The shooting death of Brown, who was unarmed, quickly became a flashpoint for protesters in St. Louis County and nationwide who were angry at the seeming impunity with which the police killed African American men and boys and the lack of accountability and transparency in the investigations of the deaths that followed (Lowery, 2017).

Leslie Ashburn-Nardo, Kecia Thomas, and Aspen Robinson (2017) described BLM as a result of the anger and frustration of African Americans who were "tired of existing in a nation whose history and present practices carry strong evidence suggesting the insignificance of black bodies, the originators of #BlackLivesMatter created a movement that has now inspired millions to become agents of change" (p. 699). These authors describe BLM as an "organization (that) raises awareness of the violations against the human rights of black persons in this country, whether they be adult or child, free or incarcerated; man, woman, or gender neutral, cis, queer, or trans; citizen or undocumented" (p. 698).

The BLM movement and organization, as represented in the #BlackLivesMatter social media hashtag, "began as a call to action in response to state-sanctioned violence and anti-Black racism" (What we believe, 2018), and came to embody the interrogation of the long-held and seldom challenged police narrative that had been employed in the explanations for and justifications of the deadly force incidents in which the victims were men and women and boys and girls of color. This narrative typically portrayed the police themselves as the victims of unprovoked violence at the hands of violent and dangerous predatory criminals, who left the police no choice but to use deadly force in order to end the violent confrontation and to bring the "criminal" to justice and protect the innocent.

The narrative most often contained descriptions of those against whom deadly force was used in pejorative terms that demonized the dead. According to *The New Yorker*, Darren Wilson, the Ferguson officer who killed Michael Brown, in testifying before the grand jury, described Brown as one who had "the most intense, aggressive face," and looked "like a demon." Wilson further described Brown as a "bad guy," and when asked if he ever thinks about the teenager who he shot and killed, responded: "Do I think about who he was as a person? Not really, because it doesn't matter at this point. Do I think he had the best upbringing? No. Not at all" (Halpern, 2015).

Osagie Obasogie and Zachary Newman (2016) have written about local news media accounts of the officer-involved deaths in light of the BLM movement. These authors describe BLM as arising in opposition to the "respectability politics" that has characterized much of the mainstream response to police violence enacted upon black bodies. The "politics of respectability" is

> the notion that minorities can best respond to structural racism by individually behaving in a "respectable" manner that elicits the esteem of Whites as a way to insulate the self from attack while also promoting a positive group image that can "uplift" the reputation of the group.
>
> (Obasogie & Newman, 2016, p. 543)

They question whether or not the public narrative of the local news reporting of deadly force incidents involving police has shifted from a narrative of respectability politics to one framed by BLM, which raises "awareness of inequality in general and police brutality in particular as part of an effort to disrupt and eradicate respectability politics" (p. 544). Obasogie and Newman argue that "the media deploys tropes, signifiers, and languages that enable consumers to read and comprehend the deaths of Michael Brown, Eric Garner, Tamir Rice, Walter Scott, Freddie Gray, and all other Black victims of police violence in particular ways" (p. 552).

Obasogie and Newman (2016) discovered that BLM's "concerns over race and respectability are not reflected in journalists' accounts," and that media stories adhered to a reporting and examination of the deaths of African Americans at the hands of police that cast the victims in light of the "politics of respectability." The media reports they reviewed continued to examine the lives of the victims in terms of whether or not they conformed to commonly accepted middle-class behavioral norms, and left unexamined the underlying issues of societal inequality, police violence, and systemic and structural racism in the criminal justice system in general and in policing in particular. They found three consistent themes that emerged in media reports of the deaths of African Americans at the hands of the police:

> (1) a strong commitment to colorblindness in discussing the race of the parties involved, (2) the dominance of the police perspective in reporting these incidents, and (3) continued use of criminalizing language unrelated to the incident itself to characterize the victim's respectability.
>
> (Obasogie & Newman, 2016)

The narrative is a familiar one: Michael Brown was a "demon," a "monster," and "menacing" who had drugs in his system (marijuana); Tamir Rice "was large for his age" (he was 12-years old), and "looked like a man" (a black man); Freddie Gray was "well known to the police" (i.e., a criminal); Eric Garner was "a very large man" (i.e., a "beast"). In other words, in the framing of the narrative led by the police, and abetted by the media, these were not "respectable" individuals who "played by the rules" and who were thus ultimately deserving of their fates. Consider this depiction of Michael Brown from *The New York Times*:

> Michael Brown, 18, due to be buried on Monday, was no angel … He lived in a community that had rough patches, and he dabbled in drugs and alcohol. He had taken to rapping in recent months, producing lyrics that were by turns contemplative and vulgar …
>
> (Eligon, 2014)

Kristin Dukes and Sarah Gaither (2017) investigated media portrayals and depictions of African Americans following their victimization at the hands of police in deadly force incidents and "how learning negative, Black racially stereotypic information versus positive, Black counter-stereotypic information about a shooting victim affects attributions of fault and blame, sympathy and empathy" (p. 792) when looking to affix blame, punishment, and exoneration. Their research looked at the media reporting following the shooting deaths of Michael Brown and Trayvon Martin by police or their proxies. Dukes and Gaither found that "when negative, Black stereotypical information was given about a victim, it significantly colored those victims as being more at fault for their own deaths compared to when positive, Black counter-stereotypical information was provided regardless of the victim's race" (p. 801).

Dukes and Gaither (2017) also found that when the race of the victims and their shooter was the same, i.e., a white police officer killing a white victim or black police officer killing a black victim, "the differences regarding levels of perceived fault and blame were not as strong" and that "the interracial nature of shooting altercations has a particularly strong effect on shaping how shooting incidences are viewed and the levels of blame that are applied" (p. 802). The researchers advise caution in that there are clearly instances where the victims of police shootings are not blameless and have engaged the police under circumstances that clearly warrant the use of deadly force. And there are also instances where the police, in using deadly force, have acted courageously, selflessly, and without malice or animus toward the target of the deadly force incident. Nonetheless, they argue that "the relative social status and perceived authority police officers have may actually exacerbate the impact of negative victim information" and that "the interracial nature of shooting altercations has a particularly strong effect on shaping how shooting incidences are viewed and the levels of blame that are applied" (p. 802).

The anthropologists Yarimar Bonilla and Jonathan Rosa (2015) have examined the use of social media platforms such as Twitter, Instagram, and Facebook as a means of channeling the discourse and challenging dominant-group narrations of the police interacting with members of communities of color (non-dominant groups). Their analysis of the use of social media hashtags following the deaths of Michael Brown and Trayvon Martin identified the means through which those who seek to establish a "livestreamed" challenge to the police narrative and the mainstream media narrative: "The increased use and availability of these technologies has provided marginalized and racialized populations with new tools for documenting incidents of state-sanctioned violence and contesting media representations of racialized bodies and marginalized communities" (p. 5).

According to Bonilla and Rosa (2015), social media platforms allow users to "filter" the information they receive and to "dial out" counternarratives that serve to contradict their experience. They caution that "this filtering process also has a distorting effect. Social media create a distorted view of events, such that we only get the perspective of the people who are already in our social network" (p. 6). Through social media campaigns, such as those that emerged following the shooting deaths of Brown and Martin, "users sought to call attention to the arbitrary nature of racialized policing, the vulnerability of black bodies, and the problematic ways in which blackness is perceived as a constant threat" (p. 8).

The challenge to the law enforcement narrative serves to recast the police-as-victim trope into a depiction of the contentiousness and confrontation that too often accompany the interactions between the police and residents of communities of color. The disconnect and the frequent animus that occurs during these interactions are largely unknown to white people, who generally have positive interactions with the police. According to *The Marshall Project*:

> It seems whites have a very different experience with law enforcement than everyone else. Studies suggest that police officers are more respectful to whites during stops and less likely to use force on white suspects. Another study found they're also less likely to stop whites or search their vehicles during traffic stops—even though white drivers were found in one study more likely to be stopped with guns and drugs in their possession.
>
> (Ramsey, 2017)

Donovan Ramsey, writing for *The Marshall Project*, interviewed criminologist Ron Weitzer who observed that

> whites tend to see the police as allies in the fight against crime. To the extent that whites associate violent crime with minorities, their support for robust crime control measures may also translate into support for police, since the white population is assumed to be largely law-abiding.
>
> (2017)

BLM and similar activist movements such as the Coalition Against Police Violence and the Black Youth Project 100 (among many others), posit a counter narrative, one that confronts and challenges "violent policing (and) systemic racism" (Day, 2015). BLM's Garza, speaking to *The Guardian*, demanded recognition for the legitimacy of claims of unjust and racist policing: "You know what? This has to stop. We cannot continue to have police kill with impunity and not face any consequences." She went on to cite the need to consider "defunding police departments with a track record of violence, introducing a national training standard for officers, and mandating psychiatric testing" (for police officers) (Hunt, 2016).

Writing of the events following the shooting of Michael Brown, Wesley Lowery, an African American journalist, spent three months in Ferguson, Missouri, followed by eight more months of traveling across the country, visiting city after city to report on and understand the social movement that vowed to awaken a sleeping nation and insisted it begin to truly value black life. Each day, it seemed, there was another shooting. In city after city, I found officers whose actions were at worst criminal and at best lacked racial sensitivity, and black and brown bodies disproportionately gunned down by those sworn to serve and protect.

(Lowery, 2017)

Lowery (2017) spoke to Brittany Packnett, a 31-year-old protester from Ferguson who, in addition to others like DeRay Mckesson, emerged as prominent spokespersons for the BLM movement in 2016, and who met with President Barack Obama several times. Following the Republican National Convention in the summer of 2016 and the elections that November, there was little cause for optimism in the movement. Nonetheless, Packnett told Lowery: "We have no choice but to keep going. If one of the central demands of the movement is to stop killing us, and they're still killing us, then we don't get to stop, either." Packnett "knew it was my job to translate the pain I had seen and experienced in the streets and bring it into these halls of power."

Jelani Cobb (2016), writing in *The New Yorker*, also spoke about Packnett and two other activists who are prominent in the BLM movement, DeRay Mckesson and Johnetta Elzie, who "quickly became the most recognizable figures associated with the movement in Ferguson." Cobb observed that "while Black Lives Matter's insistent outsider status has allowed it to shape the dialogue surrounding race and criminal justice in this country, it has also sparked a debate about the limits of protest, particularly of online activism."

Jessica Watters (2017) has written about the BLM movement and the unique and specific means through which black women are affected that are often offered less public exposure through BLM than similarly situated black men. As but one example, she observed that "although the story of Sandra Bland was widely publicized, there are so many other unknown Black women who have been victimized at the hands of law enforcement that a second campaign, #SayHerName, has arisen in response" (p. 204). The point is well taken, and what is frequently overlooked when protests and condemnation arises as a result of yet another instance of state-sponsored violence in which a black man or boy is victimized is that, as Watters argues, "Black women also face gender-specific risks from police encounters, such as an increased likelihood of sexual harassment and assault, thereby further conflating issues of race and gender" (p. 204).

Watters advocates for the participation of white women in the BLM movement, and in writing about the 2017 Women's March that took place in Washington, D.C., New York, Chicago, Boston, Seattle, and Los Angeles, where over two million women marched and not one person was arrested, she said "Women's March protesters were welcomed by cheerful officers willing to take selfies and march alongside them … (and that this) exemplifies a privilege to congregate peacefully and without threat of violence" (2017, p. 205). A privilege, she suggests, that can and should be co-opted in the service of the BLM gatherings and protests, activity that while protected under the First Amendment, is too often met with the police in riot and SWAT gear, ready for battle when those assembled are largely people of color. For Watters, "Black women are victimized in similar ways as Black men through police violence, random stops, racial profiling, and targeting of poor, disabled, and trans women" (p. 204).

Mary Angela Bock (2016) writes about the phenomenon of "cop-watching," a form of *sous-veillance* in which participants film the police in the performance of their duties as a means of challenging the police narrative. According to the Pew Research Center, in 2018: "The vast majority of Americans—95%—now own a cellphone of some kind. The share of Americans that own smartphones is now 77%" (Mobile fact sheet, 2018). This ubiquitous smart phone presence facilitates participant recording and provides "witness accounts, supported by video evidence, (that) challenge the authority of police and traditional media. Cop-watching borrows from and disrupts traditional journalistic practices while giving voice to counternarratives" (Bock, 2016, p. 14). Bock's analysis of the participant-recording of the police

> suggests that cop-watching represents a type of active citizenship that combines text and practice, resulting in embodied narratives that give voice to longstanding, previously marginalized concerns about police use of force. Cop-watching disrupts the public sphere and raises theoretical questions about accountability, journalism, and visual evidence.
>
> (2016, p. 14)

Bock refers to cop-watching as "digital democracy" whose purpose is to document instances and situations in which the police appear to engage in excessive behavior in order to hold them to an accountability that has historically been elusive and challenging to document. Even though the police had been filmed in the public performance of their duties going back to protests and marches during the 1960s, it was no doubt the video recording of the 1991 beating of Rodney King in Los Angeles by a private citizen using a hand-held video recorder that brought the public's awareness of the use of technology to provide incriminating evidence of police abuse and excess. This form of digital democracy gives witness and voice to those whose narratives, particularly as they relate to police brutality and oppression, have historically been marginalized, negated, and dismissed: "Once a monopoly for large, moneyed media institutions, today anyone can participate in this kind of storytelling. Anyone can have—materially and metaphorically—a voice" (Bock, 2016, p. 18).

Bock's findings provide authority and legitimacy to citizen-empowered counternarratives to the historically dominant narratives of the police and conventional media outlets, entities whose relationship is often mutually intertwined and co-dependent in ways that may serve to unquestionably perpetuate the prevailing, mainstream narrative, a narrative that has most often favored the law enforcement perspective. For Bock, cop-watching, in exposing certain (albeit infrequent) instances of police excess, "allow viewers to see, and therefore, (presumably) know what is happening on the street. Their looking balances the authoritarian gaze of government, turning tables on commonly accepted dystopian accounts of surveillance. It represents a form of mutual gaze" (2016, p. 28) that ultimately provides an alternative narrative and may even serve to inhibit police excess.

Joy Leopold and Myrtle Bell (2017) examined media coverage of BLM and related movements protesting police excess and violence to determine if the media exhibited bias and/or disapproval of the protests and their messages, the so-called "protest paradigm." According to Francis Lee (2014), the protest paradigm is viewed "as a pattern of news coverage that expresses disapproval toward protests and dissent" (2014, p. 2727). Leopold and Bell identify five characteristics of the protest paradigm that "have been used as a guide for researchers to draw conclusions about and recognize negative journalistic patterns in protest coverage" (2017, p. 721). The five characteristics are: news frames, reliance on official sources and official definitions, invocation of public opinion, delegitimization, and demonization.

News frames typically ground coverage of an event and in covering protests that often include "riot frames, which overemphasize any lawlessness, danger, destruction, and disorder occurring because of the protests." In relying primarily on official sources for information about protests "journalists allow those in power to define protests in and on their terms, (and) the protestors are characterized by their deviance from societal norms rather than by their struggle for representation, equality, or change." In invoking public opinion about ongoing protests in their reporting of the events journalists cite those who "generally have a limited understanding of the social movement or the social issue on which the movement is focused, so much of their commentary is negative or superficial" (Leopold & Bell, 2017, p. 722).

In delegitimizing the protests and the protesters, reporters may restrict coverage of the protests solely to the actions of the protesters themselves and these actions, rather than identifying the underlying causes of the protest, provide an incomplete portrait of the events, causing observers to judge them as pointless. And in demonizing the protesters, Leopold and Bell describe the media as focusing on "extensive and episodic coverage of any destruction wrought by protesters, listing of arrests, or highlighting altercations with police are common forms of demonization" (2017, p. 722).

The 2017 Leopold and Bell study reviewed BLM coverage in seven mainstream media outlets in the months following the shooting death of Michael Brown in August 2014. These included newspapers such as *The New York Times*, the *St. Louis Post Dispatch*, and the *Los Angeles Times*. They examined 15 articles from mainstream print and online outlets and their content analysis "did in fact heavily follow the protest paradigm, and also revealed language and coverage patterns that further negatively framed the BLM protests" (p. 725). Additionally, Leopold and Bell identified a sixth element of the protest paradigm that was consistently present in their content analysis: "blame attribution": "This characteristic manifests as the attribution of acts of violence or crime to the protests or to protesters even when there is no evidence that the protesters committed the acts" (p. 726).

Thus, as evidenced in this study, the mainstream media, either wittingly or unwittingly, serve to abet, to echo, and to amplify the message and the narrative of law enforcement and government officials to the detriment of BLM and other social movement protesters, many if not most of whom are African American, in their attempt to draw attention to social justice issues implicated in police excess and violence.

Sentineling White Space

In April of 2018, two African American men, Rashon Nelson and Donte Robinson, were arrested at a Starbucks coffee shop in Philadelphia where they had arrived for a business meeting and asked to use the restroom. They had not made a purchase in the coffee shop. The store manager, a white woman, "called the police to report 'two gentlemen in my cafe that are refusing to make a purchase or leave'" (Siegel, 2018). The police responded and immediately arrested Nelson and Robinson, charging them with trespassing and creating a disturbance. When the story went viral, the charges were dropped against the men.

Also, in April of 2018, three African American artists, Komi-Oluwa Olafimihan, Kelly Fyffe-Marshall, and Donisha Prendergast (who is the granddaughter of the late singer Bob Marley), were exiting a home that they had rented through the online service "Airbnb" in Rialto, California, and loading their suitcases into the trunk of their car. According to *The New York Times*, "within minutes, several police cars had arrived and the group was being questioned as a helicopter flew overhead. A neighbor who didn't recognize them had reported a possible burglary, the police said" (Victor, 2018). The police questioned the artists for 22 minutes before finally releasing them; "the three black people in the group are suing the Rialto Police Department, saying they were unfairly treated during the April 30 encounter" (Victor, 2018).

And on April 29, 2018, in Oakland, California, two African American men, Kenzie Smith and Onsayo Abram, were spending a Sunday afternoon having a barbecue at Lake Merritt, when a white woman called the police, complaining that the men were not allowed to use a charcoal grill in the area. According to the *San Francisco Chronicle*, the woman remained until police arrived and the ensuing dispute turned into a two-hour confrontation (Taylor, 2018). Widely circulated video recordings of the incident have been viewed over 1.5 million times on YouTube and earned the woman, Dr. Jennifer Schulte, the nickname "Barbecue Betty." (There is also a "Coupon Carl," a "Permit Patty," and a "Pool Patrol Paula.")

In May 2018, a black Yale graduate student, Lolade Siyonbola, was napping in the common room in the Hall of Graduate Studies when confronted by campus police who wanted to "verify that you belong here," according to *The Washington Post* (Wootson, 2018, May 11). A white student, Sarah Braasch, had taken a photo of Siyonbola and called police, claiming that she had "every right to call the police," since "you cannot sleep in that room." The police demanded identification from Siyonbola and that she prove to the officers that she was in fact a student at the university.

And in July 2018 an African American student and teacher's assistant at Smith College in Northampton, Massachusetts, Oumou Kanoute, was eating lunch and reading a book in a common room at the school when an employee of the college called police because Kanoute seemed "to be out of place," telling the police dispatcher that "we have a person sitting there laying down in the living room area over here" (Wootson, 2018). And again, after the story went viral, the college's president, Kathleen McCartney, offered "my deepest apology that this incident occurred" and tried to assure Kanoute that "she belongs in all Smith spaces" according to *The Washington Post* (Wootson, 2018, August 5). The college refused to divulge the identity of the caller who notified the campus police.

Instances where white privilege and racism seek to enlist, to coopt, and to exploit the public authority of the police in asserting and maintaining control over spaces and activities believed to be "white" are so commonplace that the social media hashtag #LivingWhileBlack has gained widespread adoption, traction, and recognition. This challenge to the narrative, that has long seen white racism invoke the authority of the police in the reification of racial dominance, is emerging in publicly identifying this indefensible practice and those who enable it: white people who feel entitled, privileged, authorized, and willingly abetted by law enforcement.

Doreen St. Felix, writing in *The New Yorker*, observed that "we perceive a weird and ancient adrenaline in many of the cop callers, who have internalized that the police are their personal valets, ready to treat any perceived inconvenience as violence" (2018). Of the sometimes grainy and shaky videos of these encounters that circulate so widely on the internet, St. Felix noted the absurdity of these "vignettes" that stand in stark contrast to the purported unbiased neutrality of the police body-camera videos that also swarm the internet, and in so doing depict the authenticity of the actors in the recordings: their anger, their resentment, even their bemusement. She argued that the videos serve to "skewer white privilege, dwell on its irrationality, and, in so doing, turn aggressors into mockable memes."

The sociologist Elijah Anderson offers this explanation for the phenomenon of white people calling the police on black people living their lives: "Many white people have not adjusted to the idea that black people now appear more often in places of privilege, power, and prestige—or just places where they were historically unwelcome" (2018). He observed that

> When black people do appear in such places, white people subconsciously or explicitly want to banish them to a place I have called the "iconic ghetto"—to the stereotypical space in which they think all black people belong, a segregated space for second-class citizens.

Anderson notes the "cognitive dissonance" that many white people feel in the transition from a segregated to a desegregated society, as black Americans "attend the best schools; pursue the professions of their choosing; and occupy various positions of power, privilege, and prestige." Of the role of the police in facilitating the racist proclivities of the 911 callers and affirming and enforcing racially separated public spaces, Anderson argues that "white people need to put the black interlopers in their place, literally and figuratively. Black people must have their behavior corrected, and they must be directed back to 'their' neighborhoods and designated social spaces" (2018).

The challenge to the dominant narrative continues and its interruption and interrogation are altering this emergent discourse in ways that are both intolerant of Anderson's "iconic ghetto" and disquieting to those who have long dominated and determined the racial and the criminal justice hierarchy. This hierarchy and this narrative have long privileged whiteness and the self-regarding righteousness of the law enforcement standpoint, to the overall detriment of those who have repeatedly borne the brunt of this iniquity.

Conclusion

The police have long used the authority and the commonly affirmed belief in the legitimacy of their office to control the narrative that is provided to the public regarding their activities. This has historically been accomplished with the support of middle- and working-class whites, while being viewed skeptically by many residents of communities of color. Social and political movements such as BLM and other activist organizations that have emerged in the second decade of the twenty-first century have challenged and interrogated these narratives, so much so that the law enforcement narrative and the police public reporting of events in which they are involved are no longer unquestionably accepted as truthful. The emergence of a counter-narrative has proved vexing for the police and their supporters.

NOTE

1 The video was published by WCPO.com on YouTube in 2015 and can be viewed here: www.youtube.com/watch?time_continue=93&v=ZocdejrSjyc.

REFERENCES

Anderson, E. (2018, August 10). Black Americans are asserting their rights in "white spaces." That's when whites call 911. *Vox.* Retrieved from: www.vox.com/the-big-idea/2018/8/10/17672412/911-police-black-white-racism-sociology.

Ashburn-Nardo, L., Thomas, K., & Robinson, A. (2017). Broadening the conversation: Why Black Lives Matter. *Equality, Diversity and Inclusion: An International Journal, 36* (8), pp. 698–706.

Bock, M. A. (2016). Film the police! Cop-watching and its embodied narratives. *Journal of Communication, 66* (1), pp. 13–34.

Bonilla, Y., & Rosa, J. (2015). #Ferguson: digital protest, hashtag ethnography, and the racial politics of social media in the United States. *American Ethnologist, 42*, pp. 4–17.

Cobb, J. (2016, March 14). The matter of black lives. *The New Yorker.* Retrieved from: www.newyorker.com/magazine/2016/03/14/where-is-black-lives-matter-headed.

Day, E. (2015, July 19). #BlackLivesMatter: The birth of a new civil rights movement. *Guardian.* Retrieved from: www.theguardian.com/world/2015/jul/19/blacklivesmatter-birth-civil-rights-movement.

Dukes, K. N., & Gaither, S. E. (2017). Black racial stereotypes and victim blaming: Implications for media coverage and criminal proceedings in cases of police violence against racial and ethnic minorities. *Journal of Social Issues, 73* (4), pp. 789–807.

Dwyer, C. (2017, December 7). Former S.C. officer who killed Walter Scott sentenced to 20 years in prison. *National Public Radio.* Retrieved from: www.npr.org/sections/thetwo-way/2017/12/07/569070544/former-s-c-officer-who-killed-walter-scott-will-be-sentenced-to-up-to-24-years.

Eligon, J. (2014, August 24). Michael Brown spent last weeks grappling with problems and promise. *The New York Times.* Retrieved from: www.nytimes.com/2014/08/25/us/michael-brown-spent-last-weeks-grappling-with-lifes-mysteries.html.

Elmore, C., & MacDougall, D. (2015, April 3). N. Charleston officer fatally shoots man. *The Post and Courier.* Retrieved from: www.postandcourier.com/archives/n-charleston-officer-fatally-shoots-man/article_4480489f-a733-57fc-b326-bdf95032d33c.html.

Garza, A. (2014, October 7). A herstory of the #BlackLivesMatter movement by Alicia Garza. *The Feminist Wire.* Retrieved from: www.thefeministwire.com/2014/10/blacklivesmatter-2/.

Halpern, J. (2015, August 10). The cop. *The New Yorker.* Retrieved from: www.newyorker.com/magazine/2015/08/10/the-cop.

Hersher, R. (2016, November 29). Former S.C. police officer takes the stand at his murder trial. *National Public Radio.* Retrieved from: www.npr.org/sections/thetwo-way/2016/11/29/503737818/former-south-carolina-police-officer-takes-the-stand-at-his-murder-trial.

Hunt, E. (2016, September 2). Alicia Garza on the beauty and the burden of Black Lives Matter. *Guardian.* Retrieved from: www.theguardian.com/us-news/2016/sep/02/alicia-garza-on-the-beauty-and-the-burden-of-black-lives-matter.

Lee, F. L. (2014). Triggering the protest paradigm: examining factors affecting news coverage of protests. *International Journal of Communication, 8*.

Legum, J. (2015, April 8). Everything the police said about Walter Scott's death before a video showed what really happened. *Think Progress*. Retrieved from: https://thinkprogress.org/everything-the-police-said-about-walter-scotts-death-before-a-video-showed-what-really-happened-f623b4205390/.

Leopold, J., & Bell, M. P. (2017). News media and the racialization of protest: An analysis of Black Lives Matter articles. *Equality, Diversity & Inclusion*, 36 (8), pp. 720–735.

Lowery, W. (2017, January 17). Black Lives Matter: Birth of a movement. *Guardian*. Retrieved from: www.theguardian.com/us-news/2017/jan/17/black-lives-matter-birth-of-a-movement.

Mobile fact sheet. (2018, February 15). *Pew Research Center*. Retrieved from: www.pewinternet.org/fact-sheet/mobile/.

Obasogie, O., & Newman, Z. (2016). Black lives matter and respectability politics in local news accounts of officer-involved civilian deaths: An early empirical assessment. *Wisconsin Law Review*, pp. 541–574.

Ramsey, D. (2017, July 19). White America's unshakeable confidence in the police. *The Marshall Project*. Retrieved from: www.themarshallproject.org/2017/07/19/white-america-s-unshakeable-confidence-in-the-police.

Robles, F., Blinder, A., & Grant, J. (2015, April 12). After 8 shots in North Charleston, Michael Slager becomes an officer scorned. *The New York Times*. Retrieved from: www.nytimes.com/2015/04/13/us/after-8-shots-a-quiet-officer-now-scorned.html.

Rojek, J., Alpert, G. P., & Smith, H. P. (2012). Examining officer and citizen accounts of police use-of-force incidents. *Crime & Delinquency*, 58 (2), pp. 301–327.

St. Felix, D. (2018, July 21). The summer of Coupon Carl, Permit Patty, and the videos that turn white privilege into mockable memes. *The New Yorker*. Retrieved from: www.newyorker.com/culture/culture-desk/the-summer-of-coupon-carl-permit-patty-and-the-videos-that-turn-cop-callers-into-mockable-memes.

Scott, M., & Lyman, S. (1968). Accounts. *American Sociological Review*, 33, pp. 46–62.

Siegel, R. (2018, May 3). Two black men arrested at Starbucks settle with Philadelphia for $1 each. *The Washington Post*. Retrieved from: www.washingtonpost.com/news/business/wp/2018/05/02/african-american-men-arrested-at-starbucks-reach-1-settlement-with-the-city-secure-promise-for-200000-grant-program-for-young-entrepreneurs/?utm_term=.afe77a981f42.

Taylor, O. (2018, May 17). Even in Oakland, calling the cops on black people just living their lives. *San Francisco Chronicle*. Retrieved from: www.sfchronicle.com/news/article/Even-in-Oakland-calling-the-cops-on-black-people-12920652.php.

University of Cincinnati Police Division Information Report. (2015). *University of Cincinnati Police Division*. Retrieved from: www.uc.edu/content/dam/uc/ucomm/docs/incident-report.pdf.

Victor, D. (2018, May 8). A woman said she saw burglars. They were just black Airbnb guests. *The New York Times*. Retrieved from: www.nytimes.com/2018/05/08/us/airbnb-black-women-police.html.

Watters, J. (2017). Pink hats and black fists: the role of women in the Black Lives Matter Movement. *William & Mary Journal of Women & The Law*, 24 (1), pp. 199–207.

What we believe. (2018). *Black Lives Matter*. Retrieved from: https://blacklivesmatter.com/about/what-we-believe/.

Wootson, C. (2018, May 11). A black Yale student fell asleep in her dorm's common room. A white student called police. *The Washington Post*. Retrieved from: www.washingtonpost.com/news/grade-point/wp/2018/05/10/a-black-yale-student-fell-asleep-in-her-dorms-common-room-a-white-student-called-police/?utm_term=.aa79b-b297ce2.

Wootson, C. (2018, August 5). "All I did was be black": Someone called the police on a student lying on a dorm couch. *The Washington Post*. Retrieved from: www.washingtonpost.com/news/grade-point/wp/2018/08/05/all-i-did-was-be-black-someone-called-the-police-on-a-student-lying-on-a-dorm-couch/?utm_term=.7b1cd72a64a6.

Chapter 5

The "War Against the Police"

The Fictive Response to the New Accountability

The Nascent Accountability

Following the August 9, 2014, shooting death of 18-year-old Michael Brown in Ferguson, Missouri by then-police officer Darren Wilson, protesters took to the streets in St. Louis County to denounce the killing of the unarmed African American teenager. The Black Lives Matter[1] social movement figured prominently in the protests, and it was following Brown's death that the hashtag #BlackLivesMatter gained traction and widespread recognition on various social media platforms as well as in more conventional national and international media outlets. Black Lives Matter had been founded following the 2013 acquittal of George Zimmerman, a sometime neighborhood watch member in a gated community in Sanford, Florida from the 2012 shooting death of Trayvon Martin, a 17-year-old unarmed African American high school student.

The police account of the death of Brown followed a predictable narrative: Wilson, the police officer, suspected Brown and a companion of having stolen packages of cigarillos from a local convenience store and observed the two walking in the street. Wilson then ordered Brown and his companion on to the sidewalk and drove toward them and blocked them with his department-issued Chevy Tahoe SUV. Then, according to then-officer Wilson, Brown reached into the driver side window of the police vehicle and punched Wilson and a struggle ensued. Wilson unholstered his gun and shot at Brown twice from within the SUV, hitting him in the hand. Brown then fled on foot for approximately 180 feet, during which time Wilson fired ten more shots at Brown, hitting him six to eight times, before Brown fell dead in the street, having been struck by a bullet to the head (United States Department of Justice, 2015).

Although no video footage was available for the encounter, Wilson's claim that Brown had attacked him and that he shot and killed the unarmed Brown because he was in fear for his life was an all too familiar law enforcement trope, one that was met with disbelief, anger, and outrage in the African American community in Ferguson; the highly charged emotional and visceral response moved quickly beyond Ferguson and St. Louis County, largely through social media and the internet. The law enforcement version of what had happened to Michael Brown in Ferguson was challenged; the credibility of the police was in jeopardy, and Black Lives Matter became the counter-narrative to the police's long-held representations of being in "fear for their lives" in confrontations with African American men and women, boys and girls, and particularly unarmed encounters.

In the aftermath of the death of Michael Brown, protests against police violence and excess took place in cities throughout the United States (Davey & Bosman, 2014). The police, for their part, felt as though they were under siege (Sanchez, 2015), and that there were unprecedented threats against their safety. In December 2014, two New York City police officers, Wenjian Liu and Rafael Ramos, were shot dead as they sat in their police cruiser in the Bedford-Stuyvesant section of Brooklyn. The gunman, 28-year-old Ismaaiyl Brinsley, shot and killed himself as officers closed in on him following the murders of the two officers, who never even drew their weapons (Mueller & Baker, 2014).

On July 17, 2016, a gunman shot six police officers in Baton Rouge, Louisiana, killing three. This shooting followed the July 5, 2016, police shooting of an African American man, Alton Brown, by police in Baton Rouge. The lone gunman in the Baton Rouge police killings, Gavin Long, an African American military veteran, was later shot and killed by police (Bloom et al., 2016). Following the shootings in Baton Rouge, on July 8, 2016, five police officers were shot and killed in Dallas, Texas, by a heavily armed sniper. The sniper, Micah Johnson, a 25-year-old African American military veteran, "specifically set out to kill as many white officers as he could," according to officials (Fernandez et al., 2016). He was killed by police using a remote-controlled explosive device. On July 4, 2017, another New York City police officer, Miosotis Familia, was shot and killed in an unprovoked attack in the Bronx, while she sat in a police command post vehicle. That gunman, Alexander Bonds, "who had been in and out of prisons and jails for 15 years and was slipping into severe mental illness" was also subsequently shot and killed by police (Mueller & Baker, 2017).

During the second decade of the twenty-first century, given the ubiquity of the technology capable of recording virtually any activity occurring in public spaces, and particularly the activities of law enforcement officers nationwide who were engaged in the performance of their often-public duties, there emerged an unprecedented number of police-related video and audio recordings that were often unflattering to and critical of the police in their encounters with the public, and particularly with residents of communities of color. In addition to privately recorded depictions of police activities that were (and are) widely disseminated on the internet, there were recordings that the police themselves generated from dashboard mounted cameras in police vehicles as well as recordings made from cameras that the officers wore, so-called body cameras.

The countless recordings of the police that often evidenced what many believed were objectionable and unjustifiable instances of the use of force, contributed in large part to a nascent narrative that sharply interrogated the closely-held and long-established depiction of the police as the "thin blue line" between order and chaos, safety and anarchy, good versus evil. Many of those who would default to positions of support of, respect for, and deference to the police, more and more frequently saw their sentiments waver.

The Police and Victimhood

The police responded to the increasingly strident tenor of the public condemnation of police wrongdoing and increased calls for accountability by often casting themselves in the role of persecuted victims. In August of 2017, in a controversial video posted on the internet, a New York City Police Department union official claimed that the police had become victims of what he called "Blue Racism," "claiming that police officers are the frequent victims of discrimination," and that "this strange form of racism … continues to engulf the country" (Feuer, 2017).

That the police should themselves adopt the role of victim in the "Blue Racism" trope is patently offensive for many actual victims of racism and oppression, particularly given that for many members of "otherized" racial and ethnic origin groups, it is the police themselves who are seen as the actual perpetrators of their oppression and the most visible and tangible representations of a racist and discriminatory criminal justice system in their communities. The construct of "Blue Racism" delegitimizes and subordinates claims of racism and discriminatory policing practices that have a well-documented history in communities of color, that is prominently in evidence in the many excessive and deadly force incidents perpetrated by the police in which the victims are too often men and women of color, and specifically African Americans.

The notion that the police have been subjected to oppression and maltreatment in the form of what some of the police have called "Blue Racism" ignores the reality that it is the police who have arrogated to themselves the power and the authority that is an essential element in the enactment of discrimination and oppression—racism. Men and women of color are largely powerless to oppress, mistreat, or victimize the police in any systematic or institutionalized manner. Assuming the mantle of victimhood by the police ignores this stark and clearly delineated power imbalance and serves to undermine claims by African Americans, Latinx, and LGBTQ populations that the police have been, as an institution, an instrument of racism and oppressive and often violent practices. "Blue Racism" also casts the police as a "race," something that it clearly is not, and overlooks the reality that the "blue," unlike fixed racial and ethnic origin group identification, is easily cast aside at the end of a shift with a change in clothing. Certainly not all police see themselves as victims of this faux "racism," but it is perhaps a significant enough reaction to an interrogation and re-imagination of their role in policing our communities to warrant exposure and examination.

This "Blue Racism" bromide is instrumental in examining recent efforts by state legislatures to enact so-called "hate crime" legislation that casts police officers, again, in the role of the victim. In 2016 Louisiana became the first state to enact a so-called "Blue Lives Matter" bill, that provided sentencing enhancements for those who attack police officers, Emergency Medical Technicians, and firefighters. This made police officers a protected class, similar to racial and religious groups (Craven, 2016). According to the *Huffington Post*, since the beginning of 2017, "lawmakers in 14 states have introduced at least 32 bills proposing that members of law enforcement be included in hate crime protections — like those received by people of color, religious minorities and members of the LGBTQ community" (Craven, 2017). Many see the so-called "Blue Lives Matter" laws as redundant and counterproductive, since sentencing enhancements and laws providing for the protection of police officers already exist in all 50 states and the District of Columbia (Beitsch, 2016). The police are already a protected class.

The Anti-Defamation League strongly opposes the inclusion of police officers as a protected class under hate crime laws, stating that

> Hate Crimes are designed to protect people's most precious identity categories—their "immutable characteristics" like race, religion, gender, sexual orientation, disability, ethnicity, and gender identity. Proving the bias intent is very different for these categories as it is for the bias intent of a crime against a law enforcement officer—and adding professional categories to the current Hate Crimes statue deters efforts from protecting against identity-based crimes.
>
> (Anti-Defamation League, 2016)

Most of the bills are unlikely to pass: "At least 20 of the bills introduced over the past year died by vote or at the end of the congressional session after being referred to a state legislative committee" (Craven, 2017). Nonetheless, "the truth is that including police in hate crime laws is merely a political statement—and an unnecessary one at that," says Mark Potok, a senior fellow at the Southern Poverty Law Center (Craven, 2017).

The politicization of this narrative, where crimes against the police are seen as evidence of the deterioration of the societal fabric that is only maintained and tenuously held together through the law enforcement imprint, serves to legitimize the social construct of the "Blue Lives Matter" movement as an appositive to the Black Lives Matter social movement. "Blue Lives Matter" and similar law enforcement support networks serve to position law enforcement officers and their advocates on a higher moral plane than those who would seek to hold them accountable for instances of wrongdoing. "Blue Lives Matter" arose in a large part to undermine and to delegitimize the traction and the credibility that the Black Lives Matter movement had garnered through largely peaceful protests against law enforcement violence and excess, protests that gained widespread notice and affirmation following demonstrations in Ferguson, Missouri, in the aftermath of the death of Michael Brown. In the worldview of "Blue Lives Matter" then-police officer Darren Wilson, who shot and killed the unarmed teenager, is seen as a hero and a victim (Blue Lives Matter, 2017). In this world, Black Lives Matter protesters are seen as criminals, rioters, looters, thugs—racist "dog whistle" terms depicting people of color.

For anyone who has ever seen the public spectacle of a funeral for a police officer who has been killed in the line of duty and the conspicuous display and accompanying outpouring of solemnity, reverence, and awe, there can be no doubt that police lives matter, and that they matter publicly far more than most of the rest of us. The dirge, the bagpipes, the drums, the assembly, the march, the long line of police vehicles, and lights flashing silently, even garishly, rival funeral services for heads of state in the sheer magnitude of the tribute, the farewell to a hero in the eyes of all of those assembled to pay tribute. To suggest otherwise, as is implicit in the telling of "Blue Lives Matter" adherents, is to ignore the largely widespread support and respect that the police benefit from in the Unites States, even in the aftermath of the exposure of the relatively small number of police who engage in gratuitous violence, corruption, incompetence, and other wrongdoing, activities that continue to the present.

Following the shooting death of Michael Brown in Ferguson, Missouri, in the summer of 2014 and the widespread condemnation not only of then-police officer Darren Wilson's killing of the unarmed teenager, but perhaps even more consequentially the over-the-top police response to the street demonstrations that followed Brown's death, there began a retrenchment of sorts for police departments nationwide and a re-evaluation of the necessity and prudence of the use of a heavily militarized civilian police response to street unrest in American cities.

Perhaps predictably, once the police were roundly criticized for their use of military weapons, vehicles, aircraft, and other ordnance in the frequently-violent suppression and dispersal of unarmed protesters who were engaging in constitutionally protected activity, often while dressed somewhat inexplicably in desert camouflage uniforms, they adopted the victim role, and saw themselves as unappreciated, selflessly-dedicated warriors in the perilous battle between good and evil.

The "Ferguson Effect" and the "War on Police"

St. Louis Police Chief Sam Dotson, Heather MacDonald and others, including then-Federal Bureau of Investigation (FBI) director James Comey, advanced the wholly unsubstantiated notion of something they dubbed the "Ferguson Effect" (MacDonald, 2016), wherein the police, hobbled (and emasculated) by the public condemnation of the law enforcement response to the protests in Ferguson and elsewhere, were now reluctant and afraid to do their jobs. The result, they argued, was anarchy and lawlessness and a sharp increase in the levels of violent crime in the streets of American cities, as the police, "handcuffed" and prevented from doing the crime fighting that only they knew how to do effectively, were hamstrung by "liberals" and then-President Obama so that "slandered by the media and targeted in the streets, officers reverted to a model of purely reactive policing that had been out of vogue since the early 1990s" (MacDonald, 2016, p. 6). Comey, perhaps imprudently, spoke to police administrators at Chicago Law School in 2015, and said that "the chill wind blowing through American law enforcement over the past year" (MacDonald, 2016, p. 6) had been the likely reason for a sharp increase in violent crime and homicides (an increase not substantiated by the Uniform Crime Report figures recorded by Comey's Department of Justice) (United States Department of Justice, 2016).

What of this newly coined phenomenon, the "Ferguson Effect", and its effect on an increase in violent crime in American cities? According to research conducted by Sherry Towers and Michael White at Arizona State University, "there is little statistical evidence of a Ferguson Effect in Chicago—murders and violent crime began an upward trend well before Michael Brown's death" (Towers & White, 2017, p. 29).

David Pyrooz et al. found that

the national discourse surrounding the "Ferguson Effect" is long on anecdotes and short on data, leaving criminologists largely on the sidelines of a conversation concerning one of the most prominent contemporary issues in criminal justice. Our findings are largely consistent with longstanding criminological knowledge that changes in crime trends are slow and rarely a product of random shocks (such as events in Ferguson), There is no evidence to support a systematic Ferguson Effect on overall, violent, and property crime trends in large U.S. cities.

(2016, p. 1)

Samuel Sinyangwe (2016) observed that "FBI Director Comey himself has conceded there is no evidence to support the 'Ferguson Effect,'" and that, regarding 2015 crime rates "analyses by the Marshall Project and the Justice Department have found no evidence that violent crime has significantly increased among the nation's largest cities." And as pertains to policing in communities of color and the existence of a "Ferguson Effect," Sinyangwe argued that

> The fact that a theory lacking evidentiary support could be so hastily endorsed by some of the nation's foremost institutions speaks to the enduring power of the belief that aggressive policing is the only way to keep black communities safe … In the end, the "Ferguson Effect" lacks factual basis.
>
> (p. 24)

Scott Wolfe and Justin Nix, in writing about the ubiquity of cell-phone cameras and other recording devices in the hands of ordinary citizens and their willingness to record the activities of the police, particularly following the widely-publicized deaths of Michael Brown, Eric Garner, Tamir Rice, and others "have caused such widespread negative attention that some argue it is causing police officers to withdraw from their duties in order to avoid being accused of excessive force or racial profiling—a phenomenon referred to as the 'Ferguson Effect'" (2016, p. 2). They attribute the speed with which the concept has gained traction on social media to the "social contagion effect," where "highly publicized mass killings, suicides, and other violent events tend to fuel other violence" (p. 2). Research conducted by these authors attempted to determine whether the so-called "Ferguson Effect" had effects on aspects of the law enforcement function that were not related to the concept of "de-policing," i.e., the police being not willing to perform their duties, such as the willingness of the police to engage in community partnerships, a cornerstone of the community policing philosophy.

Wolfe and Nix (2016) found that, while many officers were aware of the "Ferguson Effect," and that some were even reluctant to perform their duties in response to the widespread negative publicity that the police have seen and experienced following high-profile shootings, the Ferguson Effect "was no longer significant" (p. 2). Their

> data reveal that reduced motivation attributable to negative publicity may be counteracted if supervisors ensure fairness among subordinates. Little actions can go a long way. Fair treatment from supervisors sends the message to officers that "we are here for you" regardless of how much the public or the media tries to sully law enforcement.
>
> (p. 7)

Thus, these authors' research demonstrated that the police were not less willing to engage in community partnerships as a result of the largely social media generated phenomenon known as the "Ferguson Effect."

John Shjarback et al. (2017) sought to investigate the issue of "de-policing" in the era of social media and they examined 2015 data on motor vehicle stops in 118 of 121 police departments serving populations of over 5000 residents in Missouri, where Michael Brown was shot by police in Ferguson in 2014. These authors "found consistent evidence of a racialized de-policing effect. Departments made fewer vehicle/traffic stops, searches, and arrests in 2015 relative to 2014 in jurisdictions with larger African-American populations" (p. 50). They also "found mixed evidence of the quantity of de-policing among local Missouri agencies; departments made about 67,000 fewer vehicle/traffic stops in 2015 compared to 2014, but this pattern was not substantively significant for searches and arrests stemming from those stops," and that officers, while making fewer stops in 2015 than in 2014, "were making better stops and conducting searches that more consistently yielded contraband" (p. 50).

The results of the Shjarback et al. study "demonstrate that jurisdictions with higher percentages of minority residents are more prone to de-policing" (2017, p. 43), but that such "de-policing" does not necessarily lead to an increase in crime, and thus, they argue that there may be a positive outcome to the de-escalation of aggressive, income-driven policing, the kind of policing decried in the report of the Department of Justice on the Ferguson Police Department (United States Department of Justice, 2015).

Richard Rosenfeld's perspective on the "Ferguson Effect" analyzed a different aspect of post-Ferguson policing in St. Louis and other cities. Crime increases that may have been observed in some cities in 2015 were not owing to "de-policing" following widespread criticism of the police in 2014, but rather

> the idea that violence escalates when individuals and communities are alienated from the legitimate means of social control. When persons do not trust the police to act on their behalf and to treat them fairly and with respect, they lose confidence in the formal apparatus of social control and become more likely to take matters into their own hands. Interpersonal disputes are settled informally and often violently.
>
> (2016, pp. 18–19)

Rosenfeld goes on to suggest that the "lack of confidence in the police among African-Americans predates the recent police killings in Ferguson, Cleveland, New York and elsewhere. But it is likely to be activated by such incidents, transforming longstanding latent grievances into an acute legitimacy crisis" (2016, p. 19). So, if there is any effect on policing in the aftermath of the police shooting deaths of (mostly) African American men in America's cities, it is a crisis in the perceived failure and breakdown in the policing function and a concomitant challenge to a loss of confidence in the legitimacy of the police. Following this crisis in Ferguson, as manifested by the total breakdown of the policing function and the de-legitimacy of the police that accompanied this dysfunction, I personally advocated the abolition and disbanding of the Ferguson Police Department as well as the firing or resignation of its chief (Nolan, 2015).

According to Radley Balko, the so-called "war on cops" is a dangerous fiction, one that has the

> more pernicious effect of exaggerating the threats faced by law enforcement. When cops are constantly told that they're under constant fire, or that every interaction with a citizen could be their last, or that they're fortunate each time they come home from the job in one piece, it's absolute poison for police-community relations.
>
> (2015)

Those advancing the notion that there are individuals and groups who are waging a war on the police often use loaded terms such as "ambush" and "assassination" in describing the killings of police officers, in fearmongering and incendiary rhetoric that inflame tensions between the police and the citizenry, particularly in communities of color. ("Feloniously killed" is the term used by the FBI in describing the intentional killing of a police officer, as opposed to "accidental killings," e.g., car crashes, in official recording.) Police organizations and their supporters, in using the "war" metaphor, often cite the increase in the numbers of police officers feloniously killed in 2014 (at 51, an 80 percent increase over the previous year, when 27 officers were killed feloniously) as "evidence" that these are perilous times for police officers that are without precedent.

The year 2014 was the year that Michael Brown was killed in Ferguson, Missouri, and the year that demonstrators took to the streets nationwide to protest police violence and lawlessness. The war on police narrative is based in a large part on the unsubstantiated belief that police officers were being randomly targeted, attacked, and killed in unprecedented numbers as retribution for what police and their supporters believed were entirely justified incidents of the use of force, deadly or otherwise. This narrative saw the police as heroic, unappreciated guardians of the good, the righteous, and the moral. The war on cops narrative ignores the 27 officers killed feloniously in 2013 as being the lowest number of police officers killed feloniously since the FBI began recording these statistics (Wang, 2015).

How Dangerous Is Policing?

Balko reported that "the figure for the following year, 2014, (fifty-one officers killed) was essentially consistent with the average for the previous five years (fifty killed), and still lower than any five-year average going back to 1960" (2015). As for the dangerous world of policing in the second decade of the twenty-first century, assaults on police officers and people trying to harm officers continue at a downward trajectory that began in the mid-2000s and continues to the present (Bier, 2014). According to Bier "injuries and attacks suffered by police have been slowly declining for fifteen years. Police are dying less frequently because of better medical care, yes, but they are also being assaulted and injured less to begin with" (2014).

The FBI's Law Enforcement Officers Killed and Assaulted Program (2018) (LEOKA) reported that in 2015, 41 police officers were killed feloniously. The following year, 2016, saw 66 officers killed feloniously; in 2017 the number was 46. LEOKA also reported that four of the 46 officers killed feloniously in 2017 were "ambushed," which they describe as "premeditated entrapment," which translates as 8.6 percent of the total number of officers killed feloniously. A total of 17 of the 66 officers killed in 2016 were "ambushed," or almost 26 percent. The ten-year average for police officers killed feloniously for the year ending 2017 was 49.7.

To put this in perspective, the average number of police officers killed feloniously in the ten-year period that ended in 2007 was 55; if we were to include the 72 officers who were killed during the attack on the World Trade Center towers on September 11, 2001, the ten-year average climbs to 62. As for "ambush" killings of police officers, in the five-year period from 2000–2004, for example, the percentage of officers killed feloniously who were ambushed was

20 percent. In the years 2006–2010, the average number of police officers killed feloniously was 50; the average number of those officer killings that were classified as "ambush" deaths were 24 percent. In the five-year period from 2013–2017, the average number of police officers who were killed feloniously was 46, and the number of police officers killed feloniously who were ambushed fell to 15 percent. Simply put: since 2014, when the so-called "war on cops" supposedly commenced in earnest, the numbers of police killed, ambushed, and assaulted fell, continuing a decades long downward trajectory in assaults and killings of police officers.

An examination of assaults on police officers from 2010–2017 (the last year figures are available at the time of writing), show a strong consistency in the numbers of reported assaults and injuries to officers, as well as the type of weapons used in assaulting officers. The average percentage of police officers who reported being assaulted was 9.8 percent over the seven-year period. The average percentage of officers reporting injury during these assaults was 27.7 percent. A consistent 80 percent of the assaults involved what are referred to as "personal weapons," i.e., hands, feet, or fists. In 2014, 9 percent of officers reported being assaulted; 9.8 percent in 2015; 10.8 percent in 2016; and 10.1 percent in 2017. As a comparison, in the years 1996–2000, an average of 12.4 percent of officers reported being assaulted in a given year (13 percent in 1996; 11 percent in 1997; 13 percent in 1998; 12 percent in 1999; and 13 percent in 2000). From 2001–2005, the average number of police officers who reported assaults were 12 percent (12.2 percent in 2001; 12 percent in 2002; 12 percent in 2003; 11.9 percent in 2004; and 11.9 percent in 2005). And from 2006–2010 the average number of police officers reporting assaults fell to 10.9 percent (11.8 percent in 2006; 11.4 percent in 2007; 11.3 percent in 2008; 10.3 percent in 2009; and 10 percent in 2010).

Ronald Schouten and Douglas Brennan have observed that "longitudinal LEOKA data reveal that rates of attacks on police have decreased dramatically over the past 25 years, declining through the 1990s and then maintaining a steady level since then" (2016, p. 610). These data may be related to the overall decline in crime rates nationally, as well as

> increased availability of level I trauma services and emergency medical response; training and equipment that protect officers from assault and allow them to prevent, deter, or counter any attacks; and deterrence due to the severity of criminal penalties for assaults on police officers.
>
> (Schouten & Brennan, 2016, p. 610)

Schouten and Brennan suggest that

> this could reflect overall positive societal attitudes towards police or a general unwillingness to resort to violence, in spite of the perception of increased police bias against minority populations and use of excessive force. Instead, as one would hope in a constitutional democracy, those concerns may be expressed through peaceful protests, community action, and collective efforts to identify and resolve conflicts.
>
> (2016, p. 610)

Heather MacDonald has written about a phenomenon that she calls "The War on Cops," and she goes to considerable lengths to facilitate the police narrative of "de-policing" in the face of the continuing effort to force the police to an accountability and transparency that had long been absent in confronting police excess. An apologist for police racism, oppression, discrimination, and violence, MacDonald describes those engaged in constitutionally protected activities in assembling, protesting, and airing grievances as "savages," "looters," and "arsonists" who are torching America's cities and leaving them "in flames" (2016, p. 40). She refers to the African American teenagers and men who have been killed by police in the most pejorative light: 18-year-old Michael Brown was "a budding criminal who weighed nearly 300 pounds" who "thuggishly robbed a diminutive shopkeeper" (pp. 5–8).

For the crime of selling loose cigarettes, "in a high-crime area" (p. 31) Eric Garner "who died after a forceful police takedown, was added to the list of martyrs to racist police brutality" (p. 5), according to MacDonald (2016). New York City police officers used a long-prohibited choke hold to essentially strangle Garner to death; a man who was well known to the officers inexplicably needed to be thrown to the ground, pummeled, choked, and left to die on the sidewalk, for the most trivial of offenses, one for which a summons would have more than addressed this somehow pressing law enforcement mandate. Garner, in MacDonald's telling, had been arrested many times for not only selling loose cigarettes, but had also been arrested for possessing marijuana.

In the chapter entitled "Baltimore in Flames," MacDonald describes Freddie Gray, as a "25-year-old drug dealer with a lengthy arrest record," who was in "a high crime area" when "police reportedly claimed that he was involved in illegal activity" (2016, p. 40). Baltimore police began chasing Gray on bicycles after he "made eye contact with them and took off running." When caught, he was charged with a weapons offense after officers found a folding knife in his pocket, a knife later determined to be legal to carry. Gray died after being thrown into a police van while handcuffed and suffering a spinal cord injury. To this day it is unclear as to the reason for Gray's arrest by the Baltimore officers. Six officers were indicted and charged criminally in Gray's death, yet the officers were all subsequently either acquitted and had the charges dropped against them. Following Gray's death, demonstrators took to the streets to protest what they saw as repeated instances of social injustice in the deaths of African American boys and men, like Gray, at the hands of the police, something MacDonald (2016) referred to as "bunk." "What happened in Baltimore was simply a larger and better covered version of the flash mobs that have beset American cities in recent years, with black youths gathering via social media to steal from stores and assault whites" (MacDonald, 2016, p. 44).

For MacDonald, those who lend virtually all of what passes for substance and credence to this demonstrably fictive narrative of a "war on cops" are, predictably, the police themselves. MacDonald offers, without supporting evidence, that

> there are signs that the legal order itself is breaking down in urban areas. "There's a total lack of respect out there for the police," says a female sergeant in New York. "The perps are more empowered to carry guns because they know that we are running scared."
>
> (2016, p. 66)

"Any cop who uses his gun now has to worry about being indicted and losing his job and family" (2016, p. 57), MacDonald attests. In this war on cops: "The level of hostility has skyrocketed," and "officer morale has understandably plummeted as a consequence." She quotes Milwaukee police chief Edward Flynn: "I've never seen anything like it" (2016, p. 57).

In MacDonald's telling, bystanders in Cincinnati "loudly cursing" at officers who, in responding to the scene of a shooting in which a four-year-old girl had been shot and critically wounded, and who began checking onlookers for warrants and arresting them, were engaging in a "mini riot," and this was evidence of "the lawful use of police power being met with hostility and violence. which is often ignored by the press" (2016, p. 66). "Cops were being shot at in Ferguson" and "death threats against police officers multiplied," (p. 13) she reported. Police officers constantly "are at risk of violent attack" (p. 56) in this war, and only the restoration of "law and order" and what she calls "proactive policing" will make the streets safe again, as she believes that they were in the 1990s.

In the chapter titled "The Riot Show!" MacDonald (2016) describes media coverage of the protests in Baltimore following the death of Freddie Gray as "riot porn, in which every act of thuggery is lasciviously filmed and parsed…" (p. 47). (She refers to Gray as "the drug dealer who died of a spinal injury in police custody.") MacDonald refers to the protests in Baltimore and Ferguson as "race riots" and "urban tantrums" (p. 48), in dog whistle terms specifically meant to denigrate, demean, undermine, and delegitimize African American grievances against the police.

MacDonald casts these long-held, clearly-established, and repeated instances of unfair and disparate treatment of African Americans at the hands of police as an "incessant drumbeat," and "a seemingly constant stream of stories about alleged police mistreatment of blacks … pumped out by," she says, "the news media" (2016, p. 56). "Such lying about interactions between officers and civilians is endemic in urban areas" (p. 51), according to MacDonald, employing a well-known racist code term for African American communities.

The Mythical War

Tim Lynch, writing in *Reason*, argues that "What MacDonald calls a 'war on cops' is better described as a much-needed debate about crime, law enforcement tactics, and how to deal with systemic police misconduct" (2016, p. 58). MacDonald's "polemics" are, in his assessment, unhelpful and incendiary. Of MacDonald's "war on cops," Lynch calls her out on her hysteria:

> Beyond its analytical shortcomings, much of the book is written in an over-the-top polemical style. Barack Obama is not just misguided; he has "betrayed the nation." Black Lives Matter is a "fraud." *The New York Times* serves up "anti-police propaganda." Columbia Law School professor Jeffrey Fagan's scholarship "might be characterized as a tutorial on lying with statistics." Ending the drug war to alleviate the burden on the police, courts, and prisons is a "delusion."
>
> (2016, p. 58)

Kali Holloway, writing in *AlterNet* (2016), sees the "war on cops" as a right-wing myth, fueled in no small part by then-director of the FBI James Comey, who spoke about something he referred to as a "viral video effect," "with officers wary of confronting suspects for fear of ending up on a video." According to *The New York Times*, Comey told reporters that there's a perception that police are less likely to do the marginal additional policing that suppresses crime—the getting out of your car at 2 in the morning and saying to a group of guys, "Hey, what are you doing here?"

(Lichtblau, 2016)

Holloway has likened this mythical war and the notion that the police are now reluctant, even afraid to do their jobs to a "social panic," similar to the social panics of recent years that gave us mythical "crack babies," "welfare queens," "anchor babies," "flash mobs," and even roaming black teens playing the "knockout game" (Johnson, 2015). Holloway (2016) sees Comey's comments as suggesting "that policing without brutality is an impossibility; that police officers simply cannot do their jobs—which are difficult and challenging on the best of days—without crossing the line into abuse." Significantly, she argues that comments like Comey's, MacDonald's, and others who fan the flames of the "Ferguson Effect" and the "war on cops" serve to feed the misperception

that BLM and movements against police abuse are bigger problems than police violence; pushing the notion that activists deserve scorn for filming and calling out police misconduct when they see it; and none too subtly implying that demanding accountability for police violence somehow merits a response that jeopardizes public safety.

(Holloway, 2016)

Alice Speri, writing about the "Ferguson Effect" in *The Intercept*, also called Comey out for "suggesting that a spike in violent crime in some cities may be correlated to officers' fear of doing their jobs because of community hostility and the growing popularity of cop watching" (2016). While many, including Comey, MacDonald, then-Attorney General Jeff Sessions, and others have touted an alarming and precipitous increase in violent crime in cities across the United States, owing at least in part to the "war on cops" and the "Ferguson Effect," Speri (2016) contended that "while some cities are undoubtedly facing unacceptable levels of violence, the nationwide trend in violent crime continues to point downward, as it has for the last 25 years."

While violent crime in certain cities, such as St. Louis and Baltimore, had risen in 2014 and 2015, this has been the continuation of a long-term trend in certain cities that have a history of socioeconomic issues such as protracted poverty, substandard housing and schools, chronic unemployment and "gray-market" employment, and transient and unstable neighborhoods. Speri (2016) spoke to Jacob Crawford, who founded "We Cop Watch," a nationwide activist organization that records the police in cities across the United States (and a large contributor no doubt to Mr. Comey's "viral video" archive), who contended that "police now for the first time are having to consider the consequences of being brutal, being unethical, and doing things that for the longest time they could do and not be accountable for," he added, "But that doesn't make crime happen."

Matt Ferner, Alissa Scheller, and Nick Wing, writing in the *Huffington Post* about the "war on cops," argue that "data does (*sic*) not support claims from conservative media outlets, police union bosses and Trump, who claim that increased scrutiny of police and demand for reform has encouraged a so-called 'war on cops'" (2016). The shooting deaths of African American men and women have led to more aggressive criticism of police by the Black Lives Matter movement and other civil rights organizations. Their opponents argue that these groups have fomented a hostile environment for police. But there's no evidence to suggest that this climate is actually causing officers to be killed at higher rates.

(Ferner et al., 2016)

They interviewed David Harris, a professor at University of Pittsburgh School of Law who studies policing, and he noted that

2015 was a year with a lot of criticism of police, let's face it, and no matter how you stand on that, what we can say for sure is that does not seem to have resulted in more police officer deaths.

(Ferner et al., 2016)

Conclusion

The police have been called to an unprecedented level of accountability and responsibility for incidents in which they use force, and particularly deadly force, in marginalized communities and specifically against black and brown men and women and boys and girls. This clarion call gained momentum in the aftermath of the shooting death of Michael Brown by police in Ferguson, Missouri, in August of 2014 and continues to the present. The response on the part of certain members of the police to this interrogatory has been, at least in part, to cast themselves in the role of victim and to proclaim that there is a "war" being waged against the police by those who would call into question their strategies, tactics, and policies as they relate to the use of force and the control of acts of civil disobedience and protests. The empirical evidence that attests to and supports the notion of the existence of a "war on cops" is scant, if it exists at all.

Concomitant with the declaration that there exists a war on the police in the United States has been the identification of a so-called "Ferguson Effect," whereby the protests and calls for accountability and transparency that followed events in Ferguson that began in the summer and fall of 2014 and that continue in many cities throughout the United States to the present, have instilled in (at least some of) the police a reluctance or an inability to "do their jobs." And again, this phenomenon, in the minds of certain police, casts law enforcement officers as helpless and hapless victims to what is nothing if not the manifestation of the lack of appreciation for, deference to, and support of the heroic and selfless services that the police provide to all residents and all communities. And as with the "war on cops," the empirical evidence to support the existence of this effect is slim.

NOTE

1 For more information on the movement, you can visit the website: https://blacklivesmatter.com.

REFERENCES

Anti-Defamation League. (2016, May 2). ADL opposes "Blue Lives Matters" bill and urges Senate to vote against it. *ADL*. Retrieved from: http://neworleans.adl.org/news/adl-opposes-blue-lives-matters-bill-and-urges-senate-to-vote-against-it/.

Balko, R. (2015, September 10). Once again: There is no "war on cops." And those who claim otherwise are playing a dangerous game. *The Washington Post*. Retrieved from: www.washingtonpost.com/news/the-watch/wp/2015/09/10/once-again-there-is-no-war-on-cops-and-those-who-claim-otherwise-are-playing-a-dangerous-game/?utm_term=.3dee94c485f1.

Beitsch, R. (2016, August 3). Should killing a police officer be a hate crime? *The Pew Charitable Trusts*. Retrieved from: www.pewtrusts.org/en/research-and-analysis/blogs/stateline/2016/08/03/should-killing-a-police-officer-be-a-hate-crime.

Bier, D. (2014, August 21). By the numbers: Methodological notes on police fatalities and assaults. *The Skeptical Libertarian*. Retrieved from: http://blog.skepticallibertarian.com/2014/08/21/methodological-notes-on-police-fatalities-and-assaults/.

Bloom, J., Fausset, R., & McPhate, M. (2016, July 17). Baton Rouge shooting jolts a nation on edge. *The New York Times*. Retrieved from: www.nytimes.com/2016/07/18/us/baton-rouge-shooting.html.

Craven, J. (2016, May 25). Louisiana's new "Blue Lives Matter" law on cop killers is actually pretty redundant. *Huffington Post*. Retrieved from: www.huffingtonpost.com/entry/louisiana-hate-crime-police_us_5745ba0ee4b055bb1170c4de.

Craven, J. (2017, December 11). 32 Blue Lives Matter bills have been introduced across 14 states this year. *Huffington Post*. Retrieved from: www.huffingtonpost.com/entry/blue-black-lives-matter-police-bills-states_us_58b61488e4b0780bac2e31b8.

Davey, M., & Bosman, J. (2014, November 24). Protests flare after Ferguson police officer is not indicted. *The New York Times*. Retrieved from: www.nytimes.com/2014/11/25/us/ferguson-darren-wilson-shooting-michael-brown-grand-jury.html.

Federal Bureau of Investigation, Uniform Crime Reports, Law Enforcement Officers Killed and Assaulted Program. (2018). *2018 Law Enforcement Officers Killed*. Retrieved from: https://ucr.fbi.gov/leoka-resources.

Fernandez, M., Perez-Pena, R., & Bromwich, J. (2016, July 8). Five Dallas officers were killed as payback, police chief says. *The New York Times*. Retrieved from: www.nytimes.com/2016/07/09/us/dallas-police-shooting.html.

Ferner, M., Scheller, A., & Wing, N. (2016, October 18). Donald Trump's claim that there's a "war on police" is still bunk. *Huffington Post*. Retrieved from: www.huffingtonpost.com/entry/donald-trump-war-on-police_us_58069097e4b0180a36e7310e.

Feuer, A. (2017, August 22). Police union complains of "blue racism," then regrets word choice. *The New York Times*. Retrieved from: www.nytimes.com/2017/08/22/nyregion/nypd-union-video-discrimination.html.

Holloway, K. (2016, May 25). The numbers are in: The war on cops is a right-wing myth. *Alternet*. Retrieved from: www.alternet.org/news-amp-politics/2015-was-one-safest-years-record-be-cop.

Johnson, A. (2015, September 2). 12 stupidest racist moral panics, from crack babies to the Ferguson effect. *Alternet*. Retrieved from: www.alternet.org/media/12-stupidest-racist-moral-panics-crack-babies-ferguson-effect.

Lichtblau, E. (2016, May 11). F.B.I. Director says "viral video effect" blunts police work. *The New York Times*. Retrieved from: www.nytimes.com/2016/05/12/us/comey-ferguson-effect-police-videos-fbi.html?_r=1.

Lynch, T. (2016). There is no war on cops. *Reason, 48* (4).

MacDonald, H. (2016). *The War on Cops: How the New Attack on Law and Order Makes Everyone Less Safe*. New York: Encounter Books.

Mueller, B., & Baker, A. (2014, December 20). 2 N.Y.P.D. officers killed in Brooklyn ambush; suspect commits suicide. *The New York Times*. Retrieved from: www.nytimes.com/2014/12/21/nyregion/two-police-officers-shot-in-their-patrol-car-in-brooklyn.html.

Mueller, B., & Baker, A. (2017, July 5). Police officer is "murdered for her uniform" in the Bronx. *The New York Times*. Retrieved from: www.nytimes.com/2017/07/05/nyregion/nypd-bronx-police-shooting.html.

Nolan, T. (2015, March 9). Ferguson: The prequel. *American Constitution Society*. Retrieved from: www.acslaw.org/acsblog/ferguson-the-prequel/.

OfficerBlue. (2017, May 14). About Blue Lives Matter. *Blue Lives Matter*. Retrieved from: www.themaven.net/bluelivesmatter/pages/rF54b2VNMUOrl7wfh8vRXQ.

Pyrooz, D. C., Decker, S. H., Wolfe, S. E., & Shjarback, J. A. (2016). Was there a Ferguson Effect on crime rates in large U.S. cities? *Journal of Criminal Justice*, 46, pp. 1–8.

Rosenfeld, R. (2016, June). *Documenting and Explaining the 2015 Homicide Rise: Research Directions*. Washington D.C.: U.S. Department of Justice, Office of Justice Programs, National Institute of Justice.

Sanchez, R. (2015, September 4). Attacks leave police feeling under siege. *CNN*. Retrieved from: www.cnn.com/2015/09/04/us/us-police-feel-under-siege/index.html.

Schouten, R., & Brennan, D. V. (2016). Targeted violence against law enforcement officers. *Behavioral Sciences & The Law*, 34 (5), pp. 608–621.

Shjarback, J. A., Pyrooz, D. C., Wolfe, S. E., & Decker, S. H. (2017). De-policing and crime in the wake of Ferguson: Racialized changes in the quantity and quality of policing among Missouri police departments. *Journal of Criminal Justice*, 5, pp. 42–52.

Sinyangwe, S. (2016). Stop pretending the "Ferguson effect" is real. *University of California at Los Angeles: Ufahamu: A Journal of African Studies*, 39 (1).

Speri, A. (2016, May 12). Myth of the Ferguson effect is hard to kill. *The Intercept*. Retrieved from: https://theintercept.com/2016/05/12/myth-of-the-ferguson-effect-is-hard-to-kill/.

Towers, S., & White, M. (2017, April). The "Ferguson effect," or too many guns? *Significance*, 14 (2), pp. 26–29.

United States Department of Justice. (2015, March 4). *Report Regarding the Criminal Investigation into the Shooting Death of Michael Brown by Ferguson, Missouri Police Officer Darren Wilson*. Retrieved from: www.justice.gov/sites/default/files/opa/press-releases/attachments/2015/03/04/doj_report_on_shooting_of_michael_brown_1.pdf.

United States Department of Justice. (2016). *2015 Crime in the United States*. Retrieved from: https://ucr.fbi.gov/crime-in-the-u.s/2015/crime-in-the-u.s.-2015.

Wang, D. (2015, June 16). Data on police officers killed since 1961. *Dan Wang*. Retrieved from: http://danwang.co/statistics-on-police-fatalities/.

Wolfe, S. E., & Nix, J. (2016). The alleged "Ferguson effect" and police willingness to engage in community partnership. *Law and Human Behavior*, 40 (1).

Chapter 6

The "Immigration Police"
The Demonization of the "Other"

When Mexico sends its people, they're not sending their best. They're not sending you. They're not sending you. They're sending people that have lots of problems, and they're bringing those problems with us. They're bringing drugs. They're bringing crime. They're rapists. And some, I assume, are good people.

(Donald Trump, announcing his candidacy for president, June 16, 2015)

The Policing of Immigration: Co-Opting Local Law Enforcement

Even though immigration policy in the Unites States purports to be a process that is fair, just, and in keeping with long-held and cherished principles that endorse opportunity and democratic freedoms for those looking to immigrate, the reality has often fallen short of such lofty aspirations. The history of immigration policy in the United States has been fraught with injustices and inequalities spawned by policies often based on political expediencies. These policies have historically excluded members of certain racial and ethnic origin groups from being considered for immigration.

These exclusions, while largely abated in the latter part of the twentieth century, have been revisited and re-established with what many observers see as an unprecedented vengeance that commenced with the Trump Administration in January of 2017. This began with the signing of Executive Order 13769, which banned citizens of seven primarily Muslim countries from entering the United States. This policy became known as the so-called "Muslim Ban" and, although halted in various iterations by several federal courts, it has remained largely intact as policy in its third version as of the summer of 2018.

This administration has continued to strenuously advocate for the construction of a border wall between the United States and Mexico, as well as to reduce the numbers of legal immigrants by sharply reducing the number of green cards that will be issued (these provide lawful permanent residency in the United States). The administration has also implemented a policy of zero-tolerance for crossing the Mexican border without documentation and of separating families at the border. In addition to numerous other severe restrictions on asylum seekers and refugees, the administration has significantly stepped up deportations of those in the country without the necessary permissions and documentation.

According to *PolitiFact*,

> the Trump administration's determination to deport people in the country illegally carried over in the number of administrative arrests for civil violation of immigration laws. The number of administrative arrests went up 30 percent from fiscal years 2016 to 2017.
>
> (Valverde, 2017)

This is while apprehensions at the Southern border are at their lowest levels since 1971: "Border Patrol agents recorded 310,531 apprehensions nationwide in fiscal year 2017, the lowest since the 302,517 apprehensions in 1971. CBP tallied 415,816 apprehensions in fiscal year 2016" (Valverde, 2017).

Law enforcement at the local, county, and state levels has, in varying degrees of participation, actively engaged or participated in or facilitated Immigration and Customs Enforcement (ICE) immigration enforcement strategies. Some of the enforcement of immigration laws and policies by police has been accomplished with the knowledge and approval of affected communities; other immigration-related activities engaged in by the police are done without the awareness of or permission from elected officials, policy makers, and community residents. This co-optation of the police by immigration officials has had consequences, both intended and unintended, for immigrant communities as well as for the police.

The Trouble with So-Called "Gang Databases": No Refuge in the "Sanctuary"

I have been asked to testify in Immigration Court here in Boston several times in as many weeks on behalf of undocumented immigrant teenagers, all Hispanic and from El Salvador, who had been "verified" as gang members, purportedly belonging to either the 18th Street or MS-13 gangs. These teenagers had been "verified" as gang members in a "Gang Assessment Database" maintained by the Boston Regional Intelligence Center, aka the "BRIC," a fusion center operated and maintained by the Boston Police Department.

All were in deportation proceedings in Immigration Court, hearings based in a large part on their supposed "verified" gang membership. ICE agents had determined that these young men were in fact dangerous gang members who warranted immediate removal from the United States.

I am no expert on gangs, gang membership, gang identifiers, or gang activities. But I do have expertise in the types of data and information that can be legally entered into criminal intelligence databases, such as the ~~BRIC's Gang Assessment Database~~, and it was for this reason that my testimony was sought in Immigration Court. The operation of Criminal Intelligence Systems, such as the BRIC's Gang Assessment Database, are governed and regulated by federal law as embodied in what is known as "28 CFR Part 23" (United States Government Executive Order 12291, 1998). The Code of Federal Regulations (CFR) is essentially the codification of the rules and procedures for the administration of the federal government; they cover 50 areas and are published annually in the Federal Register. Interjurisdictional Intelligence Systems and Criminal Intelligence Systems, such as those maintained in fusion centers like the BRIC, are required by federal law to be 28 CFR Part 23 compliant. The Gang Assessment Database maintained by the BRIC is, at least in part, non-compliant with 28 CFR Part 23, and is thus in violation of the applicable federal rules as contained in the regulation.

Information concerning an individual may be "collected and maintained" in a Criminal Intelligence Database "only if there is reasonable suspicion that the individual is involved in criminal conduct or activity and the information is relevant to that criminal conduct or activity." The regulation further clarifies and defines reasonable suspicion and "criminal predicate":

> Reasonable Suspicion or Criminal Predicate is established when information exists which establishes sufficient facts to give a trained law enforcement or criminal investigative agency officer, investigator, or employee a basis to believe that there is a reasonable possibility that an individual or organization is involved in a definable criminal activity or enterprise.
>
> (1998, p. 3)

Gang membership is "verified" by the BRIC using a point system that assigns "points" for various criteria that, when met, purport to attest to gang membership. When ten points are assigned in the BRIC system, the individual is "verified" as a gang member. While there is no agreed upon national standard that has been definitively established to determine gang membership (the Department of Justice provides guidance in this area), these point systems are commonly used by law enforcement agencies nationwide.

The problem is that many of the criteria that are used to "verify" gang membership do not meet the definition of reasonable suspicion or criminal predicate as defined in 28 CFR Part 23. As such, these "identifiers" should not be collected and maintained in a Criminal Intelligence Database such as the BRIC's Gang Assessment Database. The teenagers who were subject to deportation in the hearings where I testified were "verified" for simply being seen in a photograph wearing a certain baseball hat, having a particular tattoo, or having a picture taken or being seen with another person who was a "verified" gang member. One was with a friend who was assaulted by other "known gang members" and given eight "points" in the database. Simply having a "contact" with a "known gang member" or being a "victim" of a "rival group" can get you verified as a gang member (Boston Police Department Rules and Procedures, 2017).

One of the primary issues of concern with gang databases is that they too often provide no foundation or support for the contentions and representations that the intelligence they collect is reliably indicative of gang activity, instead presenting the information as a priori determinative of gang membership. 28 CFR Part 23 requires that those collecting and maintaining information in the gang database are "responsible for establishing the existence of reasonable suspicion of criminal activity … through examination of supporting information submitted by a participating agency" (1998, p. 3). In all of the gang packets that I reviewed, that were prepared by ICE agents based on information that they received from the BRIC, there was little if any of the required "supporting information." These gang packets are presented in Immigration Court as prima facie evidence of gang membership, and the Court, in making decisions regarding bond, asylum, and deportation, is too often relying on information that has not been substantiated and is both unreliable and untrustworthy.

Thus, the police present verification as a gang member as a fait accompli for simply wearing a particular type of hat or being seen with another individual who the police believe is in a gang or being "named in documents as a gang member" (not sure what "documents," but eight points), or "participation in publications" (whatever that means, eight points). In this way, anyone, including me I suppose, can be "verified" as a gang member. This is particularly troubling because, owing to the current zeitgeist, the consequences of being perceived to be a gang member are substantial, and may include being removed from the country and being literally dropped into a perilous predicament with the potential for a grave and violent outcome.

Boston is a so-called "sanctuary city" (Annear, 2014), yet its police department is actively collaborating with ICE to facilitate the removal through deportation of those whom it may have erroneously identified as gang members, in what may be an "end run" around the sanctuary mission that the city publicly embraces. This is hardly unique to Boston and its BRIC Gang Assessment Database; databases in New York (Blitzer, 2018), Chicago (Sweeney, 2018), and Los Angeles (Winton, 2016) are similarly non-compliant. Nonetheless, this remains cause for concern if not alarm, given the current tenor regarding both documented and undocumented immigrants.

The 287(g) Program

In September 1996 Congress passed the Illegal Immigration Reform and Immigrant Responsibility Act (IIRIRA), and in so doing added a provision to the 1968 Immigration and Nationality Act that authorized the Attorney General of the United States to enter into written agreements with states and political subdivisions of states to enforce immigration laws under the authority of the federal government. These enforcement powers would be granted to an officer or employee

> who is determined by the Attorney General to be qualified to perform a function of an immigration officer in relation to the investigation, apprehension or detention of aliens in the United States, (including the transportation of such aliens across State lines to detention centers).
>
> (United States Citizenship and Immigration Services, 2006)

This language has been included in the "Immigration and Nationality Act, 8 U.S.C. 1357," at Section 287(g), a ten-part provision of the law that has come to be known simply as 287(g), and the authority that it vests in state, county, and local officers or employees as "287(g) authority" administered under the "287(g) program." Of note, and not commonly connected with the program and the formal written agreements between the Attorney General and the state, county, and local agencies that enter the agreements is language in the law that provides that no 287(g) written agreement need be in place in order for officers or employees (and these have almost exclusively been law enforcement officers) "to communicate with the Attorney General regarding the immigration status of any individual, including reporting knowledge that a particular alien is not lawfully present in the United States," or "otherwise to cooperate with the Attorney General in the identification, apprehension, detention, or removal of aliens not lawfully present in the United States" (United States Citizenship and Immigration Services, 2006).

Thus, the 287(g) "language" not only provides for the delegation of federal authority to enforce federal civil immigration laws to state and local law enforcement and the training to do so, 287(g) also encourages officers to engage in such enforcement practices whether or not they are formally authorized or trained to do so.

The Attorney General's authority to enter into 287(g) Memoranda of Agreements (MOAs) was delegated to ICE, which did not begin entering into the agreements until 2002. As of 2009, owing to increased interest in engaging in immigration enforcement at the state and local levels, ICE had entered into agreements, trained and certified 66 law enforcement agencies in 23 states and had 833 287(g) certified officers (Department of Homeland Security Office of Inspector General, 2010, p. 2). Additionally, funding for the 287(g) program had increased from $5 million in 2006 to $68 million in 2010. There were 72 287(g) certified agencies at the program's height in 2011 (Rhodan, 2017).

In 2010 the Department of Homeland Security Office of the Inspector General (OIG) conducted an audit and inspection of 287(g) and issued a special report on the program. The OIG report found "instances in which Immigration and Customs Enforcement and participating law enforcement agencies were not operating in compliance with the terms of the agreements" (2010, p. 1) and that the 287(g) program did not have adequate performance measures in place to ensure that officers met stated goals and removal priorities.

> With no specific target levels for arrest, detention, and removal priority levels, and with performance measures that do not account for all investigative work and criminal prosecutions, ICE cannot be assured that the 287(g) program is meeting its intended purpose, or that resources are being appropriately targeted toward aliens who pose the greatest risk to public safety and the community.
>
> (2010, p. 9)

The OIG report also cited a lack of ICE supervision of officers engaging in immigration enforcement activities under 287(g) authority, as well as a lack of ICE oversight of the program itself. Additionally, ICE had not performed required background checks and security clearance reviews for officers given 287(g) authority, despite a requirement of the MOAs that officer suitability for the program be determined prior to any grant of 287(g) authority.

The OIG report also cited a lack of a process for handling complaints against 287(g) officers as well as any systematic inspection process for sites where 287(g) detainees were being processed and held. Further, the four-week 287(g) training provided by ICE was determined to be inadequate to the task of preparing police officers to perform immigration enforcement duties. The OIG report made 33 recommendations for improving the implementation process and performance of the 287(g) program (2010, p. 1). According to a 2011 research study by the Migration Policy Institute, the 287(g) program was

> not targeted primarily at serious offenders, despite statements by administration officials. In assessing the implementation, enforcement outcomes, costs, and community impacts of the 287(g) program, the report finds that about half of 287(g) activity involves noncitizens arrested for misdemeanors and traffic offenses.
>
> (Capps et al., 2011)

The report also found that ICE practices "allow jurisdictions to operate the 287(g) program in fundamentally different ways across the country."

In December of 2012 the Obama Administration decided to sharply curtail the 287(g) program after persistent and ongoing complaints regarding racial profiling of Hispanics and officers abusing discretion under the 287(g) authority; the administration at that time decided not to renew any of the 287(g) agreements with state and local law enforcement agencies (United States Immigration and Customs Enforcement, 2012). Currently, ICE has 287(g) agreements with 78 law enforcement agencies in 20 states and has certified 1833 law enforcement officers as 287(g) trained and authorized. All of the agencies currently certified use the "jail enforcement model": "Under this model, 287(g) officers working in state and local detention facilities identify and process removable aliens who have been charged with or convicted of an offense" (Department of Homeland Security Office of the Inspector General, 2010, p. 3). There are currently (at least as of this writing) no police officers engaging in 287(g) enforcement activities in community settings while performing regular police duties.

Secure Communities

The "Secure Communities" (S-Comm) initiative is an information sharing program between ICE and state, county, and local law enforcement agencies in which fingerprint information that is obtained through the booking process initiated upon arrest by law enforcement is shared with ICE. Like the 287(g) program, police departments (at least indirectly) assist ICE in immigration enforcement practices, but the role of state, county, and local law enforcement is more circumscribed under S-Comm than the more active, street-level enforcement activities authorized under the 287(g) program. The police role in S-Comm is a passive one where immigration enforcement activities are facilitated by police rather than the more robust engagement seen under 287(g). S-Comm sees fingerprint information that is (and has been) routinely and historically taken, recorded and sent to the Federal Bureau of Investigation (FBI) also shared with ICE, which then reviews the information in order to determine an individual's immigration status and criminal history. Based on its review of this information, ICE may issue what it refers to as a "detainer," a request to law enforcement to hold the individual that it has arrested and booked until ICE can respond and take the individual into ICE custody.

The program has not been without controversy since its inception, including its constitutionality in detaining individuals who may have posted bail or otherwise been eligible for release from police custody being held without a warrant. ICE detainers are administrative requests for what are typically civil and not criminal infractions and the detainers do not provide the legal authority to arrest and detain that criminal warrants provide.

S-Comm began in 2008 and "ICE completed full implementation of Secure Communities to all 3,181 jurisdictions within 50 states, the District of Columbia, and five U.S. Territories on January 22, 2013" (United States Immigration and Customs Enforcement, 2018). In November 2014 the Obama Administration suspended the operational capability of S-Comm after concerted public outcry over abuses of the detainer requests by ICE. Although publicly proclaiming that "ICE prioritizes the removal of public safety and national security threats, those who have violated our nation's immigration laws, including those who have failed to comply with a final order of removal" (United States Immigration and Customs Enforcement, 2018), it had in practice repeatedly targeted for detention and deportation those with no criminal history and individuals with decades old misdemeanor convictions, leading to S-Comm's temporarily curtailing its detainer requests. However, on January 25, 2017, S-Comm was reactivated; "more than 43,300 convicted criminal aliens have been removed as a result of Secure Communities" through to the end of financial year 2017 (United States Immigration and Customs Enforcement, 2018).

The American Civil Liberties Union (ACLU) has expressed strident objections to S-Comm:

> S-Comm has disastrous and widespread impacts on civil liberties. It drives a wedge between local law enforcement agencies and the communities they serve, deterring victims and witnesses from reporting crimes and undermining community policing partnerships that keep everyone safe from crime.
>
> (2018a)

And again, despite ICE's representations that purport to prioritize the detention and deportation of violent and dangerous felons and suspected terrorists, the ACLU observed that

> despite ICE's statements that S-Comm should focus on people convicted of serious crimes, the federal government's own statistics have shown that it ensnares huge numbers of low-level offenders and non-criminals in its dragnet, fueling mass deportations of productive community members and the destruction of U.S. families.
>
> (2018a)

Thomas Miles and Adam Cox (2014) have studied the Secure Communities initiative in an effort to understand whether this enforcement strategy reduces crime. The Department of Homeland Security launched S-Comm in the latter part of 2008 and these authors examined county-wide crime data from the years 2004 through 2012. They "obtained from DHS tallies of the immigrants detained under Secure Communities during each month in each county since the program's launch" (2014, p. 969), in an effort to determine what effect, if any, S-Comm had on the rates of Uniform Crime Report (UCR) Part I crimes committed by immigrants. According to Miles and Cox "the evidence shows that Secure Communities did not cause a meaningful reduction in the FBI's overall index crime rate. Nor did it reduce the rate of any individual violent offense" (2014, p. 969).

Although the study conducted by Miles and Cox did report findings that were associated with modest decreases in two categories of property crimes, burglaries and auto theft, S-Comm's effect on overall crime reduction was negligible.

> The finding that Secure Communities does not reduce the overall rate of FBI index crime calls into question the long-standing assumption that deporting noncitizens who commit crimes is an effective crime-control strategy. Our estimates suggest that the marginal immigrant detainee is a much less serious offender than the marginal prisoner in the criminal justice system–even when that immigrant detainee has been selected for detention using a program designed to target the most serious immigrant criminal offenders.
>
> (Miles & Cox, 2014, p. 7)

Katlyn Brady (2017) has followed the demise of S-Comm and its replacement by the "Priority Enforcement Program" by the Obama Administration in November 2014. The S-Comm program was controversial from its inception in 2008 and in many states, cities, and counties, law enforcement had serious reservations regarding constitutional issues as well as civil liberties concerns. According to Brady, political leaders and community organizations frequently objected "that the program resulted in the removal of people for minor offenses, removal of victims of crimes, separation of families, and it deterred victims from reporting crimes to the police because they feared deportation" (2017, p. 27). The S-Comm program was specifically and repeatedly opposed by cities and police departments that had significant investments in community policing initiatives as well as those that had significant numbers of immigrant residents.

Another major concern for those opposing S-Comm was its potential for racial profiling by police, since

> research demonstrated that perhaps as many as 60% of people removed under Secure Communities had no criminal histories or only traffic violations. These numbers suggest that people were arrested not because of an underlying or previous crime, but because officers may have relied on race when conducting stops.
>
> (Brady, 2017, p. 28)

Brady also noted the objections of religious groups, particularly the Roman Catholic Church, to S-Comm: "its primary concern was the effect detainers had and deportations had on families and congregants" (2017, p. 29). The term "sanctuary" had originally referred to the sanctuary that immigrants would seek from deportation officials in a church, and religious groups were concerned that government initiatives such as S-Comm would violate the recognition and respect offered in the concept of sanctuary. In the aftermath of the implementation of S-Comm, entire cities would identify as "sanctuary cities."

Brady identified court litigation by civil rights groups as ensuring the demise of S-Comm and cited two cases pertaining to ICE detainers, the requests that law enforcement maintain custody of individuals sought by ICE for up to 48 hours: "The Third Circuit, in March 2014, determined that ICE detainers are not mandatory, but merely requests, and therefore jurisdictions that honored them were liable for any potential constitutional violations" (2017, p. 31). In April 2014, a federal judge in Oregon agreed that the ICE detainers were not mandatory, and that local law enforcement agencies that honored the detention requests could be held liable for constitutional violations of detainees' civil rights. The court noted that

> the primary constitutional concern surrounding Secure Communities and ICE detainers is that detainers are issued without judicial warrants, and often without probable cause, in violation of the 4th Amendment of the U.S. Constitution. That is, ICE detainers do not require probable cause to hold an individual, nor do detainers require the signature of an independent judicial officer.
>
> (Brady, 2017, p. 32)

Daniel Chand and William Schreckhise (2015) studied the discretionary aspects of S-Comm enforcement initiatives and the effects that the local political climate had on deportations under S-Comm. These authors accurately cite the ICE "detainer" policy as being the most controversial aspect of the S-Comm program. They note the "prosecutorial discretion" memorandum issued by ICE in July 2011 that sought to alleviate concerns regarding the discretionary issuance of ICE detainers, particularly as they pertain to Fourth Amendment constitutional implications and the significant expenses incurred by local jurisdictions in complying with the detainer requests. The discretion memo drove the decision-making authority for the initiation of removal proceedings to local ICE agents and prosecutors. Prosecutorial discretion "most importantly applies to whether an agent decides to issue a detainer for an individual flagged through Secure Communities and whether to execute a removal of an undocumented individual" (Chand & Schreckhise, 2015, p. 1627).

Chand and Schreckhise (2015) found that "geography and political environment are important factors predicting how the program is implemented," with areas of the country that showed more support for Republican presidential candidates seeing more detainer requests and deportations that those areas that demonstrated less support for Republican presidential candidates. These authors also found, counterintuitively, that

> more crime saw fewer deportations, while areas with less crime saw more. Because Secure Communities program targeted *criminals*, we should expect that areas that see more crime would focus more on removing undocumented immigrants who have committed crimes. The fact that higher crime areas are producing significantly fewer deportations contradicts the claim that Secure Communities is designed to control crime.
>
> (pp. 1635–1636)

Immigrants and Crime

David Green (2016) studied immigrant arrests for violent crimes and drug offenses at the state level between 2012–2014 in testing the so-called "Trump Hypothesis," i.e., "whether immigrants are responsible for higher levels of violent and drug-related crime in the United States, as asserted by Donald Trump in his 2015 presidential campaign announcement" (2016, p. 506). Green used four categories of immigrants in his analysis: "the overall foreign population, Mexican population, undocumented immigrant population, and undocumented Mexican population" (2016, p. 510), and examined UCRs submitted to the FBI.

Green found "no significant relationships between immigrant population rates, violent crime, or drug-related crime rates," and that "almost universally, foreign population size has no association with violent crime rates, murder, or rape" (2016, p. 519). He did find that poverty is correlated with overall rates of violent crime and that the male population rate is correlated with a higher frequency in sexual assault crimes. Green also reported "a positive relationship between drug arrest rates, including sales and possession, and undocumented immigrant population size at the state level according to these data," but that "the relative impact of this association appears weak" (2016, p. 519). Green concluded that "by comparing immigrant populations to violent and drug-related crime rates by state, results demonstrate little support for the 'Trump Hypothesis'" (2016, p. 521).

Garth Davies and Jeffrey Fagan (2016) have also examined the issue of immigration and crime and have found that "although immigration and crime have long been conflated, both on theoretical grounds and in the popular imagination, there is strikingly little evidence to support this nexus" (p. 104). These authors studied New York City neighborhoods populated by immigrants: African American, Asian, and Latinx, documented and undocumented, between 2004 and 2008 and the effects that immigration had on crime and enforcement in New York City.

These authors found that "total and violent crime rates are lower when concentrations of foreign-born persons of African descent are higher," and that "the effects of Latino and Asian immigration on crime are more modest. The direction of the effects is negative, but they do not reach significance in any of the models" (Davies & Fagan, 2016, p. 112). Thus, in neighborhoods populated by African and Afro-Caribbean immigrants, violent crime rates are actually lower than in non-immigrant neighborhoods, and in neighborhoods where immigrant residents are of Asian and Hispanic descent, the violent crime rates are lower, but not to a level of statistical significance.

As pertains to police enforcement and crime, Davies and Fagan reported that "enforcement for total, violent, and property crimes is substantially higher in places with greater proportions of immigrants. This effect is especially pronounced for newer immigrants, those who have been in the country for fewer than five years" (2016, pp. 112–114). Of significance in this research is that

> although crime is on balance lower in neighborhoods with higher immigrant concentrations, the ratio of stops and arrests to crime is higher in these same places. The police response per crime seems to be more aggressive and legally formal in immigrant neighborhoods, despite the lower crime rates in these neighborhoods.
>
> (2016, p. 114)

Davies and Fagan's research was consistent with other studies that found that "In New York and other cities (Sampson 2008; Martinez et al., this volume), there is no evidence that crime rates are higher in places with higher immigration rates. On the contrary, immigration often functions as a prophylactic against crime" (2016, p. 117).

Robert Sampson (2015) has argued that immigration has in fact contributed to declining crime rates in American cities, and that this is particularly true for Mexican immigrants. His research has found at least three factors that contribute to the lower rates of crime committed by immigrants. The first relates to so-called "selection bias": "it is widely recognized that most immigrants, Mexicans in particular, selectively migrate to the United States based on characteristics that predispose them to low crime, such as motivation to work and ambition" (Sampson, 2015). The second factor relates to community well-being and public health. Sampson's research in Chicago found that Mexican immigrants in particular are less prone to violence than African Americans and whites. He found that "first-generation immigrants were 45 percent less likely to commit violence than third-generation Americans, adjusting for individual, family, and neighborhood background. Second-generation immigrants were 22 percent less likely to commit violence than the third generation" (2015). Third, Sampson's study "showed that living in a neighborhood of concentrated immigration was associated with lower violence." And that "rather than generating crime, high concentrations of immigrants appear to reduce it" (2015).

John MacDonald, John Hipp, and Charlotte Gill (2013) examined immigrant concentration and its effect on crime rates in the city of Los Angeles and their "results indicate that greater predicted concentrations of immigrants in neighborhoods are linked to significant reductions in crime" (p. 191). In examining immigrant settlement patterns in Los Angeles neighborhoods, these authors found that "an increase in the concentration of immigrants in neighborhoods reduces the average amount of total and violent crime by substantial magnitudes, even after taking into account that immigrants are likely to select into neighborhoods with their existing co-ethnics" (p. 209).

According to the *Harvard Law Review* (2015), the policing of immigrants occurs at the federal, state, and local levels and that historically this "regulation has always been driven in part by an image of immigrant criminality, an image which itself has been driven by racism" (p. 1772). What has occurred in the contemporary policing model currently being adopted by law enforcement agencies nationwide are the ways that civil immigration enforcement have become "intertwined" with more traditional criminal law enforcement so that the two divergent and arguably incompatible functions become indistinguishable. To many under the ubiquitous "footprint" of this monolithic enforcement entity, the police are immigration agents, and immigration agents are police.

On February 5, 1917, Congress passed "An Act To regulate the immigration of aliens to, and the residence of aliens in, the United States," the 1917 Immigration and Nationality Act, also known as the Asiatic Barred Zone Act and the Literacy Act (United States Congress, 1917; Tucker & Creller, 2018). This act provided for deportation for "aliens" who were convicted of crimes involving "moral turpitude" and had been sentenced to a prison term of a year or more. Although Congress did not define the term "moral turpitude," these were generally treated as offenses related to prostitution.

The *Harvard Law Review* (2015) traced the establishment and the implementation of immigration laws that criminalized certain immigration-related offenses, beginning with the 1917 act and the later 1952 version, also called the Immigration and Nationality Act, which broadened the class of deportable criminal offenses, and the subsequent 1988 Anti-Drug Abuse Act, the 1990 Immigration Act, and the 1996 IIRIRA: "The immigration laws now identify broad categories of criminal 'convictions'—like 'aggravated felonies' and 'crimes involving moral turpitude'—that trigger sharp and inevitable civil-immigration consequences. Since the 1990s these categories have included many minor offenses" (2015, p. 1774), such as misdemeanor drug possession charges.

Immigration Enforcement and Fallout

In fact, it is now routine for Customs and Border Protection (CBP) officers to charge anyone entering the United States without documentation, even children, with a criminal offense in addition to a civil administrative offense. According to the *Harvard Law Review*, "immigration crimes like illegal entry and reentry did not exist before the 1980s, but since 2004 they have topped the list of federal prosecutions. Since 2009, they have constituted more than half of the entire federal criminal docket" (2015, p. 1775).

And as the lines become blurred between the enforcement of federal civil immigration laws and state criminal statutes, often by the same law enforcement officers who either have dual authorities to enforce civil immigration laws as well as the criminal laws, or police officers who work in tandem in "task force" operations with civil immigration agents, the same types of abuses that have been found to occur in communities of color across the United States are just as prevalent, if not more so, in law enforcement's dealing with undocumented immigrants. The abuse of discretion, civil rights violations, and excessive and deadly force issues are prominent features of the immigration enforcement apparatus. According to the *Harvard Law Review*, "the unique nature of immigration enforcement exacerbates these problems":

> First, immigrants are entitled to fewer constitutional protections than citizens, and the dual criminal-civil nature of immigration law limits the applicability of constitutional protections further. Second, the structure of immigration law, which is inherently racialized, political, and divided among multiple overlapping actors, limits accountability.
>
> (2015, pp. 1777–1778)

Federal law establishes the authority of CBP officers, Border Patrol agents, and ICE agents to conduct warrantless stops and searches of individuals, vehicles, aircraft, and other conveyances within 100 miles of any "external boundary of the United States" (United States Government Publishing Office, 2018, p. 721). CBP has used this broad authority to engage in joint operations with local law enforcement officers to thwart Fourth Amendment protections that severely restrict the circumstances under which police officers may conduct searches of persons and vehicles.

CBP officers conduct searches under their federal authority to search for undocumented immigrants entering the country without proper approval and documentation, and in so doing often discover contraband such as drugs or weapons, which they then surrender to local police for prosecution in state courts. Such stops, searches, and seizures, while legal according to the law, clearly run afoul of the intent of the regulation to allow for broader warrantless searches at border crossings in order to enforce immigration laws.

According to the ACLU, "roughly two-thirds of the United States' population lives within the 100-mile zone—that is, within 100 miles of a U.S. land or coastal border. That's about 200 million people" (American Civil Liberties Union, 2018b). The ACLU filed suit against the U.S. Border Patrol in 2017 after Border Patrol agents set up a temporary checkpoint on I-93 southbound in the town of Woodstock, New Hampshire, 90 miles from the Canadian border. The Border Patrol agents used drug-sniffing dogs in their warrantless searches of the vehicles that they stopped and their occupants. If the dogs "alerted" to the presence of a controlled substance, CBP directed the vehicles and their occupants to a secondary checkpoint, where they were met by police officers of the Woodstock Police Department, who placed them under arrest for drug possession. In all, 16 legal U.S. residents were arrested in this fashion in August of 2017.

In May of 2018, the New Hampshire Circuit Court threw out the arrests for drug possession that were brought in state court, finding "that while the stated purpose of the checkpoints in this matter was screening for immigration violations the primary purpose of the action was detection and seizure of drugs" (*State of New Hampshire v. Daniel McCarthy et al.*) *The New York Times* interviewed Gilles Bissonnette, the legal director for the state ACLU chapter and co-counsel on the case: "This decision is a victory for civil liberties," he said the checkpoints "'flagrantly violated' the state and federal constitutions" (Nixon, 2018, May 4).

Yet the constitutionally questionable practices by the Border Patrol continue as of this writing. In February 2018, *The New York Times* reported that

> Border Patrol officers are working without permission on private property and setting up checkpoints up to 100 miles away from the border under a little-known federal law that is being used more widely in the Trump administration's aggressive crackdown on illegal immigration.
>
> (Nixon, 2018, February 21)

In New York, Washington state, and Florida, the ACLU has protested the Border Patrol practice of boarding Greyhound buses and Amtrak trains and asking passengers for identification. According to *The New York Times*, Border Patrol "agency data shows that less than 3 percent of foreigners entering the country illegally were caught at immigration checkpoints nowhere near the border." And of the illegal drugs seized in the so-called "border checkpoints," most are "seized in small quantities—about an ounce or less—and were taken from American citizens in 40 percent of the cases" (Nixon, 2018, February 21).

Torrie Hester (2015) has written of the history of immigration enforcement and deportation in the United States as part of the "carceral state." Of relevance today is the increased focus in deportation arising out of entry at the U.S.-Mexican border.

> An important police enforcement program in this effort has been the Consequence Delivery System (CDS), in operation since 2005. The set of policies, now known as CDS, limited voluntary removal and increased criminal prosecutions for immigration violations in the U.S. states bordering Mexico. In the 1980s, then, policy makers transitioned from mass deportations of Mexicans to mass deportations of all Latin Americans, with the addition of mass incarceration.
>
> (p. 147)

She points out that the 1996 IIRIRA also eliminated the statute of limitations for deportable criminal offenses, so that immigrants who may have been brought to the United States as children and who had lived in the country for decades, or others who may have had lawful permanent resident status no longer had protected status and were now subject to deportation upon conviction of a criminal offense in state court. Hester observed that "with the broadening scope of deportable crimes and the lack of time limits, even more criminal convictions trigger deportability. Federal immigration control has now assumed a major anticrime mandate" (p. 149).

With this new mandate, state and local authorities began seeking reimbursement from the federal government for their role in housing immigrants in state prisons and county jails, both those immigrants who had been convicted of criminal offenses as well as those who were housed in "detention" awaiting deportation proceedings. This involvement of state and local officials in immigration enforcement served to further ensnare immigrants, both documented and undocumented, mainly from Latin American countries, within the carceral state.

According to Hester, the congressional response to the terrorist attacks on September 11, 2001, and the ensuing legislative response has further "heightened the national security dynamic of immigration enforcement" (2015, p. 151).

> In its efforts to protect national security, Congress folded immigration enforcement into the Department of Homeland Security, which, in turn, expanded the jurisdiction of local and state officials in immigration enforcement. Since 2004, for example, U.S. Immigration and Customs Enforcement has trained more than 1,200 state and local officials to enforce immigration law.... The addition of antiterrorism to the list of the government's goals magnified its ability to carry out mass deportations and mass incarceration.
>
> (Hester, 2015, p. 51)

Mai Thi Nguyen and Hannah Gill (2016) have studied the effects that immigration enforcement and enhancement programs such as the 287(g) program have had on relations between the local police and their constituent communities. Their research, conducted in two North Carolina jurisdictions, Alamance County and Durham City, attempted to discover the extent to which local police enforcement of federal immigration laws might lead to a so-called "chill effect," which "involves the erosion of trust, cooperation and communication between police and immigrant communities after the adoption of immigration enforcement policies" (p. 302).

Nguyen and Gill also suggest that the involvement of local police in "force multiplier" operations such as the 287(g) program in the enforcement of civil immigration laws may also be violative of the Equal Protection Clause of the Fourteenth Amendment in at least two ways. The Equal Protection Clause requires that law enforcement treat all of those with whom they come into contact equally, regardless of race, gender, ethnic origin group, immigration status, or other racial characteristics and law enforcement is prohibited from stopping, detaining, or seizing anyone based on racial or ethnic origin group characteristics (*United States v. Brignoni-Ponce*).

The second way that the Equal Protection Clause may be violated by local police participating in the 287(g) program is through discrimination based on racial characteristics in practices such as racial profiling.

There are concerns that local immigrant enforcement programs such as 287g [sic] and SCOMM make it easier for local law enforcement officials to discriminate. Reports indicate that pretextual vehicle stops (stops in which officers detain people for a traffic offence because they are suspicious of immigration status) have risen in some jurisdictions that have adopted 287g [sic].

(Nguyen & Gill, 2016, p. 306)

Nguyen and Gill (2016) found that "the ambiguity about the role of law enforcement after the adoption of 287(g) and fear of deportation have affected immigrants in a number of ways, including civic engagement, access to services and perceived vulnerability to crime." Their research also revealed effects of 287(g) policing that went beyond the "chill effect" in that "immigrant businesses have experienced a disruption in economic activity and immigrants report greater exploitation by employers and landlords. These are social and economic concerns relevant to the entire community, not just immigrants" (p. 318).

Amada Armenta and Isabela Alvarez (2017) studied local law enforcement practices relating to immigration enforcement and the effects that these enforcement practices had on the relations between the police and unauthorized immigrant communities. The authors identify the three means by which most law enforcement agencies engage in the practice of immigration enforcement:

> (a) the direct enforcement of immigration laws, (b) intermediary immigration enforcement through ad hoc cooperation with federal immigration enforcement authorities, and (c) immigrant criminalization through the day-to-day enforcement of criminal violations associated with immigrant "illegality."

(p. 2)

Armenta and Alvarez (2017) reported that "Latino immigrants are unlikely to cooperate with a criminal investigation because they believe the police can use it as an opportunity to investigate their immigration status, or the immigration status of someone close to them" (p. 7), and they also cite results from a 2008 survey conducted by the Pew Hispanic Center that "indicates that respondents who report being stopped by the police, and asked about their immigration status, report the lowest levels of confidence that police do their jobs well" (p. 7).

Nik Theodore and Robert Habans (2016) studied the effects that local law enforcement's involvement in immigration enforcement had on the relationships between the police and immigrant and non-immigrant Latinos. These researchers used surveys to determine participant attitudes regarding the police enforcement of immigration laws, participant immigration status, and the extent to which they may have had negative interactions with police in matters pertaining to immigration issues. They surveyed over 2000 individuals, 79 percent in Spanish, in Chicago, Houston, Los Angeles, and Phoenix.

They found that a significant percentage of study participants were "reluctant to voluntarily contact the police to report a crime or to provide information about crimes, specifically because they fear that police officers will inquire about the immigration status of themselves, their friends or their family members" (p. 985). They also reported that "regardless of immigration or documentation status, few Latinos feel safer because of the increased focus on immigration by law enforcement; many others are hesitant to report crimes to the police," and that their results are strongly indicative of a "link between increasing police involvement in immigration enforcement and negative attitudes among Latinos concerning social isolation and personal safety" (pp. 985–986).

Justin Pickett has studied the issue of what he has called "crimmigration," i.e., the continuing and expanding policy and practice of engaging in interior (non-border) immigration enforcement by local police through routine criminal law enforcement. His research sought to "evaluate whether perceptions of Latino economic and political threat are associated with support for granting police greater latitude in stopping, searching, and using force against suspects" (2016, p. 125).

Pickett's research results "revealed that both forms of perceived Latino threat—political and economic—were associated with greater support for expanding police powers, at least among White respondents" (2016, p. 125). He also found "that perceived Latino threat may be most consequential for public views about police policies that have clear potential to result in discrimination against Latinos." According to Pickett, the perceived threat of Latino immigrants to whites:

> may constitute an important social foundation for crimmigration. That is, by increasing public support for aggressive policing, or, at minimum, by reducing opposition to discriminatory social controls such as police profiling, threat perceptions may increase the political attractiveness and viability of crimmigration as a "solution" to the immigration problem.
>
> (2016, p. 125)

Conclusion: An Unholy Alliance

The participation of the police in the enforcement of immigration laws has created an unholy alliance between ICE and law enforcement at the local, county, and even state levels. This alliance engages in collaborative practices and strategies that are frequently at odds with well-established and long-embraced principles of community and problem-oriented policing, and in so doing may jeopardize community safety rather than enhance it. While the politicization of immigration policies at the federal level arguably make our borders less secure, the co-optation of the police by ICE serves to undermine the partnerships that the police have established with constituent communities that serve to reduce crime and to enhance community safety. ICE essentially "trades on" the hard-won legitimacy that the police have striven to maintain in immigrant communities, a legitimacy that is often held delicately in a balance that may tip precipitously close to collapse with any misstep. Police participation in the enforcement of immigration laws in this unholy alliance with ICE is just such a misstep.

REFERENCES

American Civil Liberties Union. (2018a). Secure communities ("S-Comm"). *ACLU*. Retrieved from: www.aclu.org/other/secure-communities-s-comm.

American Civil Liberties Union. (2018b). The constitution in the 100-mile border zone. *ACLU*. Retrieved from: www.aclu.org/other/constitution-100-mile-border-zone.

Annear, S. (2014, August 20). City Council passes "Trust Act." *Boston Magazine*. Retrieved from: www.bostonmagazine.com/news/2014/08/20/boston-trust-act-passed/.

Armenta, A., & Alvarez, I. (2017). Policing immigrants or policing immigration? Understanding local law enforcement participation in immigration control. *Sociology Compass*, 2.

Blitzer, J. (2018, January 1). The teens trapped between a gang and the law. *The New Yorker*. Retrieved from: www.newyorker.com/magazine/2018/01/01/the-teens-trapped-between-a-gang-and-the-law.

Boston Police Department Rules and Procedures. (2017). Rule 335—Gang assessment database. *Boston Police Department*. Retrieved from: https://static1.squarespace.com/static/5086f19ce4b0ad16ff15598d/t/593a8cb5e6f2e1d2faf8f4c3/1497009333424/rule335+%28gang+database%29.pdf.

Brady, K. (2017). Sanctuary cities and the demise of the secure communities program. *Texas Hispanic Journal of Law & Policy*, 23, pp. 21–50.

Capps, R., Rosenblum, M., Chishti, M., & Rodríguez, C. (2011, January). Delegation and divergence: 287(g) state and local immigration enforcement. *Migration Policy Institute*. Retrieved from: www.migrationpolicy.org/research/delegation-and-divergence-287g-state-and-local-immigration-enforcement.

Chand, D. E., & Schreckhise, W. D. (2015). Secure communities and community values: Local context and discretionary immigration law enforcement. *Journal of Ethnic & Migration Studies*, 41 (10), pp. 1621–1643.

Davies, G., & Fagan, J. (2016). Crime and enforcement in immigrant neighborhoods: Evidence from New York City. *The Annals of the American Academy of Political And Social Science*, 641 (1).

Department of Homeland Security Office of the Inspector General. (2010). *The Performance of 287(g) Agreements*. Retrieved from: www.oig.dhs.gov/assets/Mgmt/OIG_10-63_Mar10.pdf.

Green, D. (2016). The Trump hypothesis: Testing immigrant populations as a determinant of violent and drug-related crime in the United States. *Social Science Quarterly*, 97 (3), pp. 506–524.

Hester, T. (2015). Deportability and the carceral state. *Journal of American History*, 102, 1, pp. 141–151.

MacDonald, J., Hipp, J., & Gill, C. (2013). The effects of immigrant concentration on changes in neighborhood crime rates. *Journal of Quantitative Criminology*, 2.

Miles, T., & Cox, A. (2014). Does immigration enforcement reduce crime? Evidence from Secure Communities. *The Journal of Law & Economics*, 4, 937.

Nguyen, M. T., & Gill, H. (2016). Interior immigration enforcement: The impacts of expanding local law enforcement authority. *Urban Studies*, 53 (2).

Nixon, R. (2018, February 21). Under Trump, Border Patrol steps up searches far from the border. *The New York Times*. Retrieved from: www.nytimes.com/2018/02/21/us/politics/trump-border-patrol-searches.html.

Nixon, R. (2018, May 4). Drug arrests at immigration checkpoint violated Constitution, New Hampshire court finds. *The New York Times*. Retrieved from: www.nytimes.com/2018/05/04/us/new-hampshire-border-patrol-illegal-checkpoints-aclu.html.

Pickett, J. T. (2016). On the social foundations for crimmigration: Latino threat and support for expanded police powers. *Journal of Quantitative Criminology*, 32 (1), pp. 103–132.

Policing immigrant communities. (2015). *Harvard Law Review*, 128 (6), pp. 1771–1793.

Rhodan, M. (2017, March 17). President Trump wants sheriffs to help with deportations. Here's what sheriffs think. *Time*. Retrieved from: http://time.com/4704084/donald-trump-immigration-sheriffs-287g/.

Sampson, R. J. (2015). Immigration and America's urban revival: The evidence favors a hypothesis many Americans reject: immigration has helped reduce crime and revitalize city economies. *The American Prospect*, 3, 20.

State of New Hampshire v. Daniel McCarthy, et al. Second Circuit, District Division Plymouth, Docket #469-2017-CR-01888, et al., 2018.

Sweeney, A. (2018, June 20). Lawsuit alleges Chicago Police Department's massive gang database discriminatory, inaccurate. *Chicago Tribune*. Retrieved from: www.chicagotribune.com/news/local/breaking/ct-met-chicago-police-gang-database-lawsuit-20180619-story.html.

Theodore, N., & Habans, R. (2016). Policing immigrant communities: Latino perceptions of police involvement in immigration enforcement. *Journal of Ethnic & Migration Studies*, 42 (6), pp. 970–988.

Tucker, D., & Creller, J. (2018). *1917 Immigration Act*. Retrieved from: http://library.uwb.edu/Static/USimmigration/1917_immigration_act.html.

United States Citizenship and Immigration Services. (2006). *INA: Act 287—Powers of Immigration Officers and Employees*. Retrieved from: www.uscis.gov/ilink/docView/SLB/HTML/SLB/0-0-0-1/0-0-0-29/0-0-0-9505.html#0-0-0-357.

United States Congress. (1917). *Sixty-Fourth Congress. Session II. Chapter 29. "An Act to Regulate the Immigration of Aliens to, and the Residence of Aliens in the United States."* Retrieved from: www.loc.gov/law/help/statutes-at-large/64th-congress/session-2/c64s2ch29.pdf.

United States Government Executive Order 12291. (1998). *Criminal Intelligence Systems Operating Policies, 28 CFR Part 23*. Retrieved from: https://it.ojp.gov/documents/28cfr_part_23.pdf.

United States Government Publishing Office. (2018). *8 CRR Part 287, Field Officers Powers and Duties*. Retrieved from: www.gpo.gov/fdsys/pkg/CFR-2016-title8-vol.1/pdf/CFR-2016-title8-vol.1-part287.pdf.

United States Immigration and Customs Enforcement. (2012, December 20). *FY 2012: ICE Announces Year-End Removal Numbers, Highlights Focus on Key Priorities and Issues New National Detainer Guidance to Further Focus Resources*. Retrieved from: www.ice.gov/news/releases/fy-2012-ice-announces-year-end-removal-numbers-highlights-focus-key-priorities-and#wcm-survey-target-id.

United States Immigration and Customs Enforcement. (2018). *Secure Communities*. Retrieved from: www.ice.gov/secure-communities.

United States v. Brignoni-Ponce, 422 U.S. 873, 884, 1975.

Valverde, M. (2017, December 19). Have deportations increased under Donald Trump? Here's what the data shows. *PolitiFact*. Retrieved from: www.politifact.com/truth-o-meter/article/2017/dec/19/have-deportations-increased-under-donald-trump-her/.

Washington Post Staff. (2015, June 16). Donald Trump announces a presidential bid. *The Washington Post*. Retrieved from: www.washingtonpost.com/news/post-politics/wp/2015/06/16/full-text-donald-trump-announces-a-presidential-bid/?utm_term=.5fec5c177a6e.

Winton, R. (2016, August 11). California gang database plagued with errors, unsubstantiated entries, state auditor finds. *Los Angeles Times*. Retrieved from: www.latimes.com/local/lanow/la-me-ln-calgangs-audit-20160811-snap-story.html.

Chapter 7

"Soldier Up"

The Consequences of Police Militarization for Communities of Color

Public scrutiny and assessment of the appropriateness and justification of the police use of force, particularly deadly force, has increased dramatically and sharply in the second decade of the twenty-first century. Video recordings of the police in encounters with members of the public are routinely recorded and widely circulated on the internet, leading to ongoing tensions between the police in the United States and the communities in which they perform their duties. The ubiquity of cell phone video cameras and the dissemination of recorded police/ citizen interactions via social media have challenged the police narrative regarding use-of-force incidents, a narrative long controlled and dominated by the police subcultural standpoint and perspective. The combination of the militarization of the police in the United States through the acquisition and deployment of military grade vehicles, equipment, aircraft, weapons, and uniforms, and the shift in operational policing philosophy from community policing to "Homeland Security" policing (Oliver, 2009), combined with the proliferation of video recordings of police engaging in brutality and violence, has proven a daunting and vexing series of challenges for the police, communities of color in the United States, and those concerned with issues of social justice.

The Demise of Community Policing

The mid-1970s through the early 2000s saw a shift in the philosophy of domestic policing in the United States from one that embraced rapid response to 911 calls for service and an omnipresent, ubiquitous police imprint, one that measured police effectiveness strictly in terms of numbers: arrests, citations, crime rates, to one that endorsed principles of so-called "community policing" (Community Oriented Policing Services, United States Department of Justice, 2018), or "problem oriented policing" (National Institute of Justice, 2018). These policing philosophies advocated partnerships between the police and the communities that they served in a collaborative effort to identify problems and issues unique to a particular community and to propose solutions to these particular problems that both the police and the community "stakeholders" could work toward resolving.

Under community policing principles, community residents were seen as "co-producers" of strategies to address quality-of-life issues that both community residents and the police agreed were in need of collaborative law enforcement and community intervention. Partnerships were forged between the police and community residents to solve problems and to prevent crime. Community policing was the mantra of policing in the United States throughout the latter part of the twentieth century and into the first decade of the twenty-first century, and many attribute the sharp reduction in the rates of violent crime during the 1990s and into the early 2000s to the successful implementation and adoption of the philosophies of community and problem-oriented policing (Lawrence & McCarthy, 2013). In fact, then-President Bill Clinton promised to provide funding to law enforcement agencies to fulfill his pledge to hire 100,000 police officers nationwide, providing that the agencies would embrace community policing as an operational philosophy (United States Department of Justice, 1994).

Even though most domestic law enforcement agencies nationwide still publicly embrace community-policing principles as their operational philosophy in 2019, it is clear that the paradigm shift away from community policing began with the terrorist attacks on the World Trade Center towers and the Pentagon on September 11, 2001. Police in the United States, in response to widespread concerns regarding potential terrorist attacks on American cities and infrastructure, quickly morphed into the front-line shock troops in the inchoate domestic "war on terrorism" (Galhotra, 2012). Partnerships with the community, co-producers, and collaborators in shared community betterment were all quickly overrun and superseded by what law enforcement saw as an unprecedented threat requiring all available police, and now military, resources.

The Militarization of the Police: Civil Rights and Civil Liberties at Peril

Beginning in 1990 and 1991 with the passage of the National Defense Authorization Act, Congress authorized the Department of Defense, through the Defense Logistics Agency (DLA), to transfer surplus military equipment to domestic law enforcement agencies for their use in fighting the so-called "War on Drugs" in what became known as the "1033 Program" (Defense Logistics Agency, 2018). The belief at the time was that law enforcement agencies in the United States faced an unprecedented threat from heavily armed drug cartels and drug distributors that could only be countered by equipping police with military-grade weapons and vehicles. Since its inception, the 1033 Program has distributed over $5.1 billion worth of equipment to over 8000 law enforcement agencies. In 2013 alone, $450 million worth of equipment was distributed to local, state, and county agencies.

In the aftermath of the terrorist attacks on September 11, 2001, and in the years that followed, domestic law enforcement operations in the United States began a strategic shift toward tactical initiatives that endorsed and supported more militarized responses to routine police activities. Much of the militarization of domestic law enforcement has been facilitated and supported by the federal government through DLA's 1033 Program as well as the Department of Homeland Security (DHS) "Homeland Security Grant Program" (HSGP) and the Department of Justice (DOJ) Edward Byrne Memorial Justice Assistance Grant (JAG) program. The 1033 Program provides police agencies with M-16 and M-14 rifles, bayonets, night-vision goggles, military aircraft, tactical vehicles—such as Bearcats and Mine-Resistant Ambush Protected (MRAP) vehicles—and military watercraft. The HSGP and JAG funding allows police departments to purchase tactical weapons, military uniforms, less-lethal weapons, body armor, and SWAT equipment, all contributing in large part to the militarization of civilian law enforcement in the United States.

It became commonplace in the United States during the first and second decades of the twenty-first century to see police officers dressed in Battle Dress Uniforms (BDUs) or other military-type uniforms that were designed for use during actual combat operations and military engagement with an enemy during war. Modified M-16 and M-4 rifles are standard patrol long guns in many police departments across the country. Tactical, military vehicles are routinely used in SWAT deployments and crowd control incidents. City police and state highway patrol agencies now frequently use unmarked black SUVs with blacked out windows, such as those used by the United States Secret Service, the Federal Bureau of Investigation (FBI), and the Drug Enforcement Administration.

Dressing police as soldiers and equipping them with military weapons and body armor, having these officers perform routine patrol activities in fortified and armored vehicles, and sending these officers into our communities to engage an "enemy" causes them to adopt the mentality of warriors and the trope of soldiers engaged in a war on the battlefield. The battlefields have become our communities and we are the enemy. As any soldier will readily admit: on the battlefield there is no Constitution, and enemies do not have civil rights or civil liberties. These are the casualties that we are taking in our communities and neighborhoods. Our new policing paradigm: the "Homeland Security Police."

In late 2014 then-President Obama sought to sharply curtail federal grant and surplus military equipment programs, following public concerns in the aftermath of the police response in Ferguson, Missouri, to ongoing public protests over the shooting death of 18-year-old Michael Brown by then-Ferguson police officer Darren Wilson (Parlapiano, 2014).

However, in the summer of 2017, the Trump administration announced that it would restore the government redistribution of surplus military equipment, vehicles, aircraft, and weapons to law enforcement agencies. Speaking at a convention of the Fraternal Order of Police, then-Attorney General Jeff Sessions told the police in attendance that

> We will not put superficial concerns above public safety … The executive order the president will sign today will ensure that you can get the lifesaving gear that you need to do your job and send a strong message that we will not allow criminal activity, violence, and lawlessness to become the new normal.
>
> (Jackman, 2017, August 27)

The Militarization of the Police: SWAT Deployments

According to a 2014 report by the American Civil Liberties Union (ACLU), policing in America has become "paramilitarized" and the deployment of heavily armed SWAT teams has become routinized in the execution of so-called "no knock" search warrants, particularly in communities of color, and frequently for possessory drug offenses, along with which there is no information that there are weapons in the homes being searched. Among the findings of the ACLU:

1   Policing—particularly through the use of paramilitary teams—in the United States today has become excessively militarized, mainly through federal programs that create incentives for state and local police to use unnecessarily aggressive weapons and tactics designed for the battlefield.
2   The militarization of policing in the United States has occurred with almost no public oversight.
3   SWAT teams were often deployed—unnecessarily and aggressively—to execute search warrants in low-level drug investigations; deployments for hostage or barricade scenarios occurred in only a small number of incidents.
4   The use of paramilitary weapons and tactics primarily impacted people of color; when paramilitary tactics were used in drug searches, the primary targets were people of color, whereas when paramilitary tactics were used in hostage or barricade scenarios, the primary targets were white.
5   SWAT deployments often and unnecessarily entailed the use of violent tactics and equipment, including armored personnel carriers; use of violent tactics and equipment was shown to increase the risk of bodily harm and property damage.

(American Civil Liberties Union, 2014, pp. 5–6)

The ACLU analyzed over 800 SWAT deployments carried out by 20 law enforcement agencies during the years 2011–2012 (American Civil Liberties Union, 2014).

SWAT raids are undoubtedly violent events: numerous (often 20 or more) officers armed with assault rifles and grenades approach a home, break down doors and windows (often causing property damage), and scream for the people inside to get on the floor (often pointing their guns at them) (American Civil Liberties Union, 2014, p. 3).

The ACLU found that 79 percent of the SWAT raids that they reviewed involved the search of a person's home and that 60 percent were searches for drugs. The justifications for the use of heavily-militarized SWAT teams to execute search warrants for drugs in private homes were most often predicated on the belief that there would be firearms found in the home that could and would be used in armed confrontations with officers serving the search warrants. According to the ACLU's findings, officers discovered the presence of a weapon in only 35 percent of the cases when officers indicated a belief that occupants of the homes would be armed.

Weapons used by SWAT teams in the execution of search warrants in private homes, most often in a search for drugs, include potentially lethal flash-bang grenades (a military weapon designed for use during war-related battles), heavy battering rams for breaking down doors and smashing windows, and explosive breaching devices to blow up entryways, according to the ACLU (American Civil Liberties Union, 2014, pp. 21–22). The SWAT officers are most often dressed in military BDUs, armed with military AR-15 assault rifles, and arriving in MRAP armored personnel carriers, surplus military vehicles designed for use during the wars in Iraq and Afghanistan and distributed upon request at no cost to law enforcement agencies nationwide.

Additionally, the ACLU investigation reported significant racial disparities in the deployment of SWAT teams in the execution of search warrants: "Of the deployments that impacted minorities (Black and Latino), 68 percent were for drug searches, whereas of deployments that impacted white people, only 38 percent were for drug searches" (American Civil Liberties Union, 2014, p. 35). Adding to concerns regarding racial disparities, the ACLU "determined that of the 818 deployments studied, 14 percent involved the presence of children" (p. 40).

According to *Pro Publica*, "at least 50 Americans have been seriously injured, maimed or killed by (police using) flashbangs grenades since 2000" (Angwin & Nehring, 2015). Flashbangs "designed nearly 40 years ago to help military special forces rescue hostages, flashbangs create a stunningly bright burst of light and an ear-splitting boom that temporarily blind and deafen anyone standing within a few feet of them" (Angwin & Nehring, 2015).

On May 28, 2014, police in Habersham County, Georgia, maimed and nearly killed 18-month-old "Bou" Phonesavanh when they threw a flashbang grenade into the child's playpen during the execution of a search warrant for drugs in the home where the child lived with his family.

On October 1, 2012, a 12-year-old girl suffered first and second degree burns when a SWAT team in Billings, Montana, executed a search warrant during which "no arrests were made during the raid, but officers dropped a flashbang into the room where the girl was sleeping" (Angwin & Nehring, 2015).

At 5:30 a.m. on July 21, 2010, police in Clayton County, Georgia, severely burned Treneshia Dukes when they detonated three flashbangs in her home during the execution of a "no knock" warrant in a marijuana investigation. Dukes was asleep when 18 police officers arrived in an armored vehicle and undercover white van at the home that she shared with her boyfriend; police detonated the devices as they made forcible entry into the home. Less than one-tenth of an ounce of marijuana was discovered during the raid, but "Dukes suffered second-degree burns across her body. When later asked to describe the pain she felt that morning on a scale of one to 10, with 10 being the absolute greatest, Dukes said 100" (Angwin & Nehring, 2015).

John Lindsay-Poland (2016) suggests that the message sent to police in equipping them with military weapons, equipment, and uniforms "who may not be party to the decisions that militarize their equipment and procedures," is that they are in fact at war. Believing that they are at "war," there will necessarily need to be an identified "enemy," and in cities, counties, and increasingly suburban and rural areas, the enemy is, by default, those "others" who are perceived to be "criminally inclined." Too often these are residents of communities of color. Lindsay-Poland observed that:

> First, in the face of violent events, paramilitary police are frequently less effective than other forms of policing, and even less effective than nonviolent civilian interventions. Tragically, in the case of the San Bernardino massacre, there is not much evidence that the police response led to any reduction in killing.

Second, in equipping and training police for worst-case scenarios, military equipment and methods are inevitably used in situations that do not remotely require a military response.

Third, by focusing on violent events with little context as emergencies, the state's responsibility to address a myriad of other emergencies becomes invisible: poverty, lack of affordable housing and healthy food options, inadequate or inaccessible medical care, a dysfunctional judicial system, mental health crises—that in some cases precipitate the same violent events that policing purports to neutralize.

(2016, p. 155)

During the first two decades of the twenty-first century the deployment of heavily armed and militarized SWAT teams had become so routinized that they attracted little attention. It became difficult if not impossible, as the ACLU discovered, to determine even approximate numbers of SWAT deployments, since most police departments did not keep records specifically related to SWAT activations, and statewide figures were not compiled, save for a handful of states nationwide: Maryland, Connecticut, and Utah were states that enacted some form of oversight and reporting laws regarding SWAT use (Balko, 2014, February 17).

According to Radley Balko (2014),

by the end of the decade (2000s), state and local SWAT teams were regularly being used not only for raids on poker games and gambling operations but also for immigration raids (on both businesses and private homes) and raids on massage parlors, cat houses, and unlicensed strip clubs … If the government wants to make an example of you by pounding you with a wholly disproportionate use of force, it can. It's rare that courts or politicians even object, much less impose consequences.

Militarization and the First Amendment

As relates to the constitutional protections contained in the First Amendment, and particularly to the Assembly Clause, Hiram Emmanuel Arnaud (2016) argued that, following the Occupy Movements that began to emerge throughout the United States in 2011, "militarized police units signified the norm when responding to prolonged periods of protest. In fact, police brutality spurred substantially larger protests across the country" (2016, p. 778). He further observed that "militarized police activity in the midst of an otherwise peaceable protest is an implicit violation of the right to peaceably assemble" (2016, p. 807).

Using the examples of the Occupy Wall Street protests in New York City in 2011 and the protests in Ferguson, Missouri, following the shooting death of Michael Brown in 2014, Arnaud (2016) suggests a "balancing scheme" in determining whether the police response to each was lawful and appropriate. The criteria used in the balancing scheme are: "whether or not the assembly was peaceable" (p. 807); a weighing of the parties' respective interests (i.e., the protesters and the city); examining "prospective burdens" (e.g., occupying a park for a year versus other routine use of the park); the use of police force (i.e., appropriate to the threat encountered).

Using this balancing scheme, Arnaud concludes that the police were justified in evicting the Occupy Wall Street protestors after they had occupied a city park for over a year, but that the highly militarized response of the police in Ferguson, Missouri, to protests there that

> the protestors have every right to sue the local government for an implicit infringement of their right to peaceably assemble. This conclusion is based entirely on two factors: (1) the fact that the protestors are assembled in a permissible area, as previously discussed, and (2) the use of militarized police tactics in quelling the peaceful protests.
>
> (2016, p. 810)

When the police engage in a militarized response to First Amendment protected activity, the effect, whether intentional or not, may be to curtail or suppress the activity, whether it be speech, assembly, the right to petition government for redress, and to have the activity reported by the press. We have seen the police use weapons and implements designed for military use on the field of battle in suppressing oftentimes nonviolent, peaceful protests; this is of particular and alarming concern when the protests involve the actions of the police themselves, as we have seen in Baltimore, Chicago, New York, Ferguson, Missouri, Phoenix, Philadelphia, and elsewhere.

Balko (2014), in writing about the Occupy movement and associated protests, observed that "police across the country met protesters in riot gear, once again anticipating—and in too many instances seemingly even craving—confrontation" (p. 286). Balko recounted the notorious incident involving Occupy protesters at the University of California Davis and then-campus police Lieutenant John Pike, who discharged a canister of pepper spray at a group of over 20 student protesters who were seated on the ground with their arms locked, a widely recognized tactic that conveys the protesters' message to law enforcement that "we will do no harm; we will break no laws; we are peacefully protesting." That message was apparently not conveyed to the woefully unprepared University of California Davis campus police in any training that they may have (or more likely have not) received on crowd control strategies during protests. The video depicting Pike brutalizing the students he was sworn to protect will no doubt be a prominent feature in law enforcement training on protests and crowd control in police academies across the country for years to come—training on how *not* to respond to peaceful protests.

We have seen instances where the police have used tear gas and Long-Range Acoustic Devices (LRADs) in dealing with unarmed protesters. According to the Organization for the Prohibition of Chemical Weapons, since the use of such gases has been condemned and prohibited for use during war and "that this prohibition shall be universally accepted as a part of International Law, binding alike the conscience and the practice of nations" (Organization for the Prohibition of Chemical Weapons, 1928), it seems wholly incompatible with and inimical to contemporary, enlightened, and progressive police practices. Yet the use of tear gas continues in domestic law enforcement operations in 2019.

Likewise, LRADs are sound cannons that were developed by the U.S. military following the 2000 attack on the *U.S.S. Cole* in Yemen. The devices were designed to ward off small vessels from approaching larger ships, as had been the means of attack on the *Cole*. When used for "crowd control" in domestic law enforcement operations, the devices can cause severe headaches, nausea, extreme pain, and hearing loss (Baldwin, 2014).

The police have also used water cannons, rubber bullets, wooden projectiles, MRAP vehicles, assault rifles, police dogs, riot shields, and Tasers in confronting protesters who have been, for the large part, peaceful and unarmed, and these practices continue to raise alarm and concern among civil rights and civil liberties advocates.

According to The Constitution Project (2015),

> Local law enforcement's use of military surveillance techniques and military equipment, from armored personnel carriers to Long Range Acoustic Devices ("LRADs"), can implicate an individual's right to free speech under the First Amendment. This threat arises from two potential sources: one, the chilling effect that visible firepower can have on a protester or a potential protester; and two, the fact that the use of such equipment may not be narrowly tailored to meet a significant governmental interest.
>
> (pp. 1–2)

Regarding the first threat, that of visible firepower, The Constitution Project (2015) describes two types of strategies that the police employ that may have a chilling effect on the freedoms to assemble and to engage in free speech activities. The first is what is described as "preemptive policing," a recent practice "cover(ing) a number of police activities that occur prior to a law being broken, from shutting down meetings to arresting protesters." The second tactic is what The Constitution Project refers to as the "weapons effect," whereby police make protesters aware that they will be met by a highly militarized law enforcement response, including heavily armed officers in MRAP vehicles, equipped with tear gas, LRAD sound cannons, rubber bullets, etc., and that the police also intend to use sophisticated surveillance technologies to collect "intelligence" on the individuals and groups intending to protest.

As to the second threat to the protections contained in the First Amendment, the fact that the police may invoke a response to citizens engaging in protected activity that is not tailored to meet "a significant government interest," is what I have called a "hyper-exaggerated" response that exceeds the proportionality necessary to meet the identified and pre-articulated interests of public safety. Law enforcement may, in context-specific circumstances, have a compelling public safety (i.e., government) interest in curtailing or limiting certain activities relating to speech and assembly, and in certain circumstances they may need to use force or a show of force to do so. The police infringe on activities protected under the First Amendment when their response to those engaged in acts of civil disobedience exceeds a proportional, necessary, and justifiable threat to public safety.

We have seen such disproportionate police responses to events in Ferguson, Missouri, in the summer and fall of 2014 as well the Boston Marathon bombing on April 15, 2013, and the days that followed. The militarization of the police response to incidents and situations involving civil rights and civil liberties protections and constitutional implications, while on prominent display in communities of color and in dealing with protesters representing movements such as Black Lives Matter, is by no means restricted to those types of events and incidents, as observations and analyses regarding the police response to protests in cities across the United States will show.

The Militarization of the Police: Events in Ferguson, Missouri

On August 9, 2014, Ferguson, Missouri, police officer Darren Wilson shot and killed an unarmed African American teenager, Michael Brown, after an altercation following Officer Wilson's order to Brown to refrain from jaywalking. That Brown was unarmed and that his body lay on the ground for over four hours infuriated residents of St. Louis County, and they took to the streets in protest. The law enforcement response to the largely peaceful protests was a hyper-exaggerated, hysterical, and highly militarized juggernaut. Thousands of police officers from Ferguson and surrounding municipalities, the St. Louis County Police Department, the St. Louis Metropolitan Police Department, and the troops of the Missouri National Guard, were assembled in Ferguson to meet the threat posed by several hundred largely peaceful and unarmed protesters.

The law enforcement footprint was monolithic: police dressed as soldiers stood atop gun turrets in Bearcat and MRAP military vehicles pointing M-16 and M-4 rifles at unarmed protesters. Police used LRADs (sonic sound cannons developed for military defense), and fired upon protesters using rubber bullets, tear gas (banned by the Geneva Conventions except for use during war), smoke bombs and grenades, stun grenades, wood bullet projectiles, pepper pellet rounds, and beanbag rounds. For most people in the United States, and the world, this was the first glimpse into the newly emergent and highly militarized "Homeland Security" police, resplendent in their military uniforms and gear, riding in their fortified MRAP vehicles, flying above in their military aircraft, while shooting, gassing, deafening, bombing, and stunning members of the community who were engaging in constitutionally protected activities. The police in Ferguson, Missouri, roundly trounced the First Amendment guarantees of freedom of speech, freedom of assembly, freedom to petition government for redress, as well as freedom of the press. These constitutionally protected freedoms were ignored and trampled by police forces that had adopted a highly militarized posture and response to a situation that was wholly the result of police misconduct: the excessive force that caused the death of Michael Brown, the secrecy and lies in the aftermath of the shooting, and the unilateral suppression of civil rights and civil liberties and the First Amendment to the Constitution.

Consider the report issued by the DOJ on March 4, 2015 (United States Department of Justice), that roundly condemned not only the Ferguson Police Department (FPD), but also the entire system of criminal justice as administered in the City of Ferguson. The DOJ report found that the FPD regulated the activities and behavior of Ferguson's African American residents, workers, students, and visitors through petty stops and harassment and enforcement strategies designed to raise revenue rather than to protect the public, and that it did so in collusion with the municipal court and the city government. These practices are wholly inimical to commonly accepted and widely supported community policing principles that are endorsed by virtually all of the almost 18,000 legitimate police agencies protecting and serving our communities in the United States. These procedures, combined with race-based and pervasive violations of the First, Fourth, and Fourteenth Amendments to the Constitution, served to de-legitimize the FPD in the eyes of many (Apuzzo, 2015).

The FPD had a dysfunctional history of operating beyond the margins of commonly accepted twenty-first century police practices and it was a department that had become a renegade and outlaw menace. The recommendations contained in the DOJ report somewhat optimistically presume that the FPD is a department that can be rehabilitated and reborn into one that respects the law and the Constitution and that will ensure the safety of the members of the community through respectful and just treatment.

The Police Response to Protests in North Dakota, Baton Rouge, and St. Louis

Protesters in North Dakota at the site of the Dakota Access pipeline construction had been staging demonstrations for months beginning in the spring of 2016, not far from the Standing Rock Sioux Reservation and had repeatedly been met with a highly militarized response from law enforcement officers who were charged with protecting the construction of the 1170-mile, $3.7 billion pipeline. The pipeline would bring natural gas from North Dakota to Illinois and the activists, many of them Native Americans, had objected to the project for years, convinced that the pipeline "threatens the region's water supply and would harm sacred cultural lands and tribal burial grounds" (Skalicky & Davey, 2016). According to *The New York Times*, Amnesty International had sent observers to the site of the demonstrations, concerned with law enforcement's excessive and violent response to the protests.

The protesters, who call themselves "water protectors," were met by a heavily armed law enforcement response with officers converging on the site near Cannon Ball, North Dakota, a response that could be described as nothing short of hysteria and overkill on the part of the police, in a presence that was wholly out of proportion with the "threat" they confronted. The largely peaceful protests at the contested site (indigenous people "consider the land unceded territory belonging to them under the 1851 Laramie Treaty") (Carpenter, 2016), were met with a law enforcement show of force that was unprecedented in its sheer scope and magnitude against Native American and other activists: police used fire hoses against protesters in sub-freezing temperatures, injuring as many as 300 protesters. Police also used chemical weapons, police K9 dogs, concussion grenades, Taser weapons, rubber bullets, and beanbag and sponge rounds. A young woman attending the protest had her arm blown off when police fired a concussion grenade into the crowd. According to the ACLU, there were 75 law enforcement agencies from ten states, some as far away as Louisiana, that had sent officers to the scene, where the protesters numbered in the thousands at one point, representing 200 Native American tribes (American Civil Liberties Union, 2016).

More typically, as the confrontation wore on, the protesters numbered in the low hundreds. Over 700 protesters were arrested by police, beginning in August of 2016 through February 2017, when the police arrested 47 people and finally broke up the camp where protesters stayed (Jackman, 2017, February 8). Many journalists were also arrested by police during the seven months that the standoff took place. At its height in November, the camp, called the *Oceti*

Sakowin, contained an estimated 10,000 people (Beaumont, 2017). When finally broken up, the camp had approximately 70 remaining protesters.

The public outcry and anger at this fearsome and hyper-exaggerated response to civil disobedience and protest in North Dakota had been largely muted compared with the strident display of public indignation seen in places like Ferguson, Baltimore and Chicago only two years earlier. The police in North Dakota were protecting property, not people, and in so doing violated the constitutional rights and civil liberties protections of those whom they were duty bound to protect.

In Baton Rouge, Louisiana, protesters took to the streets following the July 5, 2016, shooting death of Alton Sterling, a 37-year-old African American man shot by Baton Rouge police during a struggle. Police had responded to a report of a man selling CDs outside of a convenience store being armed with a handgun and officers shot Sterling several times after they pinned him to the ground. Protesters, largely peaceful and never exceeding more than 200, gathered, chanted and marched for several nights following the shooting death of Sterling. They were met by a heavily militarized response from police and sheriff's deputies dressed in so-called "Ninja" riot gear, armed with assault rifles and gas masks, driving armored Bearcat vehicles. They used an LRAD device to disperse the protesters.

Over 180 protesters were arrested, including, again, journalists who were on the scene to report on the protests. "An officer just pointed a machine gun at me," a reporter for *Huffington Post* said, as he captured the moment on camera (Workneh & Lohr, 2016).

According to *The Washington Post*, when "riot police appeared, their faces (were) covered with plastic masks. Protesters couldn't understand a word of what they were supposed to do, or where police wanted them to go" (Hauslohner et al., 2016). *The New York Times* reported that "images racing across social media of protesters facing police officers clad in riot gear are from here (Baton Rouge), as are those of SWAT trucks rolling down residential streets and of journalists being arrested" (Robertson & Robles, 2016). One protester, Donney Rose, 35, said, "What you're seeing is a situation much like Ferguson and other places where you have a majority-white force policing a majority-black city" (Robertson & Robles, 2016).

One woman, 22-year-old Kira Marrero, "said a police officer pointed an assault rifle at her shortly before her arrest," and that, according to observers, "when protesters moved their demonstration to the street outside of police headquarters on Friday night, police met them in riot gear, pounding on shields with their batons to make a deafening and repetitive thud" (Hauslohner et al., 2016).

In September 2017, in St. Louis, Missouri, the police prepared for protesters to take to the streets following the acquittal of former police officer Jason Stockley in the shooting death of a 24-year-old unarmed African American man, Lamar Smith, in 2011. In August 2016, some five years after the shooting, Stockley had been charged with first degree murder in Smith's death and he was acquitted in a bench trial on September 15. The protests continued in the streets of St. Louis for several weeks and the police were repeatedly accused of using unnecessary force against the protesters and of violating their constitutional rights and civil liberties. In November 2017, a federal judge ruled that the St. Louis Police Department had in fact violated protesters' constitutional rights and granted a preliminary injunction that placed restrictions on the department's responses to continued protests. U.S. District Judge Catherine Perry found sufficient evidence that police arbitrarily declared an assembly unlawful even when there was no violence, and that there was "no credible threat of force or violence to officers or property" when police rounded up citizens, including journalists, on Sept. 17. After those arrests, the acting head of the St. Louis MPD declared that his department had "owned" the night, as his officers mocked protesters by chanting "Whose streets? Our streets!"

(Reilly, 2017)

The St. Louis Metropolitan Police Department had been under a federal court order from 2015 that placed restrictions on when the police could use tear gas and other chemical weapons in dealing with protesters (*Templeton, et al. v. Sam Dotson, Chief of Police, City of St. Louis, et al.*), but they appear to have acted in violation of that order when dealing with protesters in 2017. This order should serve as a national model for law enforcement and should certainly guide police policy when they are dealing with protesters engaged in constitutionally protected activity. Judge Perry's incisive and comprehensive order prohibits the police from using their authority or discretion to:

1 Declare an unlawful assembly under St. Louis Code of Ords. §15.52.010 when the persons against whom it would be enforced are engaged in expressive activity, unless the persons are acting in concert to pose an imminent threat to use force or violence or to violate a criminal law with force or violence;

2 declare an unlawful assembly under St. Louis Code of Ords. §15.52.010 or enforce St. Louis Code of Ords. §17.16.275(A) and (E) for the purpose of punishing persons for exercising their constitutional rights to engage in expressive activity;

3 use chemical agents, including, but not limited to, mace/oleoresin capsicum spray or mist/pepper spray/pepper gas, tear gas, skunk, inert smoke, pepper pellets, xylyl bromide, and similar substances (collectively "chemical agents"), whatever the method of deployment, against any person engaged in expressive, non-violent activity in the City of St. Louis, in the absence of probable cause to arrest the person and without first issuing clear and unambiguous warnings that the person is subject to arrest and such chemical agents will be used and providing the person sufficient opportunity to heed the warnings and comply with lawful law enforcement commands or as authorized in paragraph 5 below;

4 use or threaten to use chemical agents, whatever the method of deployment, against any person engaged in expressive, non-violent activity in the City of St. Louis, for the purpose of punishing the person for exercising constitutional rights; and

5 issue orders or use chemical agents, whatever the method of deployment, for the purpose of dispersing person(s) engaged in expressive, non-violent activity in the City of St. Louis without first: specifying with reasonable particularity the area from which dispersal is ordered; issuing audible and unambiguous orders in a manner designed to notify all persons within the area that dispersal is required and providing sufficient warnings of the consequences of failing to disperse, including, where applicable, that chemical agents will be used; providing a sufficient and announced amount of time which is proximately related to the issuance of the dispersal order in which to heed the

warnings and exit the area; and announcing and ensuring a means of safe egress from the area that is actually available to all person(s).

(*Ahmad, et al. v. City of St. Louis, Missouri*, 2017, pp. 46–47)

When the police themselves engage in what has been dubbed "police rioting," a term coined after the disastrous police response to protests in Chicago during the 1968 Democratic National Convention (Davis, 2018), where protesters chanted at the police "The whole world is watching," their actions serve not only to undermine their legitimacy, but convey to those present and to those watching that the police cannot control the situation and that they have ultimately failed in their public safety mission.

The 1968 Chicago police riots saw live television broadcasts in their earliest incarnation, and the whole world watched in shock, disgust, and awe—the police had indeed crossed a line that had been heretofore unseen and unknown. Given the ubiquity of recording and broadcasting technology, combined with social media and the internet in the current era, the whole world is now always and already watching, and saw that in the second decade of the twenty-first century, out of control police in North Dakota, St. Louis, Ferguson, and elsewhere repeatedly rode roughshod over the Constitution and the civil rights and civil liberties of those whom they were duty-bound to protect and to keep safe.

The Militarization of the Police: The Response to the Boston Marathon Bombing

I will preface this perspective with the recognition and acknowledgment that some may find my analysis and observations objectionable and, in some cases, even offensive. The Boston Marathon bombing remains for many throughout Boston, Massachusetts, and beyond a source of anguish, pain, and a jarring psychic injury that endures, even as of this writing. I have been a lifelong resident of Boston, and member of its police department for 27 years—I was here in the city when the bombs exploded.

On April 15, 2013, two bombs were detonated near the finish line of the Boston Marathon, killing three spectators and injuring over 260 others. The response of the law enforcement community to this attack was without precedent in contemporary U.S. history and included thousands of police officers, both on- and off-duty, from all over New England, as well as federal agents of the FBI, ATF, DHS, CIA, and others. Additionally, 19,000 National Guard troops moved into the city to assist in the search for the bombing suspects, who were identified from surveillance photos taken on Boylston Street as Tamerlan and Dzhokhar Tsarnaev.

Then-Governor Deval Patrick ordered residents to remain in their homes and to "shelter in place," a term ordinarily used in reference to remaining indoors during a chemical or biological weapons attack in order to avoid contamination. Reports of the law enforcement response at the time of the bombing attack characterized it as "mayhem" and "chaos" (Kamp, 2015). The police, dressed in military uniforms, equipped with military long rifles, dogs, body armor, and driving heavily militarized vehicles, cordoned off a 20-square block section in the town of

Watertown and parts of the city of Cambridge, and conducted warrantless house-to-house searches of hundreds of homes in the days following the bombing attack, often ordering residents out of their homes at gunpoint.

These warrantless searches of homes were conducted in clear violation of the Fourth Amendment to the Constitution, and to date there has been no public accounting for or explanation from the police in their riding roughshod over the unequivocal mandates contained in the Fourth Amendment. No law enforcement official has provided any rationale or justification for the decision to dispense with the provisions of the U.S. Constitution in the search for the surviving bombing suspect who was found hiding in a boat after a resident called 911 and reported seeing a hand moving the boat's covering. Officers converging on the boat fired hundreds of rounds into the vessel and the suspect, Dzhokhar Tsarnaev, was found to be unarmed (his brother Tamerlan had already been killed). Tsarnaev has since been convicted of crimes related to the Boston Marathon bombing and has been sentenced to death.

Presumably, the police in the aftermath of the bombing and their search for the suspects relied upon an exception to the Fourth Amendment warrant requirement when forcefully entering the hundreds of homes that they searched in vain for the bombing suspects. Since the homes were searched by police who were armed with dogs and pointing rifles at residents, ordering them out of their homes (there are many videos on YouTube and elsewhere attesting to this practice having in fact occurred in Watertown and Cambridge), claims of "consent" searches are not sustainable. (One police official commented to me privately that the searches were "community safety searches," a term that I was then and now unfamiliar with.) The "fresh pursuit" exception to the warrant requirement was likewise inapplicable, since officers were not actively engaged in any specific pursuit.

That would seem to leave the "exigent circumstances" exception to the warrant requirement as the one exemption to be offered and argued in defense of the searches. (A justification, it should be pointed out, that has not been offered as of this writing.) The Legal Information Institute at Cornell Law School defines the "exigent circumstances" exception to the warrant requirement as:

> circumstances that would cause a reasonable person to believe that entry (or other relevant prompt action) was necessary to prevent physical harm to the officers or other persons, the destruction of relevant evidence, the escape of the suspect, or some other consequence improperly frustrating legitimate law enforcement efforts.
>
> (Cornell Law School, Legal Information Institute, 2018)

Thus, it would seem extraordinarily difficult to provide a legal justification for the warrantless searches of hundreds of homes in what are essentially "house-to-house" searches under the circumstances known to law enforcement officers at the time that the searches were conducted. They had no specific (or even generalized) knowledge of where the suspects were or had fled; there was no information that police officers or other persons were in imminent danger if the searches weren't conducted; there was no knowledge on the part of law enforcement regarding the imminent destruction of evidence; the suspects had already made good their escape; and there is no information that failing to carry out the house-to-house searches would facilitate the further escape of the suspects.

An analysis of the police response to the Boston Marathon bombing, released by the Massachusetts Emergency Management Agency in December 2014, found that thousands of police officers from across Massachusetts, New England, and New York "self-deployed" to the town of Watertown, Massachusetts, where it was believed that Dzhokhar Tsarnaev was hiding. These officers had not responded to any mutual-aid request and did so without authorization. The after-action report found "that there was no command or management structure formally assigned to manage incoming mutual aid personnel" (Massachusetts Emergency Management Agency, 2014), and that this disproportional, heavy-handed, disorganized, and disquieting response likely exacerbated an already dangerous situation and posed a serious threat to the safety of the officers on the scene who did in fact have the legal authority to respond to the incident and subsequent search.

The report also cited a lack of "weapons discipline" in officers randomly firing their weapons without identifying targets and creating dangerous and potentially deadly crossfire situations. In fact, one transit police officer was shot by a fellow officer and nearly died. The officer, Richard Donahue, was permanently disabled from his injuries and was forced to retire from his police position. The officer who shot Donahue has never been identified.

The police response to this horrific incident was so fearsome, menacing, frightening, and intimidating, that voices objecting to the warrantless searches or questioning Fourth Amendment and other constitutional issues fell silent, lest they be labeled unpatriotic or terrorist sympathizers. For 108 hours in Boston, chaos and mayhem were the (dis)order of the day, and the Fourth Amendment to the Constitution was shelved as the police morphed into the military, and civil rights and civil liberties were struck down with the butt of an M-16 rifle. No one was surprised and few objected when a year later, for the running of the 2014 Boston Marathon, the police announced that they would be conducting searches—warrantless searches—of anyone carrying a backpack on the street in the vicinity of the marathon finish line.

Militarization, Technology, and the Erosion of the Police Narrative

Concomitant with the escalation of police strategies and policies that privilege the acquisition of military equipment, vehicles, aircraft, weapons, and uniforms, as well as military operational tactics in routine engagement with the civilian population, is the memorialization and dissemination of video and audio recordings of the police engaged in these activities by members of the public. This militarization, coupled with the widespread distribution of video footage evidencing police violence and brutality via social media and other outlets, contributes to an erosion of trust in the police and a tangible sense of dread, danger, and peril in many of our communities, particularly communities of color (communities where the legacy of police-community "relations" is already characterized by suspicion and mistrust that is based on a history of oppression, racism, and discrimination).

Historically, it has been the police who have maintained a firm grip and almost complete control of the law enforcement narrative in the United States. The police version of events and incidents that they were involved in was always and already accepted as factual, truthful and without question, at least by the white working and middle classes. The police routinely hold press conferences to display the drugs and guns that they had "taken off the streets" in order to convince us that they are effective at and dedicated to keeping our communities safe from criminals. When the police used deadly force and killed men, women, and children, we accepted their version of the events leading up to the deadly encounters (one inevitably fraught with danger, violence, bravery, and heroism—for the police), without question. And after all, the police themselves meticulously and methodically investigated these instances of the use of deadly force and always came to the "proper" conclusion.

Conclusion

Only with the emerging ubiquity of video footage depicting police actions that stand in stark contrast to familiar and long-practiced police narratives, tales that describe the life-threatening peril and danger of police encounters that too often result in serious injuries and death to men, women, and children of color, do we begin to imagine a shift in the discourse and challenges to the credibility that has long been accorded to the police by default. It would have been unimaginable even a few years ago to see police officers charged with murder for killing unarmed black men, as has occurred in North Charleston, South Carolina; Cincinnati, Ohio; and Balch Springs, Texas.

The militarization of the police in the United States, coupled with the exposure of the police using deadly force against unarmed African American men, women, and children without justification, has caused those concerned with issues involving social justice to interrogate the police narrative. It is fair to say that the police version of events will continue to be viewed skeptically and to be questioned and not accepted as truthful or factual without corroboration and substantiation.

The police very much see themselves as the victims in this emergent narrative. This "self-victimization" of the police will prove inimical and detrimental to engaging in the productive dialogue and relationship building that needs to occur between the police and communities of color before this fractured and ruptured trust and confidence can be re-established (and if it ever existed at all necessarily needs to be part of that dialogue).

Those of us who remember the Chicago police riot at the 1968 Democratic National Convention or the May 4, 1970, shooting deaths of four students at Kent State University by the Ohio National Guard may have thought that the days of law enforcement repression of those engaged in activities protected by the Constitution was a phenomenon studied in history books as a legacy of the bad old days. The increased militarization of the almost 18,000 police forces in the United States reminds us that we must remain vigilant and that we must continue to challenge and to cross examine those in law enforcement who arrogate to themselves the authority to interpret the Constitution and to impose arbitrary limitations to our civil rights and civil liberties.

REFERENCES

Ahmad, et al. v. City of St. Louis, Missouri. United States District Court, Eastern District of Missouri. Case No. 4:17 CV 2455 CDP, 2017.

American Civil Liberties Union. (2014). War comes home: The excessive militarization of American police. *ACLU.* Retrieved from: www.aclu.org/report/war-comes-home-excessive-militarization-american-police.

American Civil Liberties Union. (2016). Stand with Standing Rock. *ACLU.* Retrieved from: www.aclu.org/issues/free-speech/rights-protesters/stand-standing-rock.

Angwin, J., & Nehring, A. (2015, January 12). Hotter than lava: Every day, cops toss dangerous military-style flash-bang grenades during raids, with little oversight and horrifying results. *Pro Publica.* Retrieved from: www.propublica.org/article/flashbangs.

Apuzzo, M. (2015, June 30). Justice department report says police escalated tensions in Ferguson. *The New York Times.* Retrieved from: www.nytimes.com/2015/07/01/us/draft-justice-dept-report-says-police-escalated-tensions-in-ferguson.html.

Arnaud, H. E. (2016). Dismantling of dissent: Militarization and the right to peaceable assemble, *Cornell L. Review,* 101, pp. 777–812.

Baldwin, R. (2014, August 14). What is the LRAD sound cannon? *Gizmodo.* Retrieved from: https://gizmodo.com/what-is-the-lrad-sound-cannon-5860592.

Balko, R. (2014). *Rise of the Warrior Cop: The Militarization of America's Police Forces.* New York: Public Affairs Books.

Balko, R. (2014, February 17). Shedding light on the use of SWAT teams. *The Washington Post.* Retrieved from: www.washingtonpost.com/news/the-watch/wp/2014/02/17/shedding-light-on-the-use-of-swat-teams/?utm_term=.158d2da67411.

Beaumont, H. (2017, February 23). Cleared: Police arrest 47 while emptying Standing Rock protest camp. *Vice News.* Retrieved from: https://news.vice.com/en_us/article/a3jmq4/police-arrest-47-while-emptying-standing-rock-protest-camp.

Carpenter, Zoe. (2016, October 26). Militarized police are cracking down on Dakota Access Pipeline protesters. *The Nation.* Retrieved from: www.thenation.com/article/militarized-police-are-cracking-down-on-dakota-access-pipeline-protesters/.

Community Oriented Policing Services, United States Department of Justice. (2018). *Problem Solving.* Retrieved from: https://cops.usdoj.gov/Default.asp?Item=2558.

Cornell Law School, Legal Information Institute. (2018). Exigent circumstances. *Cornell Law School.* Retrieved from: www.law.crnell.edu/wex/exigent_circumstances.

Davis, R. (2018). The 1968 Democratic National Convention. *Chicago Tribune.* Retrieved from: www.chicagotribune.com/news/nationworld/politics/chi-chicagodays-democraticconvention-story-story.html.

Defense Logistics Agency. (2018). *Law Enforcement support office.* Retrieved from: www.dla.mil/Disposition-Services/Offers/Reutilization/LawEnforcement.aspx.

Galhotra, S. (2012, September 17). Domestic terror: Are we doing enough to combat the threat from within? *CNN.* Retrieved from: www.cnn.com/2012/09/16/us/domestic-terrorism/index.html.

Hauslohner, A., Samuels, R., & Cusick, A. (2016, July 10). As arrests mount in Baton Rouge, protesters question police tactics. *The Washington Post.* Retrieved from: www.washingtonpost.com/national/as-arrests-mount-in-baton-rouge-protesters-question-police-tactics/2016/07/10/8d695124-46f1-11e6-bdb9-701687974517_story.html?utm_term=.b8959344ffdo.

Jackman, T. (2017, February 8). Sheriffs ask Trump for federal help with Dakota Access pipeline protesters. *The Washington Post.* Retrieved from: www.washingtonpost.com/news/true-crime/wp/2017/02/08/sheriffs-ask-trump-for-federal-help-with-dakota-access-pipeline-protesters/?utm_term=.a31df4b63838.

Jackman, T. (2017, August 27). Trump to restore program sending surplus military weapons, equipment to police. *The Washington Post.* Retrieved from: www.washingtonpost.com/news/true-crime/wp/2017/08/27/trump-restores-program-sending-surplus-military-weapons-equipment-to-police/?noredirect=on&utm_term=.556ae6d2a3d8.

Kamp. J. (2015, April 3). Boston Marathon bombing marked by bravery and chaos, report finds. *The Wall Street Journal.* Retrieved from: www.wsj.com/articles/boston-marathon-bombing-marked-by-bravery-and-chaos-report-finds-1428088945.

Lawrence, S., & McCarthy, B. (2013). What works in community policing? A best practices context for measure Y efforts. *The Chief Justice Earl Warren Institute on Law and Social Policy University of California, Berkeley School of Law.* Retrieved from: www.law.berkeley.edu/files/What_Works_in_Community_Policing.pdf.

Lindsay-Poland, J. (2016). Understanding police militarization in the global superpower. *Peace Review,* 28 (2), pp. 151–157.

Massachusetts Emergency Management Agency. (2014). After action report for the response to the 2013 Boston Marathon bombings. *National Police Foundation.* Retrieved from: www.policefoundation.org/critical-incident-review-library/after-action-report-for-the-response-to-the-2013-boston-marathon-bombings/.

National Institute of Justice. (2018). Practice profile: Problem-oriented policing. *Crime Solutions.* Retrieved from: www.crimesolutions.gov/PracticeDetails.aspx?ID=32.

Oliver, W. (2009). Policing for homeland security: Policy & research. *Criminal Justice Policy Review,* 20 (3), pp. 253–260.

Organization for the Prohibition of Chemical Weapons. (1928). Protocol for the prohibition of the use in war of asphyxiating, poisonous or other gases, and of bacteriological methods of warfare. *OPCW.* Retrieved from: www.opcw.org/chemical-weapons-convention/related-international-agreements/chemical-warfare-and-chemical-weapons/the-geneva-protocol/.

Parlapiano, A. (2014, December 1). The flow of money and equipment to local police. *The New York Times.* Retrieved from: www.nytimes.com/interactive/2014/08/23/us/flow-of-money-and-equipment-to-local-police.html.

Reilly, R. (2017, November 15). Federal judge Reins in St. Louis Police, finding protest crackdown unconstitutional. *Huffington Post.* Retrieved from: www.huffingtonpost.com/entry/st-louis-police-protest-unconstitutional_us-59ef8960e4b0bf1f88365466.

Robertson, C., & Robles, F. (2016, July 11). Escalating discord between police and protesters strains Baton Rouge. *The New York Times.* Retrieved from: www.nytimes.com/2016/07/12/us/protests-police-baton-rouge.html.

Skalicky, S., & Davey, M. (2016, October 28). Tension between police and Standing Rock protesters reaches boiling point. *The New York Times.* Retrieved from: www.nytimes.com/2016/10/29/us/dakota-access-pipeline-protest.html.

Templeton, et al. v. Sam Dotson, Chief of Police, City of St. Louis, et al. United States District Court, Eastern District of Missouri, Cause No. 4:14cv-2019CEJ, 2015.

The Constitution Project. (2015). The constitutional implications of the use of military equipment by law enforcement. *The Constitution Project.* Retrieved from: https://constitutionproject.org/wp-content/uploads/2015/01/TCP-Use-of-Military-Equipment.pdf.

United States Department of Justice. (1994). *President Clinton Announces New Crime Bill Grants to Put Police Officers on the Beat.* Retrieved from: www.justice.gov/archive/opa/pr/Pre_96/October94/590.txt.html.

United States Department of Justice. (2015). *Investigation of the Ferguson Police Department.* Retrieved from: www.justice.gov/sites/default/files/opa/press-releases/attachments/2015/03/04/ferguson_police_department_report.pdf.

Workneh, L., & Lohr, D. (2016, July 10). Baton Rouge cop points assault weapon at HuffPost reporter, protesters. *Huffington Post.* Retrieved from: www.huffingtonpost.com/entry/baton-rouge-assault-weapon-huffpost-reporter-protesters_us_5782415be4b0c590f7e9b48e.

Chapter 8

"Taking Off the Cuffs"
Police Retrenchment and Resurgence

The "Narrative"

In the early morning hours of January 25, 1995, Boston police officers who were assigned to the Youth Violence Strike Force were getting ready to finish their shift at approximately 2:00 a.m. when they heard a broadcast on one of the police radio channels that they monitored regarding a shooting at a local restaurant and that a suspect vehicle was being pursued by officers. The gang unit officers, who operated in plainclothes and who drove unmarked police vehicles, decided to join in the chase for the suspects who had fled the scene of the shooting in a Lexus and who were heading in the general direction of their unit headquarters. Initial police radio broadcasts regarding the shooting had erroneously reported that a police officer had been shot.

The pursuit was joined by over a dozen police vehicles from across the city and ended several miles away in the Mattapan neighborhood of the city when the suspects attempting their escape in the Lexus bailed out of their vehicle and fled on foot. The officers, including the plainclothes officers in the gang unit, were close behind and gave chase on foot. The suspects, all described as African American males, began to scale a tall chain-link fence as they fled and one of the gang unit officers, Michael Cox, an African American officer, began scaling the fence as well.

Other police officers, not recognizing the plainclothes officer Cox, mistakenly believed that Cox was one of the suspects and dragged him down from the fence. Officers then beat Officer Cox with heavy metal flashlights and truncheons and stomped on him and kicked him with the steel-toed boots favored by many of the officers. When the officers saw Cox's badge, handcuffs, and the familiar semi-automatic pistol that they all carried, they realized their mistake. Instead of calling for an ambulance and administering aid to their colleague, virtually all of the officers, 21 of them, fled the scene. Only Cox's police partner remained to offer assistance and to call for help. Cox was knocked unconscious in the beating and seriously injured, suffering severe organ damage and head wounds.

News of the beating of the plainclothes officer garnered national attention, particularly given the racial angle to the compelling narrative and the exposure that it provided to racialized police excess and brutality. Not surprisingly, the initial narrative of the event provided by the police described Officer Cox's injuries as having occurred when he "hit his head on the ice" in a fall (Lehr, 2009, p. 136). In all, 21 police officers who had been involved in the pursuit of the Lexus and who had been at the termination point of the chase filed the required reports of their involvement in the incident. Not one officer reported seeing Officer Cox being beaten or dragged down from the fence. There was ample evidence that the police officers present had conspired and colluded in constructing a narrative that would evidence blamelessness and innocence on their part, the truth elusive, as slippery as a fall on the ice.

The public outcry and the scandal that followed the widespread reporting of the beating critically challenged the police narrative. Federal trials, appeals, and civil lawsuits followed; criminal investigations dragged on without closure. Not one Boston police officer was ever convicted of charges in the beating of Officer Cox. The case went on internally in the Boston Police Department and in the federal court system for nearly ten years with no positive outcomes for any of those involved (unless one counts the officers who brutalized Cox keeping their jobs—they all did). All Cox wanted at the time of the beating was an apology; this was never forthcoming. But not since the 1991 beating of Rodney King in Los Angeles by police, a beating captured on video for the world to see, had the police seen such tangible recrimination for their brutality and ensuing cover-up.

Even though he sought no retribution from his colleagues and was far from strident in condemning what had happened to him, Cox refused to go along with the narrative crafted by his fellow officers. For this he was transferred from the elite gang unit and ostracized and outcast by his fellow officers. He and his family were harassed and had their home and car vandalized; lives forever altered by police officers who had nearly killed a fellow officer who was African American and who refused to "lie down" for it.

For many observers, the 1990s provided the foregrounding for the challenges to the police narrative that would continue to the present day. And as technology has advanced and evolved since George Holliday purchased his Sony CCD-F77 camcorder in 1991, the camcorder that he used on March 2, 1991, to record the police beating of Rodney King (Skolnick and Fyfe, 1993), the police have continued to grapple with the acceleration and ubiquity of the recordings, depictions, and the various media that have continued to expose officer-involved wrongdoing, brutality, and violence. Having historically exerted firm control over the narrative renderings and depictions of their exploits, virtually always portraying their activities in the most flattering and often heroic light, the police have seen their credibility eroded and viewed with increasing skepticism by a public that has grown doubtful and wary of what many see as self-serving and duplicitous accounts of law enforcement activities.

The "Pattern-or-Practice" Investigations and the Consent Decrees

It was during the period beginning in the mid-1990s that the police began to see the Department of Justice (DOJ) investigating police departments for "pattern-or-practice" violations of the Constitution, specifically the First, Fourth, and Fourteenth Amendments. In a pattern-or-practice investigation, the DOJ will investigate

> whether the police department has engaged in a pattern or practice of stops, searches, or arrests that violate the Fourth Amendment; use of excessive force; discriminatory policing; violation of the constitutional rights of criminal suspects; or violation of First Amendment rights.
>
> (United States Department of Justice, 2018a)

The authority to conduct such investigations lies in 42 U.S.C., Section 14141, which authorizes the Attorney General to initiate a civil action into "unlawful conduct":

> It shall be unlawful for any governmental authority, or any agent thereof, or any person acting on behalf of a governmental authority, to engage in a pattern or practice of conduct by law enforcement officers or by officials or employees of any governmental agency with responsibility for the administration of juvenile justice or the incarceration of juveniles that deprives persons of rights, privileges, or immunities secured or protected by the Constitution or laws of the United States.
>
> (United States Department of Justice, 2018b)

If the DOJ finds that a particular police department has engaged in systemic practices that are violative of the Constitution or civil rights and civil liberties protections of individuals and groups that are based on race, ethnic origin group, religious affiliation, or other protected status, then the DOJ will seek to enter into voluntary consent decrees or Memoranda of Agreements (MOA) that are overseen by a federal court or an appointed outside monitor. Should a particular department refuse to voluntarily enter into an agreement with the DOJ, then the DOJ has the right to bring suit against the department and to force compliance with the policy and practice changes necessary to bring the law enforcement agency into constitutional compliance. Many in the police community saw DOJ investigations and the ensuing consent decrees and MOAs as essentially "handcuffing" the police and preventing them from doing their jobs.

The DOJ "pattern-or-practice" investigations primarily involve use of force issues, discriminatory police practices and unlawful searches, seizures, and arrests, interfering with individuals recording the police in the performance of their duties, and the unlawful police restrictions on individuals and groups engaging in constitutionally protected activity, such as speech, assembly, association, and petitioning government for redress of grievances. Should a DOJ investigation determine that a pattern-or-practice violation has occurred, "it responds by defining, prohibiting, and reforming the unlawful practice" (United States Department of Justice, 2017).

According to the DOJ,

> the reform process initiated by a pattern-or-practice investigation can enable law enforcement agencies to remedy identified problems; repair mistrust between the community and the police; and bring about policing that is lawful, effective, and responsive to community needs.
>
> (United States Department of Justice, 2018)

In pushing back on federal oversight of policing practices that are constitutionally suspect, leaders of some departments have voiced concerns and skepticism of the policies, practices, and training that they are required to change or implement under the decrees. According to *The Washington Post*, police in New Orleans are reluctant to initiate stops of those who officers believe are acting suspiciously, or to engage in so-called "proactive" policing. The paper interviewed Capt. Mike Glasser, head of the Police Association of New Orleans, who described the officer reluctance thus: "Yes, he looks suspicious. Yes, he might be up to no good. But you know what? I don't have to do that," Glasser said, "Because you don't get in trouble for what you don't do" (Kelly et al., 2015).

Part of the judgment in the lawsuit that the DOJ brought against the New Orleans Police Department (NOPD) required the officers to wear body cameras and to record their interactions with the people who they come into contact with. The NOPD superintendent in 2015, Michael Harrison, told *The Washington Post* that "officers are somewhat reserved about their levels of aggression toward fighting violent crime because of the oversight" (Kelly et al., 2015).

The DOJ entered into its first consent decree in 1997 with the Pittsburgh Police Department. In Pittsburgh, the DOJ "identified a pattern or practice of excessive force; unlawful stops, searches and arrests, linking these findings to insufficient accountability systems and failure to supervise officers" (United States Department of Justice, 2017). By 2004 the DOJ had entered into MOAs or consent decrees with 15 police departments nationwide, including those in Newark, New Jersey; Washington, D.C.; Los Angeles; Buffalo, New York; Cleveland and Columbus, Ohio; and Detroit. And from 2009 through 2017, the DOJ entered into 25 MOAs, consent decrees, and settlement agreements with law enforcement agencies that included police departments in Baltimore; New Orleans; Portland, Oregon; Seattle; Maricopa County, Arizona; and three in Missoula, Montana, with its county attorneys' office, police department, as well as the University of Montana Campus Police Department (United States Department of Justice, 2017).

The most recent consent decree was entered into in 2017 and involved the Baltimore Police Department (BPD), which had sought to initiate a collaborative process with the DOJ's Office of Community Oriented Policing Services in 2014. The BPD's request preceded the widespread condemnation and protest directed at the BPD following the death of Freddie Gray at the hands of Baltimore officers on April 12, 2015. The DOJ initiated its pattern-or-practice investigation in May 2015. The DOJ

> found that BPD made stops, searches and arrests without the required justification; used enforcement strategies that unlawfully subjected African Americans to disproportionate rates of stops, searches and arrests; used excessive force; and retaliated against individuals for their constitutionally-protected expression.
>
> (United States Department of Justice, 2017)

Of note: the DOJ's investigation found patterns and practices in 2017 in Baltimore that echoed findings made by the DOJ in Pittsburgh—20 years earlier, in 1997.

Zachary Powell, Michele Meitl, and John Worrall (2017) have conducted research on the efficacy of consent decrees in reducing the number of lawsuits filed against the police for officer misconduct under 42 U.S.C. § 1983, the federal statute that allows individuals and groups to file tort actions against government agencies for wrongdoing. Their study "offers preliminary evidence that consent decrees may reduce civil rights violations" (p. 575). In studying 23 police departments that entered into consent decrees with the DOJ between 1990 and 2013, the authors found that litigation filed against police departments dropped by as much as 36 percent during the period of time that the consent decrees were in effect, but that litigation began to increase once the departments studied were no longer bound by the decrees. They observed that

> reductions in such filings may signal increased satisfaction with police agencies and a move toward reduced systemic police misconduct. As such, consent decrees should continue to be considered as a possible tool for correcting problematic police departments, but additional research in this area is critical.
>
> (Powell et al., 2017, p. 575)

David Douglass (2017) has seen that "consent decrees constitute a compendium of best practices for constitutional, effective, community-oriented policing." He argues that consent decrees "can empower communities to initiate police reform and to educate communities concerning the elements of effective, constitutional policing, and establish agreement with the police concerning the elements of constitutional and effective policing" (p. 322). Going forward, Douglass suggested that consent decrees "serve as the foundation for an agreed-upon roadmap for reform, including measures of progress, accountability, and results" (p. 322).

Floyd v. City of New York

Not all of the remedial efforts to reform the dozens of police departments nationwide that were found to have engaged in pattern or practice violations of the Constitution and racial profiling were contained in the form of settlement agreements or MOAs with the DOJ. And perhaps conspicuous in its absence from the list of the many dozens of police departments that have entered into consent decrees with the DOJ is the nation's largest and, in many ways, the most notoriously noxious police department: the New York City Police Department (NYPD). The NYPD coined and advanced the concept of "Blue Racism" and solidly embraced "zero-tolerance," "order maintenance," and "broken windows" policing, policies and practices (derisively referred to by many in New York's communities of color as "broken kneecaps" policing) (*The Nation*, 1999). The city of New York was also the named defendant in *Floyd v. City of New York*, an August 2013 case in which federal Judge Shira Sheindlin found that "the NYPD engages in unconstitutional stop and frisk practices, including racial profiling against Black and Latino New Yorkers" (Center for Constitutional Rights, 2013, p. 1). Judge Sheindlin found that the NYPD's unconstitutional policing practices "resulted in the disproportionate and discriminatory stopping of blacks and Hispanics in violation of the Equal Protection Clause. Both statistical and anecdotal evidence showed that minorities are indeed treated differently than whites" *(Floyd v. City of New York*, p. 16).

The judge ordered the appointment of an independent monitor who would report to the court and be responsible for overseeing the remedies mandated by the court to halt the unconstitutional practices. The court also ordered that the remedies would first include revisions to the NYPD's training in the laws pertaining to the authority to stop and frisk and second, to "revise its policies and training regarding racial profiling to make clear that targeting 'the right people' for stops, as described in the Liability Opinion, is a form of racial profiling and violates the Constitution" *(Floyd v. City of New York*, p. 17).

Among the findings of fact in the *Floyd* case, which were not contested by the NYPD, were the following:

Between January 2004 and June 2012, the NYPD conducted over 4.4 million Terry stops.

The number of stops per year rose sharply from 314,000 in 2004 to a high of 686,000 in 2011.

52% of all stops were followed by a protective frisk for weapons. A weapon was found after 1.5% of these frisks. In other words, in 98.5% of the 2.3 million frisks, no weapon was found.

8% of all stops led to a search into the stopped person's clothing, ostensibly based on the officer feeling an object during the frisk that he suspected to be a weapon, or immediately perceived to be contraband other than a weapon. In 9% of these searches, the felt object was in fact a weapon. 91% of the time, it was not. In 14% of these searches, the felt object was in fact contraband. 86% of the time it was not.

6% of all stops resulted in an arrest, and 6% resulted in a summons. The remaining 88% of the 4.4 million stops resulted in no further law enforcement action.

In 52% of the 4.4 million stops, the person stopped was black, in 31% the person was Hispanic.

In 2010, New York City's resident population was roughly 23% black, 29% Hispanic, and 33% white.

In 23% of the stops of blacks, and 24% of the stops of Hispanics, the officer recorded using force. The number for whites was 17%.

Weapons were seized in 1.0% of the stops of blacks, 1.1% of the stops of Hispanics, and 1.4% of the stops of whites.

Contraband other than weapons were seized in 1.8% of the stops of blacks, 1.7% of the stops of Hispanics, and 2.3% of the stops of whites.

Between 2004 and 2009, the percentage of stops where the officer failed to state a specific suspected crime rose from 1% to 36%.

(Floyd v. City of New York, p. 9)

In the wake of the 198-page decision by Judge Sheindlin, NYPD union representatives attempted to discredit the decision and to weigh in on the threatened appeal of the court order. In a familiar refrain, the NYPD Patrolmen's Benevolent Association (PBA) issued a statement decrying the decision and blaming constitutional, race profiling, and civil rights issues with stop, question, and frisk practices on quotas and a lack of funding and inadequate staffing. The PBA pleaded for the NYPD "to allow police officers to exercise their professional discretion and judgment" in deciding when and where to make stops. The court's decision, the PBA asserted, "will do nothing more than make the toughest policing job in the world even more difficult and dangerous," referring to an "unwieldy judicially created regime" that is apparently the root cause of what the court determined were race-based practices employed by the NYPD (Patrolmen's Benevolent Association, 2013). Even the city's then-Mayor, Michael Bloomberg, and then-Police Commissioner Ray Kelly "blasted" the court's decision. According to the *Huffington Post*, Bloomberg held a press conference following the decision and claimed that "this is a dangerous decision made by a judge who I think does not understand how policing works and what is compliant with the U.S. Constitution as determined by the Supreme Court"; at the same press conference Kelly lambasted what he called the court's "disturbing disregard" for the "good intentions" of "police officers who do not racially profile" (*Huffington Post*, 2013).

The court's decision in *Floyd* continued the interrogation and the skepticism of the police narrative that began in its latest iteration in the 1990s, as the internet began its ascendency and its omnipresence. No longer would the police version of events in which they were implicated be unquestioningly and unwaveringly accepted as invariably truthful. As a young police officer in the 1970s and 1980s, my version of and testimony regarding incidents in which I became involved in my official capacity were believed verbatim and without question; they were carefully scripted, sculpted, and crafted in the ways that I had been schooled on as a novice by colleagues, superiors, and even prosecutors. I could likely have testified in court that the moon was made of green cheese and I would have been believed by all present, with the possible exception of defense counsel.

The Police and the "Others"

The police response to the ongoing challenge to their construction of a world that is framed in a duality of lightness and darkness, good versus evil, us against them, has been to assume the posture of defensiveness, defiance, and recalcitrance. Those "others" who seek to challenge the police worldview and their narrative, occupy the evil darkness that exists in a stark binary to the world of light, the good, the law-abiding, the deferential—those who unequivocally support the police in all that they do, regardless of the fallout for those whose constitutional rights and civil liberties may be trammeled in the process.

It is hardly the case that significant (or even moderate) reforms have been initiated in the wake of the federal court decision in *Floyd*. The Police Reform Organizing Project (PROP) conducted field research in New York City courtrooms as recently as 2018, several years after the *Floyd* decision, and found that the NYPD continued to process defendants of color through the court system for petty misdemeanor crimes, such as possession of marijuana, at rates that far outpaced their proportional representation in the general population of New Yorkers.

The Nation reported that "PROP sent researchers to attend misdemeanor arraignments in every borough from January through August 2017, witnessed more than 1,600 proceedings, and observed that across all five boroughs, 1,438, nearly 90 percent, involved New Yorkers of color" (Chen, 2018). This is despite repeated assurances from Manhattan's District Attorney Cyrus Vance and New York Mayor Bill DiBlasio that marijuana citations, arrests, and prosecutions would be sharply curtailed (Hannon, 2018). PROP reported that "compared to the total population of the city—which is about 44 percent white, 25 percent black, 25 percent Latino and 13 percent Asian American—the prevalence of non-whites among the arraigned was vastly disproportionate" (Chen, 2018).

Van Maanan's (1978) analysis of the police world view and subculture was published in the year that I began my career in law enforcement and it is as insightful and relevant a resource for understanding the prism through which the police view those with whom they come into contact today as it was some 40 plus years ago. His analysis entitled "The Asshole," describes the three-part typology that the police use as a form of "cognitive shorthand" to categorize citizens whom they encounter:

> (1) "suspicious persons"—those whom the police have reason to believe may have committed a serious offense; (2) "assholes"—those who do not accept the police definition of a situation; and (3) "know-nothings"—those who are not either of the first two categories but are not police and therefore, according to the police, cannot know what the police are about.
>
> (p. 225)

Van Maanan's conceptualization may be instructive in understanding (at least in part), the reasons why black and brown people so frequently bear the brunt of the police "imprint": in discriminatory enforcement practices, excessive violence, their disproportionate targeting in criminal proceedings for trivial offenses (such as those reported by PROP and others), and in deadly force incidents involving the police where the victims are unarmed.

For "suspicious persons" are those, whether they be drug dealers, burglars, bank robbers, or prostitutes, who share an understanding with the police regarding the "code of the street," the code that acknowledges that while most crimes and criminal activity will remain undetected by the police and thus unsanctioned, when confronted and apprehended by the police in the commission of a criminal offense, the "suspicious person" will defer immediately to the authority of the police to control and to dictate the terms of the encounter. It is thus, to a large extent, a mutually respectful engagement in which all parties present understand the rules, i.e., that the police are always and already in charge.

"Assholes" on the other hand "are stigmatized by the police and treated harshly on the basis of their failure to meet police expectations arising from the interaction situation itself" (Van Maanan, 1978, p. 226). The term of art that most immediately comes to mind from my days in policing is an individual's "flunking the attitude test," i.e., displaying a confrontational tone or posture in response to a police intervention, a response that could lead to a violent outcome or arrest for the individual displaying a non-deferential or "disrespectful" attitude. The police see "assholes" as "unworthy human beings" who are undeserving of fair treatment and whose constitutional rights and civil liberties are unacknowledged and denied, forfeited for being an "asshole."

Too often it is people of color who are relegated by the police to this category of "asshole" for failing to conspicuously and obsequiously display immediate deference and respect to the police when stopped, questioned, or frisked. For "it is the asshole category which is most imbued with moral meaning for the patrolman—establishing for him a stained or flawed identity to the citizen upon which he can justify his sometimes-malevolent acts" (p. 226).

Most people fall into the "know nothing" category in the police worldview; they are crime victims, witnesses, onlookers, motorists, office workers, students, laborers, and others who have little regular contact with the police. They are not police or members of police families or their friends; they may generally be supporters of the police who can usually be counted upon to accept the police version of events and the police narrative. In the eyes of the police then, they know nothing.

Much of what confronts the police and the communities they serve today has little changed from Van Maanan's prescient sentiments of several decades ago: "And, since the police view their critics as threatening and as people who generally should be taught or castigated, one could argue that the explosive potential of police-citizen encounters will grow" (p. 233). It is clear that much of what currently transpires between the police and communities of color is a manifestation of this explosive potential that has often driven a wedge between the police and those with whom they interact. Consider that

> If the police become more sensitive to public chastisement, it could be expected that something of a self-fulfilling prophecy might well become a more important factor in the street than it is presently. That is to say, if the police increasingly view their public audience as foes—whose views are incomprehensible if not degenerate or subversive—it is likely that they will also magnify clues which will sustain the stereotype of citizen-as-enemy, escalating therefore the percentage of street interactions which result in improper arrest and verbal or physical attack.
>
> (Van Maanan, 1978, pp. 232–233)

The ongoing "public chastisement" of certain practices of some of the police that have been the subject of observation throughout this text can thus be seen as at least in part the rationale for and the justification of (at least in the minds of the police) interactions in the street that have had violent and occasionally fatal and tragic outcomes. If the police continue to consider their communities and their public as "others" and as foes or enemies, then the disconnect will continue unabated.

The Cuffs Come Off: Revanche

Many police: line patrol officers, supervisors, managers, and administrators, believed that their operations had in fact been hamstrung by the consent decrees and that they had been "handcuffed" by the DOJ and prevented from doing their jobs effectively (as only they knew how to do). The President of the Chicago branch of the Fraternal Order of Police (FOP), as an example, in writing about a consent decree that had been years in the undertaking by the Chicago Police Department and the DOJ, suggested that violence in Chicago

> is a direct and chilling refutation of the entire argument posed by the talking heads from the city, attorney general and from groups like the ACLU to impose this proposed consent decree. It (violence) also may very well be a hint of what is to come if the war on the police continues.
>
> (Spielman, 2018)

On March 31, 2017, then-Attorney General Jeff Sessions, in a memorandum to United States Attorneys and to DOJ department heads, identified the priorities of the Trump DOJ in "Supporting Federal, State, Local, and Tribal Law Enforcement." In the memo, Sessions downplayed a federal role in addressing crime rates, securing public safety, protecting the civil rights and civil liberties of citizens, and determining best police practices, stating "that these are, first and foremost, tasks for state, local, and tribal law enforcement." Sessions went on to state that "local control and local accountability are necessary for effective local policing. It is not the responsibility of the federal government to manage non-federal law enforcement agencies" (Office of the Attorney General, 2017). Sessions then ordered the Deputy Attorney General and the Associate Attorney General to commence an immediate review of all existing and pending consent decrees between the DOJ and local law enforcement agencies.

On April 17, 2017, then-Attorney General Sessions reinforced the stance of the Trump Administration on the consent decrees that had been entered into by the DOJ and dozens of police departments during the Obama Administration. Penning an op-ed piece in *USA Today*, Sessions (2017) saw the consent decrees as "harmful federal intrusion" into local law enforcement operations. Sessions wrote of a "plague of violence" that saw "violent crime surging in American cities" and stated that "too many people believe the solution is to impose consent decrees that discourage the proactive policing that keeps our cities safe." Acknowledging the need for the rebuilding of confidence in law enforcement, Sessions said that "such reforms must promote public safety and avoid harmful federal intrusion in the daily work of local police." The DOJ, under Sessions, "will not sign consent decrees for political expediency that will cost more lives by handcuffing the police instead of the criminals."

Dara Lind (2017), writing in *Vox*, has described the metamorphosis of the police in the Trump era and their emergence as "culture war heroes." Beginning in 2017, the nascent administration, with the enthusiastic support of law enforcement, had championed a vision of the police "in which rank-and-file officers are an embattled group standing up for their rights, and 'public safety' means deferring to the interests of those officers."

She observed that the culture war advocates of unbridled police authority see that "rules imposed from the outside … could render officers unable to defend themselves. They are, or could be, threats to officers' lives" (Lind, 2017). This perceived "threat" quickly morphs into the notion "that criticism of police officers puts their lives in danger." In the paradigm shift to "taking the handcuffs off" of the police, there is a reimagining (or eliminating) of the oversight role that the DOJ and bedrock community policing principles had brought into contemporary policing policies beginning in the late 1980s. In a throwback to the bad old days of police excess and abuse, what is emerging is a quietly radical vision of policymaking. It's a vision in which, because rank-and-file law enforcement officers know best what it takes to keep communities safe (after all, they live it) everyone else—including the public and their own superiors—should yield to their judgment. It's a vision of policymaking made on the front lines.

(Lind, 2017)

Lind described the transformation of policing that began with the 2016 presidential campaign and election, one that bore fruit in a retrenchment of unchecked federal oversight of police authority: "That's not what public safety meant in 2017. It meant a gift bestowed by law-enforcement officers on grateful Americans—and one that would disappear, poof, the minute anyone dared to examine it too closely" (2017).

On July 28, 2017, President Donald Trump traveled to New York to speak to a group of police officers to express his admiration and support for the police. During his speech he encouraged the officers in attendance to treat those suspects that they took into custody without apparent regard for the provisions of the Constitution or with civil rights or civil liberties. According to *The Washington Post*, Trump told the police that "we have your backs 100%. Not like the old days. Not like the old days" (Bump, 2017). He also spoke about "weak policing, and in many cases because the police weren't allowed to do their job." He made several mentions about the police having "the laws stacked against you," and then this:

> you see these thugs being thrown into the back of a paddy wagon—you just see them thrown in, rough—I said, please don't be too nice. (Laughter.) Like when you guys put somebody in the car and you're protecting their head, you know, the way you put their hand over? Like, don't hit their head and they've just killed somebody—don't hit their head. I said, you can take the hand away, okay? (Laughter and applause.).

(Bump, 2017)

Many interpreted Trump's remarks as encouraging police violence and extrajudicial punishment and imparting the not so subtle message to law enforcement nationwide that the oversight of the DOJ into local law enforcement misdeeds and civil rights violations were "stacking the laws against" the police, "like the old days." The police rank and file could be assured that "throwing thugs into the back of the paddy wagon" would meet with no inquiry from his DOJ, no review from meddlesome government lawyers, no pattern-or-practice investigations. (Completely lost on Trump was the offensive ethnic slur contained in his "paddy wagon" reference, an affront to many of the men and women in law enforcement of Irish descent who were no doubt in the audience of police.) (Mulvaney, 2017).

So it was in the words of Donald Trump and his then-Attorney General Jeff Sessions, and the policy proclamations, orders, policies, and memoranda that followed this rhetorical flourish, that the message to law enforcement was clear: policing where heads were cracked would be encouraged; civil rights were for the privileged; those without privilege (black and brown people) were thugs, rapists, vermin, and criminals; the federal government would not interfere in local law enforcement matters; the police themselves knew best as to how to engage in policing.

But would there be a resurgence of violent, discriminatory, and unlawful police practices? Would police policy makers, leaders, and practitioners be encouraged by the incendiary and inflammatory exhortations of the revanchists who now occupied positions of authority and influence in the DOJ and the White House? According to *The New York Times*, many police chiefs and other law enforcement policy makers and administrators were alarmed and frustrated by Trump's remarks and the new-found and unsolicited encouragement of troubling and unfettered police excess, excess that many progressive police executives had worked years if not decades to abate and eliminate (Eder et al., 2017).

The New York Times reported that "some of the chiefs said the new direction was out of step with a growing consensus that rebuilding community trust is essential to fighting crime, particularly after a spate of high-profile police shootings spurred a national debate on policing…" (Eder et al., 2017). Chris Magnus, the Police Chief in Tucson, Arizona, told the paper that

> I kind of resist the attorney general's narrative that the Department of Justice has been this oppressive presence in law enforcement, I actually think it's exactly the opposite, there are far more examples when they have really supported us to do innovative things.
>
> (Eder et al., 2017)

Police chiefs in Spokane, Washington; North Charleston, South Carolina (where Walter Scott was killed by police); St. Anthony, Minnesota (where Philando Castile was killed by police); Baltimore, Maryland (where Freddie Gray was killed by police); St. Louis County, Missouri; Tulsa, Oklahoma; and Fort Pierce, Florida have all requested DOJ assistance in reforming their often-troubled departments and in collaborating on necessary police reforms (Eder et al., 2017). These "technical assistance" requests were routinely accommodated by the DOJ during the Obama Administration. The requests for federal guidance and oversight of troubled police departments, that are initiated by the chief executive officers of the affected departments, are now routinely denied by the Sessions DOJ, rejections that are publicly denounced by local police chiefs who very much see the need for federal assistance and who have little interest in or support for a return to the often lawless policing practices of the latter decades of the twentieth century.

Chuck Wexler, the executive director of the Police Executive Research Forum, told *The Washington Post* that "it's the wrong message, the last thing we need is a green light from the president of the United States for officers to use unnecessary force" (Wootson & Berman, 2017). Darrel Stephens, the executive director of the Major City Chiefs Association, also spoke to the paper, and said, of Trump's urging

> Over the past two or three years, police departments have worked very, very hard to restore the loss of confidence and trust that people, particularly in the African-American community, have in the police, based on what happened in Ferguson and the other high-profile shootings. Maybe not just what the president said, but the reaction of the police officers standing behind him, I think that complicates that.
>
> (Wootson & Berman, 2017)

Police chief executives from police departments across the country also expressed reservations and concerns with Trump's remarks. In New York City; Boston; Portland, Oregon; Los Angeles; Suffolk County, New York; Gainesville, Florida; Houston; and even Woodburn,

Oregon, Trump's sentiments were roundly and repeatedly condemned (Wootson & Brennan, 2017). Executives of the International Association of Chiefs of Police and the Police Foundation also voiced objections to the remarks. Thus, it was clear that police leadership would not embrace a return to law enforcement's often troubled and violent past. What remained to be determined was the extent to which rank-and-file officers would act on this newfound incitement to belligerence. That the crowd of uniformed police officers in attendance during Trump's remarks were seen laughing and applauding was hardly a source of encouragement.

Andrew Cohen (2018), writing for the Brennan Center for Justice at the New York University School of Law, describes "National Police Week," the annual federal commemoration of police heroism and sacrifice, as a "false dichotomy," given that while police line-of-duty deaths remain at historically low rates, concerns, complaints, and reports about police excess and violence, specifically against people of color, continue to increase. This has been particularly true under the Trump Administration. The administration's continued misrepresentations and false statements of fact that rates of violent crime are increasing exponentially across the United States serve to exacerbate and perpetuate the false narrative that American cities are unsafe, and that there is a "war" against the police (Grawert & Cullen, 2018). Among the foremost acolytes of the "violent crime fiction" are the police themselves.

Consider Cohen's findings in the days leading up to "National Police Week" in 2018 as evidence of this false dichotomy: on May 8, five days before the "National Police Week" kickoff, a police union president in Miami staunchly defended an officer caught on video apparently kicking a handcuffed man in the head, calling the assault a "de-escalation technique" and that the officer "showed great restraint" (Iannelli, 2018). Or the report issued in Indianapolis two days prior to the opening ceremonies for "National Police Week" in 2018 that exonerated two Indianapolis police officers in the shooting death of an unarmed 45-year-old black man, and the public outrage and condemnation that followed. On that same day *The Washington Post* reported that a police officer in Alpharetta, Georgia was forced to resign after dashcam video footage recorded him brutalizing a 65-year-old African American grandmother while arresting her for "disorderly conduct" (Bever, 2018).

For Cohen (2018), the white Wisconsin police officer caught on video punching a black teenager repeatedly in the face (Politi, 2018), and the black teenager in Warsaw, North Carolina, who was choked by a police officer at a Waffle House restaurant while dressed in his prom tuxedo, the prom he had just taken his sister to (Molina & Bennett, 2018), support the contention that the police continue to employ violence, brutality, and oppression, particularly against people of color, while claiming victimhood and the disdain of the public. This while enacting a national commemorative week championing their bravery and heroism. He argues that

> we should reject the false dichotomy offered by Trump and Sessions and the police unions. It's not a with-us-or-against-us proposition. The truth is that we can both love the police and also seek to hold accountable those cops who sully the profession.
>
> (Cohen, 2018)

Though many police chief executives expressed dismay and frustration with the DOJ's 2017 policy of allowing local law enforcement to self-regulate and to self-monitor as well as its refusal to supply necessary and badly-needed "technical assistance" resources to local law enforcement (Community Oriented Policing Services, United States Department of Justice, 2018), those sentiments were not necessarily shared by rank-and-file police officers and their representatives. Prior to the 2016 elections, the FOP, the "the world's largest organization of sworn law enforcement officers" (Fraternal Order of Police, 2018), submitted a series of positions on criminal justice related issues and accompanying questions for the presidential candidates. This document memorialized and repeated the police narrative that cast line officers in the role of victim and included strident language condemning the exponential increase in the number of "assassinations" and "ambushes" of police officers, despite the lack of any empirical evidence to support these contentions.

The public posture of the FOP would have its supporters and candidates for president believe that

> law enforcement is facing a high level of hostility from the communities we protect and serve. Hateful rhetoric and those calling for violence are having an impact—ambush attacks on law enforcement and police shootings have spiked tremendously in the past few years. Fringe organizations have been given a platform by the media to convey the message that police officers are a "militarized" enemy and it is time to attack that enemy.
>
> (Fraternal Order of Police, 2016)

According to the FOP:

> Social media accounts are full of hatred and calls to target and kill police officers. The vitriol, the hateful screeds and statements of those we are sworn to protect and defend, as well as public calls to kill and injure police officers, are horrifying.
>
> (Fraternal Order of Police, 2016)

Portraying police officers as defenseless victims of some hidden conspiracy, we are told that "there is a very real and very deliberate campaign to terrorize our nation's law enforcement officers and no one has come to our defense" (Fraternal Order of Police, 2016, p. 5).

Among many issues contained in its pleading, the FOP calls upon presidential candidates to: reinstitute the Department of Defense 1033 program (the donation program that supplies surplus military equipment to local law enforcement agencies); reactivate the Immigration and Customs Enforcement 287(g) Program (the program that deputizes local police officers as immigration agents); support legislation classifying crimes against police officers as so-called "hate crimes"; commence the re-negotiation of extradition treaties with Cuba in the belief that violent criminals are eluding police apprehension by fleeing to the island nation, this in the aftermath of the thaw in relations between the United States and Cuba undertaken during the Obama administration.

While by no means a complete listing of the FOP issues and grievances, it is worthy of note that nowhere in this enunciation is there language pertaining to the reactivation of technical assistance programs that offered the support, guidance, and oversight that so many law enforcement chief executives saw as essential and invaluable in the continuation of their ongoing efforts to establish the partnerships and collaborations necessary to ensure the viability of community policing and problem-oriented policing practices and principles. These promising strategies had undergone repeated challenges and near-constant interrogation in the aftermath of the many instances of documented and widely-reported police violence and excess that had occurred most notoriously from 2014 to the present.

Prudent observers of the police narrative presented in the FOP "Presidential candidate questionnaire" (2016) may see the language as shrill and even alarmingly hyperbolic. In my earlier police career, I held many elected police union positions: member of the House of District Representatives of the Boston Police Patrolmen's Association (the first police union to be established in the United States); Executive Board member of the Boston Police Superior Officers Federation; and Vice-President of the Boston Police Superior Officers Federation, among others. In the police subculture and in the worldview of the police, the assertions and representations contained in the FOP narrative are all too real an expression of their long-held, inviolable, unwavering, and sacrosanct beliefs about the world and its public.

The media, "fringe organizations" (see Black Lives Matter), an unknowing and unappreciative public (see "assholes"), the Federal courts, immigrants, and "liberals" who use "buzzwords" such as "racial profiling," are all seen as ongoing, ever-present threats to the police themselves as well as to the rule of law and to the maintenance of order. The police's is often a binary view of the world of the street that only they inhabit and understand, a world that the they firmly believe is the so-called "real world," where there is good versus evil, right versus wrong, lightness and, yes, darkness. This is an especially closely-held perspective in the police union milieu.

One need go no further than "lawofficer.com," a website popular with police officers, to glimpse the mindset of the rank-and-file. In the days leading up to "National Police Week" in 2018 for example, one police officer posted a screed entitled "POLITICIANS, MEDIA AND THUGS":

> ENOUGH, for crying out loud! Let's start with the thugs. Groups like Black Lives Matter, MoveOn.org, By Any Means Necessary and Antifa want to bring change to this country but they are not American values that they uphold.... The media is another group of left wing (*sic*) goofballs that have been exposed for their lack of American values.
>
> (Barfield, 2018)

Of the police themselves, this author writes: "These are American heroes going where other (*sic*) will never and could never."

Conclusion

There exists a tension in law enforcement that was exacerbated following the presidential election in 2016 that continues to the present. The tension exists between many rank-and-file police officers who have chafed under the decades-long oversight (or at least threat of oversight) of law enforcement policies and operation by the DOJ, and police chiefs, administrators, and policy makers who have often seen the benefit and necessity of such oversight.

The police have long held taut and rigid control over the narrative through which they craft and release information to the public regarding their activities and the conduct of their officers.

This control has been at least in part eroded and fractured through the widespread release, largely through the internet and the 24-hour news cycle, of counternarratives that serve to interrogate the police narrative, often stridently. The police are attempting, with varying degrees of success, to regain control of the narrative, having been emboldened in part by public declarations by representatives of the Trump Administration that federal law enforcement and the DOJ have little interest in continuing oversight of local police departments.

REFERENCES

Barfield, T. (2018, May 7). Politicians, media and thugs. *Law Officer*. Retrieved from: http://lawofficer.com/special-topics/politicians-media-thugs/.

Bever, L. (2018, May 11). Video shows Georgia officer shouting, cursing at 65-year-old grandmother during a traffic stop. *The Washington Post*. Retrieved from: www.washingtonpost.com/news/post-nation/wp/2018/05/11/video-shows-georgia-officer-shouting-cursing-at-65-year-old-grandmother-during-a-traffic-stop/?utm_term=.9e754f89918d.

Bump, P. (2017, July 28). Trump's speech encouraging police to be "rough," annotated. *The Washington Post*. Retrieved from: www.washingtonpost.com/news/politics/wp/2017/07/28/trumps-speech-encouraging-police-to-be-rough-annotated/?utm_term=.f287ff82045c.

Center for Constitutional Rights. (2013). Summary of remedial opinion and order in *Floyd, et al. v. City of New York*, 08-cv-1034 (SAS). *CCR*. Retrieved from: https://ccrjustice.org/sites/default/files/attach/2015/09/Floyd-Remedy-Decision-Summary-8-12-13.pdf.

Chen, M. (2018, May 17). Want to see how biased Broken Windows Policing is? Spend a day in court. *The Nation*. Retrieved from: www.thenation.com/article/want-to-see-how-biased-broken-windows-policing-is-spend-a-day-in-court/.

Cohen, A. (2018, May 16). The false dichotomy of "Police Week." *The Brennan Center for Justice*. Retrieved from: www.brennancenter.org/blog/false-dichotomy-police-week.

Community Oriented Policing Services, United States Department of Justice. (2018). *Technical Assistance*. Retrieved from: https://cops.usdoj.gov/technicalassistance.

Douglass, D. (2017). Department of Justice consent decrees as the foundation for community-initiated collaborative police reform. *Police Quarterly*, 20 (3), pp. 322–336.

Eder, S., Protess, B., & Dewan, S. (2017, November 21). How Trump's hands-off approach to policing is frustrating some chiefs. *The New York Times*. Retrieved from: www.nytimes.com/2017/11/21/us/trump-justice-department-police.html.

Editorial. (1999, October 11). *The Nation*, 269, 11.

Floyd v. City of New York, 959 F. Supp. 2d 540, 2013.

Fraternal Order of Police. (2016). Presidential candidate questionnaire. *FOP*. Retrieved from: https://fop.net/CmsDocument/Doc/016PresidentialQuestionnaire.pdf.

Fraternal Order of Police. (2018). About the Fraternal Order of Police. *FOP*. Retrieved from: https://fop.net/CmsPage.aspx?id=223.

Grawert, A., & Cullen, J. (2017, December 19). Crime in 2017: Updated analysis. *Brennan Center for Justice*. Retrieved from: www.brennancenter.org/analysis/crime-2017-updated-analysis.

Hannon, E. (2018, May 15). Manhattan DA announces it will no longer prosecute marijuana possession to correct racial disparity in arrests. *Slate*. Retrieved from: https://slate.com/news-and-politics/2018/05/manhattan-da-announces-it-will-no-longer-prosecute-marijuana-possession-to-correct-racial-disparity-in-arrests.html.

Iannelli, J. (2018, May 8). Miami police union says head-kicking cop "used great restraint," shouldn't be charged. *Miami New Times*. Retrieved from: www.miaminewtimes.com/news/miami-police-union-says-head-kicking-cop-showed-restraint-10332957.

Kelly, K., Childress, S., & Rich, S. (2015, November 13). Forced reforms, mixed results. *The Washington Post*. Retrieved from: www.washingtonpost.com/sf/investigative/2015/11/13/forced-reforms-mixed-results/?utm_term=.843bf604e440.

Lehr, D. (2009). *The Fence: A Police Cover-up along Boston's Racial Divide*. New York: Harper Collins.

Lind, D. (2017, December 29). How police officers became the culture-war heroes of the Trump era. *Vox*. Retrieved from: www.vox.com/policy-and-politics/2017/12/29/16826152/trump-police-immigration-blue-lives-matter.

Molina, C., & Bennett, A. (2018, May 12). Waffle House says employees' role in NC police-choking incident wasn't "race" issue. *The News & Observer*. Retrieved from: www.newsobserver.com/news/local/article211020544.html.

Mulvaney, J. (2017, August 1). President Trump's reference to "paddy wagon" insults Irish Americans like me. *The Washington Post*. Retrieved from: www.washingtonpost.com/news/posteverything/wp/2017/08/01/trumps-use-of-paddy-wagon-insults-irish-americans-like-me/?utm_term=.181e0eae7793.

Office of the Attorney General. (2017). *Memorandum for Heads of Department Components and United States Attorneys. Supporting Federal, State, Local and Tribal Law Enforcement*. Retrieved from: www.document-cloud.org/documents/3535302-AG-Memorandum-Supporting-Federal-State-Local-and.html.

Patrolmen's Benevolent Association. (2013, August 12). PBA reacts to federal stop and frisk decision. *NYCPBA*. Retrieved from: www.nycpba.org/press-releases/2013/pba-reacts-to-federal-stop-and-frisk-decision/.

Politi, D. (2018, May 12). White Wisconsin police officer caught on camera punching black teen in face. *Slate*. Retrieved from: https://slate.com/news-and-politics/2018/05/white-wisconsin-police-officer-caught-on-camera-punching-black-teen-in-the-face.html.

Powell, Z. A., Meitl, M. B., & Worrall, J. L. (2017). Police consent decrees and Section 1983 Civil Rights Litigation. *Criminology & Public Policy*, 16, pp. 575–605.

Sessions, J. (2017, April 17). Avoid harmful federal intrusion. *USA Today*. Retrieved from: www.usatoday.com/story/opinion/2017/04/17/jeff-sessions-avoid-harmful-federal-intrusion-editorials-debates/100579848/.

Skolnick, J., & Fyfe, J. (1993). *Above the Law*. New York: Free Press.

Spielman, F. (2018, August 8). FOP ties weekend violence to "war on police" that includes consent decree. *Chicago Sun Times*. Retrieved from: https://chicago.suntimes.com/news/chicago-fraternal-order-police-union-ties-weekend-violence-crime-murders-shootings-war-cops-consent-decree/.

Stop and frisk violated rights of New Yorkers, judge rules. (2013, August 12). *Huffington Post*. Retrieved from: www.huffingtonpost.com/2013/08/12/stop-and-frisk-violated-rights-new-york-city-judge-rules_n_3743236.html.

United States Department of Justice. (2017). *An Interactive Guide to the Civil Rights Division's Police Reforms*. Retrieved from: www.justice.gov/crt/page/file/922456/download.

United States Department of Justice. (2018a). *How Department of Justice Civil Rights Division Conducts Pattern-or-Practice Investigations*. Retrieved from: www.justice.gov/file/how-pp-investigations-work/download.

United States Department of Justice. (2018b). *Law Enforcement Misconduct Statute 42 U.S.C. § 14141*. Retrieved from: www.justice.gov/crt/law-enforcement-misconduct-statute-42-usc-14141.

Van Maanan, J. (1978). "The asshole" in Van Maanan, J. & Manning, P. (eds.). *Policing: A View from the Streets*. New York: Random House, pp. 221–237.

Wootson, C., & Berman, M. (2017, July 30). U.S. police chiefs blast Trump for endorsing "police brutality." *The Washington Post*. Retrieved from: www.washingtonpost.com/news/post-nation/wp/2017/07/29/u-s-police-chiefs-blast-trump-for-endorsing-police-brutality/?utm_term=.30df12d16afd.

Chapter 9

Fusion Centers

An Unholy Alliance of Federal, State, and Local Law Enforcement[1]

Fusion Centers: Institution and Rationale

Originally established in response to the terrorist attacks on the World Trade Center towers and the Pentagon on September 11, 2001, "fusion centers" were intended to "blend relevant law enforcement and intelligence information analysis and coordinate security measures to reduce threats in their communities" (Department of Homeland Security, 2006, p. 1). H.R.1—the Implementing Recommendations of the 9/11 Commission Act of 2007 directed the secretary of the Department of Homeland Security (DHS) "to establish a State, Local, and Regional Fusion Center Initiative." It further directed: "(1) the Under Secretary to assign officers and intelligence analysts from DHS components to such centers; and (2) the Secretary to develop qualifying criteria for a fusion center to participate in assigning DHS officers or intelligence analysts" (United States Congress, 2007, p. 1). The act provided funding, personnel, and policy infrastructure for the establishment of fusion centers nationwide.

There are currently 54 so-called "primary fusion centers" that have been established in each of the 50 states, as well as in the District of Columbia, Guam, Puerto Rico, and the U.S. Virgin Islands. These are referred to by DHS as "state and major urban area fusion centers." These primary fusion centers receive the bulk of DHS resources that are allocated to fusion centers and have personnel from the DHS Office of Intelligence and Analysis (I&A) assigned there. The DHS I&A is required to provide intelligence officers to each primary (and some recognized) fusion centers, and the undersecretary for the I&A is the executive agent for federal support to fusion centers.

Additionally, there are 25 so-called "recognized fusion centers" that have been established by state and local governments. According to the DHS:

Primary fusion centers serve as the focal points within the state and local environment for the receipt, analysis, gathering, and sharing of threat-related information and have additional responsibilities related to the coordination of critical operational capabilities across the statewide fusion process with other recognized fusion centers.

(Department of Homeland Security, 2016, p. 1)

California has six fusion centers (one "primary" and five "recognized"); Texas has seven fusion centers (one "primary" and six "recognized"); Florida, Missouri, Ohio, and Pennsylvania have three fusion centers; Massachusetts, Michigan, Wisconsin, Illinois, Virginia, and Nevada each have two fusion centers. There are currently 79 fusion centers in the United States that constitute the National Network of Fusion Centers.

According to the General Accounting Office (GAO):

Recognition as a fusion center within the National Network generally requires that the governor of the state make this formal designation; a state or local governmental agency oversees and manages the center; the center has plans and procedures to function as a focal point for sharing law enforcement, homeland security, public safety, and terrorism information; and the center has achieved requisite baseline capabilities as DHS—on behalf of federal interagency partners—determines through an annual assessment of each fusion center's capabilities. A state or local law enforcement official generally serves as the center director … Analyst positions within these centers often make up a substantial portion of the staffing and typically include a combination of state, local, and federal personnel.

(United States General Accounting Office, 2014, p. 6)

Fusion centers operate in what is known as the Federal Information Sharing Environment (ISE). The "environment" is a virtual one that is "designed to facilitate the sharing of terrorism and homeland security information among all relevant entities through the combination of information sharing policies, procedures, and technologies" (Department of Homeland Security, 2015b, p. 1). Participation in the ISE requires the establishment of an agency privacy policy in order to engage in the exchange of intelligence and other information in the ISE. Fusion centers are also required to have a trained privacy officer.

Fusion centers are "owned" by the state and local governments that have established them and they are funded in part by federal grant monies, specifically through the Homeland Security Grant Program (HSGP). Fusion centers do not receive funds directly through the HSGP; rather designated agencies at the state level that are responsible for the allocation of funds received through the HSGP, as well as local or county departments with similar grant disbursement responsibilities, determine the allocation of funds to the state and major urban area fusion centers. Fusion centers request the funds through the appropriate state or local designated entity, articulating and justifying its request through a process referred to as an "investment justification" (United States General Accounting Office, 2014, p. 10).

For example, in 2010 the GAO reported that of the 52 fusion centers out of 72 that responded to a budgetary survey conducted by the DHS, the federal government funded 61 percent ($62 million) of their operating budgets, states funded 29 percent ($30 million), with 10 percent of fusion center operating budgets being locally funded ($10 million) (United States General Accounting Office, 2010, p. 16).

Fusion Center Tradecraft and the Intelligence Community

David Carter (2009) has written extensively about intelligence collection at the state, local, and tribal law enforcement (SLTLE) level and describes two broad classes of intelligence: first as a "discipline, which refers to the set of rules, processes, and lexicon of the intelligence function" (p. 10). He identified three types of intelligence that SLTLE and fusion center analysts may collect: "1. Law enforcement (or criminal) intelligence, 2. Homeland security—also known as 'all-hazards'—intelligence, and 3. National security intelligence" (p. 10).

The second broad class of intelligence, according to Carter, refers to the "application of intelligence," i.e., the articulation of the particular nexus to a specific criminal activity that the intelligence provides. For example, analysts who receive intelligence regarding activities of outlaw motorcycle gangs (OMGs) must be familiar with the culture, inner workings, symbols, jargon, history, and other relevant characteristics of OMGs generally and specific OMGs in particular in order to link the intelligence to criminal activity.

Carter has defined law enforcement intelligence as "the product of an analytic process that provides an integrated perspective to disparate information about crime, crime trends, crime and security threats, and conditions associated with criminality" (2002, p. 9). He advises careful distinction between the uses of the terms "information sharing" and "intelligence sharing," as intelligence and information have differing procedural and legal requirements and safeguards, for example, intelligence collection is governed by the provisions of 28 CFR Part 23 regulations regarding intelligence collection. "Intelligence" necessarily contains analysis, assessment, estimation, and prediction or "forecasting." "Information," on the other hand, is raw data, such as driver's records, motor vehicle, watercraft, and aircraft registration information, surveillance reports, transcripts of interviews and interrogations, and banking and financial record information, data that must be analyzed and synthesized in order to create an intelligence product (2009, p. 12).

Homeland Security, or "all hazards" intelligence is, according to Carter, "the collection and analysis of information concerned with noncriminal domestic threats to critical infrastructure, community health, and public safety for the purpose of preventing the threat or mitigating the effects of the threat" (2009, p. 14). This type of intelligence may overlap with law enforcement intelligence when pertaining to criminal activity that may also pose a threat to critical infrastructure or public health, e.g., intelligence related to a biological or chemical attack on the civilian population or intelligence pertaining to the use of explosives to blow up a bridge.

National Security Intelligence (NSI) is not ordinarily within the purview of state and major urban area fusion centers; nonetheless fusion center personnel need be knowledgeable about what constitutes NSI should they become aware of intelligence or information that may have value to the Intelligence Community (IC). One of the main reasons I&A personnel are assigned to fusion centers is to identify NSI information (Intelligence Information Reports, or IIR) and to ensure it is provided to the IC. Also, fusion center personnel who are working Organized Crime Drug Enforcement Task Forces with Drug Enforcement Administration (DEA) personnel or those working with Federal Bureau of Investigation (FBI) personnel on Joint Terrorism Task

Forces may have access to NSI, since both the DEA and the FBI are members of the IC (Carter, 2009).

> NSI embodies both policy intelligence and military intelligence. Policy intelligence is concerned with threatening actions and activities of entities hostile to the U.S., while military intelligence focuses on hostile entities, weapons systems, warfare capabilities, and order of battle.
>
> (Carter, 2009, p. 15)

The IC consists of 17 member agencies:

1   Air Force Intelligence
2   Army Intelligence
3   Central Intelligence Agency
4   Coast Guard Intelligence
5   Defense Intelligence Agency
6   Department of Energy
7   DHS
8   Department of State
9   Department of the Treasury
10   DEA
11   FBI
12   Marine Corps Intelligence
13   National Geospatial-Intelligence Agency
14   National Reconnaissance Office
15   National Security Agency/Central Security Office
16   Navy Intelligence
17   Office of the Director of National Intelligence

(United States Intelligence Community, 2016)

As we shall see in Section III, fusion center analysts and law enforcement personnel assigned to state and major urban area fusion centers should be aware of the potential for constitutional implications in the use of NSI for criminal investigative and criminal intelligence purposes, since the procedural safeguards that protect individuals and groups as articulated in 28 CFR Part 23 as well as in the Constitution and the well-established body of U.S. Supreme Court and appellate court case law do not necessarily apply to the collection of NSI.

Fusion Center Governance, Regulation, and Operations

Fusion centers, like other "criminal intelligence systems," are governed and regulated by what is known as 28 CFR Part 23. The CFR is the Code of Federal Regulations and these are a series of 50 permanent rules, procedures, and policies that form a body of administrative law promulgated by the executive branch of government. The code provides official government policy for dealing with areas ranging from fisheries and wildlife to banking and to the operating policies in the collection of criminal intelligence. Fusion center personnel are required to undergo extensive training in the provisions of 28 CFR Part 23 and the regulations contained therein provide the foundation for the collection of criminal intelligence to insure that "all criminal intelligence systems operating through support under the Omnibus Crime Control and Safe Streets Act of 1968 … are utilized in conformance with the privacy and constitutional rights of individuals" (Institute for Intergovernmental Research, 2016, p. 1).

According to 28 CFR Part 23.3, the following definitions apply to the policies contained therein:

1 Criminal Intelligence System or Intelligence System means the arrangements, equipment, facilities, and procedures used for the receipt, storage, interagency exchange or dissemination, and analysis of criminal intelligence information
2 Interjurisdictional Intelligence System means an intelligence system which involves two or more participating agencies representing different governmental units or jurisdictions
3 Criminal Intelligence Information means data which has been evaluated to determine that it:

    i   is relevant to the identification of and the criminal activity engaged in by an individual who or organization which is reasonably suspected of involvement in criminal activity
    ii meets criminal intelligence system submission criteria

4 Participating Agency means an agency of local, county, State, Federal, or other governmental unit which exercises law enforcement or criminal intelligence information through an interjurisdictional intelligence system. A participating agency may be a member or a nonmember of an interjurisdictional intelligence system
5 Intelligence Project or Project means the organizational unit which operates an intelligence system on behalf of and for the benefit of a single agency or the organization which operates an interjurisdictional intelligence system on behalf of a group of participating agencies
6 Validation of Information means the procedures governing the periodic review of criminal intelligence information to assure its continuing compliance with system submission criteria established by regulation or program policy.

(Institute for Intergovernmental Research, 2016, p. 1)

Thus 28 CFR Part 23.3 refers to the definition of criminal intelligence systems and interjurisdictional intelligence systems, what qualifies as criminal intelligence data, what agencies are covered by the policy, what an intelligence project is, as well what procedures apply to the ongoing review of intelligence data collected.

The operating principles governing the collection of intelligence data by criminal intelligence systems are contained in 28 CFR Part 23.20. A partial list of these principles establishes that:

1   A project shall collect and maintain criminal intelligence information concerning an individual only if there is reasonable suspicion that the individual is involved in criminal conduct or activity and the information is relevant to that criminal conduct or activity.

2   A project shall not collect or maintain criminal intelligence information about the political, religious or social views, associations, or activities of any individual or any group, association, corporation, business, partnership, or other organization unless such information directly relates to criminal conduct or activity and there is reasonable suspicion that the subject of the information is or may be involved in criminal conduct or activity.

3   Reasonable Suspicion or Criminal Predicate is established when information exists which establishes sufficient facts to give a trained law enforcement or criminal investigative agency officer, investigator, or employee a basis to believe that there is a reasonable possibility that an individual or organization is involved in a definable criminal activity or enterprise. In an interjurisdictional intelligence system, the project is responsible for establishing the existence of reasonable suspicion of criminal activity either through examination of supporting information submitted by a participating agency or by delegation of this responsibility to a properly trained participating agency which is subject to routine inspection and audit procedures established by the project.

4   A project shall not include in any criminal intelligence system information which has been obtained in violation of any applicable Federal, State, or local law or ordinance. In an interjurisdictional intelligence system, the project is responsible for establishing that no information is entered in violation of Federal, State, or local laws, either through examination of supporting information submitted by a participating agency or by delegation of this responsibility to a properly trained participating agency which is subject to routine inspection and audit procedures established by the project.

5   A project or authorized recipient shall disseminate criminal intelligence information only where there is a need to know and a right to know the information in the performance of a law enforcement activity.

(Institute for Intergovernmental Research, 2016, p. 1)

Thus, the operating principles dictate the circumstances under which federally funded criminal intelligence systems are allowed to collect, analyze, store, and disseminate intelligence information on individuals and groups. There must be reasonable suspicion of criminal activity and the information collected must relate to that activity. Information shall not be collected regarding political, religious, or social beliefs or activities unless those activities are related to criminal activity. Reasonable suspicion and criminal predicate is defined. Information that is obtained illegally cannot be included in any intelligence product or stored in any intelligence database. And the articulations of the "need to know" and "right to know" principles are provided. It should be noted that 28 CFR Part 23, originally issued in 1980, has not been updated since 1993, with the exception of the release of a 1998 clarification from the Office of Justice Programs regarding identifiable information and the definition of criminal intelligence systems (Office of Justice Programs, 1998, pp. 1–2).

Fusion Centers and Privacy

The Homeland Security Act of 2002 called upon the secretary of DHS to appoint a "privacy officer" whose responsibilities include:

(1) assuring that the use of technologies sustain, and do not erode, privacy protections relating to the use, collection, and disclosure of personal information; (2) assuring that personal information contained in Privacy Act systems of records is handled in full compliance with fair information practices as set out in the Privacy Act of 1974.

(United States Congress, 2002; see also United States Government Printing Office, 2009)

The DHS Privacy Office is responsible for privacy training and compliance with privacy policies in the collection of information and intelligence at fusion centers and for the protection of so-called "personally identifiable information" (PII) and for ensuring that information is collected in accordance with Fair Information Practice Principles. The DHS defines PII as:

(A)ny information that permits the identity of an individual to be directly or indirectly inferred, including any information that is linked or linkable to that individual, regardless of whether the individual is a U.S. citizen, legal permanent resident, visitor to the U.S., or employee or contractor to the Department.

(Department of Homeland Security, 2012a, p. 4)

PII includes such obvious information such as one's name, telephone number, email address, or home address, and fusion centers are required by law to have privacy policies in place that protect PII and place restrictions upon the circumstances under which PII may be collected and stored in fusion center databases. DHS further identifies "Sensitive Personally Identifiable Information" (SPII) as "Personally Identifiable Information, which if lost, compromised, or disclosed without authorization, could result in substantial harm, embarrassment, inconvenience, or unfairness to an individual" (Department of Homeland Security, 2012a, p. 4). Examples of SPII are passport number, driver's license or social security number, bank account numbers, alien registration numbers, or biometric identifier. Examples of identifiers that, if paired with another identifier, become SPII are criminal history, mother's maiden name, date of birth, account passwords, medical information, last four digits of a social security number, or sexual orientation (p. 4).

Every state and major urban area fusion center has a designated "privacy officer" whose responsibility it is to ensure compliance with the privacy provisions of the Privacy Act of 1974 as well as other applicable federal laws and regulations relating to privacy in the collection of PII and SPII. Records collected by a federal government agency on individuals are required under the Privacy Act to be published and available to the public in what is generally referred to as a System of Records Notice or SORN. The relevant SORN provides the authorization for fusion center personnel operating under federal authority to search federal databases for PII. A list of DHS and DHS component SORNs can be found online (Department of Homeland Security, 2018).

In the collection of PII at fusion centers, federally authorized personnel are required to use the information solely for certain purposes that are approved by the DHS I&A. They are also required to identify the SORN that authorizes the collection of the PII and to share the PII only if the SORN authorizes such sharing. They must also minimize the PII when sharing it and keep a record of agencies and personnel with whom the PII was shared and record the justification for the sharing (Department of Homeland Security, 2012a).

Fusion Centers: The Research

Priscilla Regan, Torin Monahan, and Krista Craven (2015) have researched so-called "suspicious activity reports" (SARs) that are collected, analyzed, classified, and stored on DHS databases in the ISE by fusion center intelligence analysts. Law enforcement has long collected information on "suspicious" activity and persons, but SARs have emerged as troublesome and questionable to those concerned with civil rights, civil liberties, and privacy. Additionally, security issues have been raised with the multiple levels of access to SAR information across the spectrum of agencies in the ISE. SARs are reports of activities and behaviors that are believed to be related to terrorist or criminal activities often generated through the observations of those with little if any training or experience in identifying terrorist-related or criminal activities. Illustrative is DHS's "If you see something, say something" campaign.

Regan, Monahan, and Craven see four privacy concerns with fusion centers' collection, retention, storing, and dissemination of information contained in SARs: First, "these reports are often the result of the reporting person's stereotypes or fears, resulting in racial or ethnic profiling" (Regan et al., 2015, p. 749). Second, the individuals (e.g., delivery people, landlords, neighbors) who are supplying the information to authorities, information that may have been gleaned through access points that are protected from government intrusion and observation without a search warrant. The third area of privacy concern relates to the storage of PII that may be contained in a SAR database that is searchable by others in the ISE. Information such as names, license plate numbers, smart phone data, and credit card numbers that are linked to a particular individual who has been identified as being possibly involved to terrorist or criminal activities "without that person's knowledge or opportunity to challenge the classification or interpretation" (Regan et al., 2015, p. 750). Their final privacy concern identified by Regan et al. (2015) involves law enforcement and DHS compliance with the provisions of the Fourth Amendment as they pertain to information that purports to establish the existence of a "suspicious activity." In particular, they observe that SARs have "inherent limitations":

> Fundamentally, they remain tips, based on the impressions of individuals—ordinary citizens, service personnel, commercial employees, and law enforcement—who make a judgment that something seems "suspicious" and are motivated to report the activity.
>
> (p. 757)

According to these authors, the information aggregation and analysis process generally fails to scrutinize these sources with the constitutional rigor courts would apply when assessing whether information from these sources is sufficient to provide grounds for a finding of reasonable suspicion.

Further, there is the definitional problem of what actually constitutes "suspicious activities." The Congressional Research Service has reported that among the activities that have been labeled as suspicious are the following "suspect actions": "Uses binoculars or cameras, takes measurements, takes pictures or video footage, draws diagrams or takes notes, pursues specific training or education that indicate suspicious motives (flight training, weapons training, etc.), espouses extremist views" (Regan et al., 2015, p. 29). According to the 2014 National Network of Fusion Centers Final Report, "the percentage of Suspicious Activity Reporting submitted by fusion centers that resulted in the initiation or enhancement of a FBI investigation increased from 3.3 percent in 2013 to 5.5 percent in 2014" (Department of Homeland Security, 2015a, p. iv). Critics who call into question the value of the SARs in identifying potential terrorist-related activity may be justifiably concerned that the FBI is discounting almost 95 percent of state, local, tribal, and territorial (SLTT) fusion center SAR submissions as having any investigatory value. The report offers: "The Nationwide Suspicious Activity Reporting Initiative continues to mature" (Department of Homeland Security, 2015a, p. v).

Torin Monahan and Neal Palmer (2009) analyzed media reports on DHS fusion centers from 2002–2008 in order to understand the evolving roles and functions that emerged for the nascent multijurisdictional intelligence gathering agencies in the aftermath of the 9/11 attacks and the "War on Terror." Having originally been established to gather intelligence related to potential terrorist activities, most fusion centers had morphed into more traditional law enforcement oriented criminal intelligence gathering entities, the "all crimes and all hazards" model, reported on activities that had at best a tenuous connection to terrorism (Monahan & Palmer, 2009, p. 625).

These authors discovered three major problems plaguing fusion centers, problems that, it will be argued further in this chapter, have remained chronic to the present. The first category of concern, according to Monahan and Palmer (2009), lies in the overall ineffectiveness of fusion centers. Operating expenses for fusion centers are shared between state and local governments and the DHS. DHS grants funnel federal funds that are frequently directed at terrorist threats that are not specified or national issues that are unrelated to local or state issues in a particular area; "In 2007, for instance, Massachusetts received funding that required the state to develop a plan for responding to improvised explosive devices (IEDs), even though local and state authorities had no existing intelligence pointing to such a threat" (p. 622).

Monahan and Palmer argue that fusion centers could be more effective if states had more say in how allocated funds were used. DHS funding mandates contribute to fusion center ineffectiveness: For example, "on the West Coast, authorities were charged with developing hurricane-evacuation plans in reaction to the muddled government response to Hurricane Katrina on the Gulf Coast, even though states in the West face little danger from hurricanes" (2009, p. 622).

State and local authorities also complain that federal resources are not being directed where they are needed, and thus represent unfunded mandates. For example: "medically related projects, such as mass-casualty response and hospital-patient tracking in the event of an attack, were bypassed in a Virginia grant application to the DHS to the chagrin of hospital representatives" (Monahan & Palmer, 2009, p. 622).

A second issue of concern regarding fusion centers for Monahan and Palmer is so-called "mission creep," which is the extension of the activities of fusion centers in intelligence gathering related to terrorist activities to an "all crimes, all threats, all hazards" model that gathers intelligence related to gangs, drugs, human trafficking, computer fraud, racketeering, and organized crime—all tenuously related to the original mandate in the establishment of fusion centers. The authors observe that

> the way fusion centers are organized also appears to encourage mission creep. Minimal guidelines at the federal level mean that fusion centers develop with different foci and different organizational emplacements. Because police personnel and other employees at fusion centers draw upon their local contexts and perceptions of need, this has led to greater police involvement in counter-terrorism development, as well as to police agencies utilizing counter-terrorism tools against more traditional crimes.
>
> (2009, p. 626)

A final issue of concern raised in this research is the one most frequently cited regarding fusion centers and the activities they routinely engage in: widespread, extensive, and ubiquitous surveillance. Surveillance and the pervasive practice across the spectrum of fusion center tradecraft of collecting, analyzing, storing, and disseminating untold amounts of information and data on private individuals and groups is of paramount concern to observers and critics. The potential for the violation of the civil rights and civil liberties as well as the privacy of individuals and groups engaging in constitutionally protected activities cannot be overstated.

The embedding of corporate and private security personnel in fusion centers only adds to this concern, particularly when these individuals are not vetted properly or lack requisite government security clearances (Monahan and Palmer, 2009, p. 623). Further, Monahan and Palmer emphasize that

> the range of people who now have access to sensitive information, and the expansion of access to people who previously did not have access to files without concurrent ethics guidelines, particularly at local and state levels, provides further credence to fears of intelligence abuse and privacy violations.
>
> (2009, p. 629)

Priscilla Regan and Torin Monahan (2014) examined the issue of accountability in fusion centers, given the multiple layers of jurisdictional authority that exist in fusion centers: federal, state, regional, county, tribal, and local. They sought answers to two primary questions: "What types of information sharing are occurring with—or enabled by—fusion centers?" and "What factors contribute to the information-sharing practices of fusion centers?" (p. 478). These authors point to the uniqueness of each of the fusion centers examined and the fact that there are no governing federal policies regarding staffing, organizational structure, or the responsibilities of the various agencies staffing the fusion centers, and thus no two are alike. They did find that most of the fusion centers studied were controlled by state or local law enforcement agencies: "Most fusion centers in our study emerged from a law enforcement context, are directed by someone with law enforcement background, are co-located with local law enforcement entities, and focus on local law enforcement activities" (p. 480).

Personnel assigned to fusion centers vary considerably from state to state, although all centers in the study had DHS and FBI personnel assigned. Some fusion centers had Customs and Border Protection (CBP), Bureau of Alcohol, Tobacco, Firearms, and Explosives, DEA, and Immigration and Customs Enforcement (ICE) agents assigned to them.

> But the great majority of staff at the fusion centers were from local law enforcement, with other staff from a range of state agencies such as public health, corrections, parole and probation, fire, emergency management, environmental protection, highway, and gaming and fishing.
>
> (Regan & Monahan, 2014, p. 481)

This organizational model most closely resembles "opportunistic (or dispersed) federalism ... where hierarchical notions are de-emphasized and instead the focus is on more flexible collaborations involving many parties with different roles and responsibilities determining goals, priorities, and implementation regimes" (Regan & Monahan, 2014, p. 477). Thus, in order to forge a productive and functioning collaboration among federal, state, county, local, and tribal (mostly law enforcement) entities, a "top down," vertical, and hierarchical organizational model was seen as counterproductive to the cooperation, lateral communication, and sharing seen necessary to "fuse" and synthesize intelligence.

What suffered in the trade-off, according to Regan and Monahan (2014), was accountability. The fusion centers have been criticized for having little transparency, public or private oversight, or accountability. They have also been cited for failing to share available information with agencies having a clear operational interest in relevant intelligence. This was made clear in the aftermath of the bombing attack at the Boston Marathon on April 15, 2013, when it was revealed that the FBI had investigated one of the bombers and had failed to share this information with state or local authorities. The Boston Regional Intelligence Center (BRIC, a "recognized" fusion center), prepared a threat assessment of the marathon that revealed no discernable terrorist threat, despite having FBI personnel assigned to the BRIC.

Regan and Monahan conclude that there is little managerial control of fusion centers at the DHS level and little substantive guidance provided to fusion centers nationwide. The attempt by DHS "to strengthen the role of the national government in relation to that of state and local government ... has been unsuccessful" as a result of resistance on the part of state and local government, the complex and nuanced relationships among personnel and the agencies staffing fusion centers, and the history of the interaction among law enforcement agencies at the federal, state, and local levels (2014, p. 494). The authors call for some measure of "shared professional norms" in order for fusion centers to be successful in the future. Since fusion centers are dominated by local law enforcement, with its long tradition of local control over training, funding, priorities, staffing, and organization, such sharing of professional norms seems unlikely. And without such sharing "the collaborating units that constitute fusion centers will not be able to establish a common means of achieving accountability" (Regan & Monahan, 2014, p. 494).

Accountability and Performance

A 2012 report from the U.S. Senate Permanent Subcommittee on Investigations found that fusion centers nationwide had largely failed to deliver any useful intelligence relating to terrorist-related activities and that the centers had collected information on individuals and groups that frequently violated civil rights and civil liberties protections. The report also concluded that the DHS and the fusion centers resisted congressional oversight and often wasted tax dollars. According to the Senate report: "The Department of Homeland Security estimates that it has spent somewhere between $289 million and $1.4 billion in public funds to support state and local fusion centers since 2003, broad estimates that differ by over $1 billion" (2012a, p. 1). The Senate investigation

> found that DHS intelligence officers assigned to state and local fusion centers produced intelligence of uneven quality—oftentimes shoddy, rarely timely, sometimes endangering citizens' civil liberties and Privacy Act protections, occasionally taken from already-published public sources, and more often than not unrelated to terrorism.
>
> (2012a, p. 1)

The investigation also sharply questioned the DHS oversight of expenditures at state and major urban area fusion centers, finding that in five of the fusion centers examined

> federal funds were used to purchase dozens of flat screen TVs, two sport utility vehicles, cell phone tracking devices and other surveillance equipment unrelated to the analytical mission of an intelligence center. Their mission is not to do active or covert collection of intelligence.
>
> (2012a, p. 1)

The two-year investigation sought answers to three basic questions regarding the operation of the fusion centers: did the DHS coordinate with the fusion centers to obtain useful intelligence that it then shared with relevant and affected federal, state, and local agencies? Did the DHS effectively oversee the distribution of federal funds to the fusion centers? And were the fusion centers effective in collecting timely and accurate intelligence relating to counter terrorism activities? In response to the first question, the subcommittee found that "DHS's involvement with fusion centers appeared not to have yielded timely, useful terrorism-related intelligence for the Federal intelligence community" (United States Senate, 2012b, p. 8). As to the second issue, the Senate investigation revealed, "DHS did not adequately monitor the amount of funding it directed to support fusion centers" (2012b, p. 8). As for the third question posed, the investigation reported that "many centers didn't consider counterterrorism an explicit part of their mission, and Federal officials said some were simply not concerned with doing counterterrorism work" (2012b, p. 8).

In response to a request from Congress, the GAO conducted a performance audit of DHS fusion centers in 2014 in response to a request from the Congress and reported the following. In 2010 the fusion centers, in collaboration with DHS and the Department of Justice (DOJ) established a set of four criteria to evaluate the performance of fusion centers called the "Baseline

Capabilities for State and Major Urban Area Fusion Centers." The criteria (or capabilities) were: receive (the ability to receive classified and unclassified information from federal partners); analyze (the ability to conduct relevant threat assessment from the intelligence received; disseminate (the ability to disseminate and distribute threat information throughout the jurisdiction to affected agencies); and gather (the ability to receive information locally, conduct threat assessments, and to prepare intelligence products for distribution).

The 2014 audit found that an assessment conducted in 2013 on the identified baseline capabilities found that

> the average overall capability score reported for the National Network was 91.7 out of 100 in 2013. This score represents an improvement of about 3 points from the 2012 average score of 88.4 and continues an upward trend from the average national score of 76.8 identified in 2011.
>
> (United States General accounting Office, 2014, p. 11)

Thus, the GAO found continued improvement for the four identified baseline capabilities but raised questions as to its applicability to the wide range of other functions performed at fusion centers, particularly since the responsibilities, functions, and duties of fusion centers vary considerably from jurisdiction to jurisdiction. The GAO called for the inclusion of other performance measures in future iterations of the assessment process, particularly as they relate to planning and subsequent outcomes.

The GAO audit reported that the federal government had assigned 288 personnel to fusion centers in 2013, and that by 2014 the federal agencies that had deployed personnel to the fusion centers: the DHS I&A, FBI, CBP, and ICE, had provided adequate guidance and support to the fusion centers to ensure that federal personnel were being utilized appropriately and provided with clear direction as to their responsibilities and roles.

What the GAO audit identified as an area of concern was that "FEMA could not reliably report on the amount of federal grants used to support centers, which is needed to help inform future investment decisions" (United States General Accounting Office, 2014). The Federal Emergency Management Agency (FEMA) is the lead DHS component responsible for the distribution of funds through the HSGP to the fusion centers and found that in 2012 that numerous states had at least $60 million in grant funds with accounting questions. The Congress and many other officials, as well as the media have called the disbursement of funds through the HSGP and state and local sources to the fusion centers into question.

By 2014 the number of federal personnel assigned to state and major urban area fusion centers had risen to 366, with 116 DOJ personnel so assigned, along with 241 DHS representatives (nine were from other deferral agencies). According to the 2014 National Network of Fusion Centers Final Report, fusion centers received an average score of 96.3 out of 100 in the Fusion Center Performance Program (FCPP), a self-assessment tool that "evaluates fusion centers' achievement of capabilities critical to the fusion process. It also strives to ensure functional consistency across the National Network, regardless of the fusion center size, scope, geography, or mission" (Department of Homeland Security, 2015a, p. iv). The average FCPP score in 2013 was 91.7, and the DHS points to this increase as evidence of the increased effectiveness of fusion centers.

The 2014 National Network of Fusion Centers Final Report also described the primary mission of the National Network of Fusion Centers as "counterterrorism" and "all-crimes" in 96.2 percent of fusion centers and "all-hazards" in 73.1 percent of fusion centers. Thus, by 2016, virtually all of the SLTT fusion centers have adopted an "all crimes" mission in addition to their original mandate for being "stood up" (to use the relevant federal jargon, i.e., "fed speak")—counterterrorism. Additionally, almost three-quarters of SLTT fusion centers have an "all hazards" mission that includes areas such as fish and wildlife, chemical, biological, nuclear, and radiological threats, critical infrastructure, healthcare and public health, tribal, emergency management, and maritime security (Department of Homeland Security, 2015a, p. 10).

Questions about Efficacy, Privacy, and Compliance with Civil Rights and Civil Liberties Protections

Jason Barnosky (2015), writing for the Brookings Institute, described the evolution of fusion centers from their initial stated mission of counter terrorism-related intelligence gathering to one in which intelligence pertaining to non-terrorist threats such as criminal activity and natural disasters is collected, analyzed, and disseminated. He observed the value potential for fusion centers' adoption of responsibilities in this area and the nationwide network of fusion centers' ability to channel information directly to the federal government as well as to affected local and regional communities. Barnosky also cited the benefit to state and major urban area fusion centers in having the support of more than 300 representatives from the DEA, FBI, Transportation Security Administration, and the DHS I&A assigned to duties at the centers. He did acknowledge that problems with FEMA oversight of federal funds distributed to fusion centers continue to plague fusion centers. Barnosky also agreed with other observers who have criticized the fusion centers for deficiencies in adhering to privacy policies respecting civil rights and civil liberties protections when collecting information on individuals and groups.

The American Civil Liberties Union (ACLU) filed a lawsuit in the July of 2014 in California challenging the SARs program at fusion centers on behalf of five plaintiffs who "were all engaging in innocuous, lawful, and in some cases First Amendment-protected activity, such as photographing sites of aesthetic interest, playing video games, and waiting at a train station" (American Civil Liberties Union, 2014, p. 1). In that case, a federal judge has ruled that the federal government will have to produce information regarding the SAR program and to defend the practice and its legality in a public court proceeding, something that the ACLU has long sought. Earlier court decisions regarding SARs having largely shielded the government and fusion centers from having to publicly defend the program or disclosing information regarding SARs practices, which shroud the program in secrecy. Julia Harumi Mass and Hugh Handeyside, writing for the ACLU, note that because "the government's loose standards define practically anything as suspicious, SARs end up targeting innocent, First Amendment-protected conduct and inviting racial and religious profiling" (2015, p. 1).

Fusion centers have engaged in the collection of information on individuals and groups that have been criticized as having strayed from an "all crimes" and "all hazards" mission to monitoring protests such as the "Occupy" events that took place in scores of locations across the United States beginning in 2011. *The New York Times* obtained over 4000 pages of documents in 2014 through Freedom of Information Act (FOIA) requests and discovered that, in Washington, "officials circulated descriptions of plans in Seattle for an anti-consumerist flash mob to dance to the rock anthem 'Invincible' ":

> The Boston Regional Intelligence Center, one of the most widely recognized fusion centers in the country, issued scores of bulletins listing hundreds of events including a protest of "irresponsible lending practices," a food drive and multiple "yoga, faith & spirituality" classes.
>
> (Moynihan, 2014, p. A12)

Fusion center responses to Occupy activities and other public gatherings varied from one location to another, as do much of the intelligence gathering activities across the spectrum of the 78 fusion centers nationwide, resulting in a lack of consistency and uniformity in the gathering of information that critics often cite as evidence of flawed and inconsistent policies and practices. Supporters of local and regional variations in information gathering practices counter, however, that issues and mandates vary considerably across the spectrum of information gathering areas, and that such divergence in practice is solid intelligence gathering tradecraft.

According to *The New York Times*, the Delaware fusion center, in responding to an inquiry regarding its monitoring of Occupy protests said, "Our fusion center has distanced itself from the movement because of 1st Amendment rights and because we have not seen any criminal activity to date" (Moynihan, 2014, p. A12). Meanwhile, "in Milwaukee, officials reported that a group intended to sing holiday carols at an undisclosed location of high visibility," whilst "In Tennessee, an intelligence analyst sought information about whether groups concerned with animals, war, abortion or the Earth had been involved in protests" (Moynihan, 2014, p. A12).

Other critics have questioned the role that the federal government is playing in local law enforcement operations in assigning federal law enforcement personnel and federal intelligence analysts to fusion centers and in providing the majority of funding for what are essentially state and local police department information "fishing" expeditions. Sanchez, writing for the Cato Institute about fusion centers, found it "absurd" that "the federal government is throwing 'homeland security' funds at institutions that, having proven hilariously incapable of making any contribution to counterterror efforts, instead busy themselves trawling Google for information about political rallies" (2014, p. 1).

Critics of fusion centers have also questioned the secrecy surrounding operational practices and policies in the data collection, intelligence analysis, and product dissemination enterprise at fusion centers. German, writing for the Brennan Center for Justice, observed, "the excessive secrecy shrouding intelligence activities means Americans have little public information from which to evaluate whether the intelligence enterprise is worth the investment" (2015, p. 1).

In 2013 the Brennan Center for Justice issued a report on information sharing by law enforcement on the federal, state, and local level entitled "National security and local police." The center conducted a study of 19 fusion centers that were affiliated with 16 "major police departments" and 14 Joint Terrorism Task Forces. The report followed the April 14, 2013 terrorist attack at the Boston Marathon and the revelation that the FBI had investigated one of the bombers, Tamerlan Tsarnaev, and may not have shared that information with the local fusion center, the BRIC. What the report "found was organized chaos—a sprawling, federally subsidized, and loosely coordinated system designed to share information that is collected according to varying local standards" (Price, 2013, p. 1). Finding "serious flaws" that "may jeopardize both our safety and our civil liberties" the Brennan Center discovered an information sharing system plagued by an inability to effectively engage in even basic intelligence collection, analysis and sharing. The center found that:

1   Information sharing among agencies is governed by inconsistent rules and procedures that encourage gathering useless or inaccurate information. This poorly organized system wastes resources and also risks masking crucial intelligence.
2   As an increasing number of agencies collect and share personal data on federal networks, inaccurate or useless information travels more widely. Independent oversight of fusion centers is virtually non-existent, compounding these risks.
3   Oversight has not kept pace, increasing the likelihood that intelligence operations violate civil liberties and harm critical police-community relations.

(Price, 2013, p. 1)

The Brennan Center study called for a "fundamental overhaul of the standards for collecting and sharing intelligence and an oversight upgrade" (p. 1). It observed that "we need a consistent, transparent standard for state and local intelligence activities" and that "state and local governments should require police to have reasonable suspicion of criminal activity before collecting, maintaining, or disseminating personal information for intelligence purposes. The same rules should apply for data shared on federal networks and databases" (p. 1). In advocating for "stronger oversight," the center suggested, "Elected officials should consider establishing an independent police monitor, such as an inspector general. Fusion centers should be subject to regular, independent audits as a condition of future federal funding" (p. 1).

The Electronic Privacy Information Center (EPIC) raised concerns beginning in 2008 regarding privacy issues at fusion centers. EPIC discovered a "Memorandum of Understanding" (MOU) between the Virginia Fusion Center (VFC) and the FBI that bound the VFC not to disseminate "FBI information extracted from investigative and intelligence files ... outside the fusion center ... or use as a basis for investigative or law enforcement activity by Fusion Center partners without the approval of the FBI Fusion Center representative." The MOU further required that the VFC in receiving "request(s) for information under the Freedom of Information Act, the Privacy Act, or a Congressional inquiry, (that) such disclosure may only be made after consultation with the FBI" (Memorandum of Understanding, 2008).

In a lawsuit filed by EPIC in Virginia (Electronic Privacy Information Center, 2008), the Virginia court ruled that the Virginia State Police must provide all documents related to the MOU in response to its FOIA request, thus affirming EPIC's contention that fusion centers are required to comply with FOIA requirements.

Threat Assessments: Controversy and Condemnation

Fusion centers have gained notoriety in the controversial dissemination of intelligence products that describe individuals and groups who are engaging in constitutionally protected activities and describing them as potentially dangerous extremists. One particularly noteworthy report prepared and circulated by the Missouri Information Analysis Center in 2009 entitled "The modern militia movement" described supporters of presidential candidates Bob Barr, Ron Paul, and Chuck Baldwin, as evidenced by the display of bumper stickers or "political paraphernalia," as "right-wing extremists" (Nixon et al., 2009, pp. 3–7). The report also described members of so-called "anti-abortion" groups and those displaying the Gadsden Flag[2] as militants and potential extremists. The report caused much embarrassment for then Missouri Governor Jay Nixon as well as then Secretary of Homeland Security Janet Napolitano until it was discredited and pulled in the March of 2009.

Similarly, also in 2009, the DHS's I&A released a threat assessment report through its "Extremism and Radicalization Branch" that categorized "groups and individuals that are dedicated to a single issue, such as opposition to abortion or immigration" as rightwing extremists (2009b, p. 2). The DHS threat assessment also stated that "the return of military veterans facing significant challenges reintegrating into their communities could lead to the potential emergence of terrorist groups or lone wolf extremists capable of carrying out violent attacks" (2009b, p. 2). This report was widely condemned by veterans groups and criticized by political leaders and the media, resulting in a public apology by then Secretary of Homeland Security Janet Napolitano.

This threat assessment followed an earlier intelligence assessment by the DHS's I&A through its "Strategic Analysis Group, Homeland Environment and Threat Analysis Division" that described so-called "leftwing extremists" as "animal rights and environmental extremists (that) seek to end the perceived abuse and suffering of animals and the degradation of the natural environment perpetrated by humans" (2009a, p. 8). The report went on to describe what it labeled "anarchist extremists" as those who "generally embrace a number of radical philosophical components of anticapitalist, antiglobalization, communist, socialist, and other movements" (2009a, p. 8), otherwise known as political ideologies or beliefs that are protected under the First Amendment to the Constitution. Once, again, the DHS found itself under the glare of the public spotlight for disseminating controversial intelligence products that it believed might be shielded from public scrutiny through its printed admonition: "For Official Use Only."

A 2009 "threat assessment" report compiled by the VFC linked the Muslim American Society and the Council on American Islamic Relations, to the Muslim Brotherhood, a suspected Middle East terrorist organization in undocumented and unsubstantiated "suspected associations" (2009, p. 41). According to a "tip" received by the VFC, "there are indications the Virginia Commonwealth University chapter of the Muslim Student Association is a front organization for the MB (Muslim Brotherhood) and is possibly involved with terrorism financing and recruitment" (2009, p. 41). The VFC also cited "environmental or animal rights movements" as potential extremist threats, and in particular the "Garbage Liberation Front," which the threat assessment reported engaged in "dumpster diving, squatting and train hopping" (2009, p. 45).

The VFC assessment also described the Nation of Islam as posing a potential terrorist threat and linked the religious group to the "New Black Panther Party," who it described as "engaging in organiz(ing) demonstrations across the nation that calls (*sic*) for black empowerment and civil rights but include inflammatory, racist commentary" and, according to the report, the group "is actively attempting to recruit college students" (2009, p. 49).

In February 2016, following the shooting death of LaVoy Finicum by law enforcement in Oregon after the lengthy occupation of the Malheur Wildlife Refuge in Harney County by Finicum and others, the Utah Statewide Information and Analysis Center (SIAC, Utah's fusion center), issued a "situation report" in which it stated that although

> The SIAC assesses no credible threat to law enforcement or to public safety … Caravans of individuals traveling to the funeral services may be comprised of one or more armed extremists. Law enforcement should remain vigilant and aware that confrontation with these potentially volatile persons, may include more than one individual.
>
> (2016, p. 2)

The report goes on to cite "visual indicators of these potential extremist and disaffected individuals" (2016, p. 3) and, once again, the Gadsden Flag, the 1775 symbol of American freedom, civil rights, and civil liberties: "Don't tread on me."

Fusion Centers and "Countering Violent Extremism"

The role of fusion centers in the field of so-called "Countering Violent Extremism" (CVE) has also been called into question and sharply criticized, particularly by organizations such as the Council on American-Islamic Relations (CAIR). Citing the general lack of agreement as to what actually constitutes CVE, CAIR defines CVE as "the use of non-coercive means to dissuade individuals or groups from mobilizing towards violence and to mitigate recruitment, support, facilitation or engagement in ideologically motivated terrorism by non-state actors in furtherance of political objectives" (2015). CAIR's report found "that the current program exclusively targets American Muslims and that claims that the government is targeting all forms of violent extremism are inconsistently supported."

The CAIR report was highly critical of a document generated by the National Counterterrorism Center (2014) that offered "a scoring system for measuring an individual's susceptibility to violent extremism." These include measures such as "Parent-Child Bonding, Empathic Connection," "Presence of Emotional or Verbal Conflict in Family," and "Talk of Harming Self or Others," all inherently subjective and somewhat common aspects of the human condition and family relationships present in most Americans and their families at some point. Another so-called "risk factor" for involvement in "violent extremism" contained in the NCTC bulletin (and of concern to CAIR) is "'Family Involvement in Community Cultural and Religious Activities,' (that) are problematic as the person filling out the form may subjectively perceive mosque attendance itself as a risk factor" for involvement in violent extremism.

The CVE mission is a shared mandate among member agencies of the IC and while DHS fusion centers do not have sole responsibility for collecting intelligence on individuals and groups suspected of potential involvement in violent extremism, CVE does remain part of the core mission of the National Network of Fusion Centers. According to the DHS, "fusion centers play an important role in countering violent extremism and protecting local communities from violent crime through their daily operations, including gathering, analyzing, and sharing threat information" (2012b).

The CAIR report raised several objections and concerns to CVE strategies as they pertain to Muslims, mosques, and Muslim organizations, which CAIR contends, are the primary targets of CVE initiatives:

1   CAIR believes government-led CVE is not an effective use of public resources.
2   CVE often relies on subjective measures and its efficacy is questionable.
3   CVE is generally driven by news events.
4   The current program exclusively targets American Muslims.
5   Claims that the government is targeting all forms of violent extremism are inconsistently supported at best.
6   The current CVE initiative undermines our national ideals.

(Council on American-Islamic Relations, 2015)

CAIR observed, according to its report, "that a key to diminishing the appeal of extremist inspired violence, which preys on the hopelessness and helplessness and perceived injustices of the disenfranchised, is to empower communities with means of expressing their dissent and criticism in healthy ways" (2015, p. 1).

Conclusion

Writing for the Center for Strategic and International Studies, Nelson and Wise chart the way forward for fusion centers. They see that the greatest challenges ahead lie in the area of cybersecurity. Fusion centers "represent a valuable means of bringing federal counterterrorism agencies together with the state and local entities who are most likely to observe suspicious terrorism-related activity" (2013, p. 1) and see the need for transparency increasing as more information becomes available on U.S. persons. They argue that the "DHS must take steps to ensure that increased controversy over how these centers are employed does not threaten their continued utility" (2013, p. 1). Of critical import, according to Nelson and Wise, is the need for "standardized intelligence training, in order to better equip those on the ground with a better understanding of the intelligence process and equalize some of the disparities between various fusion centers" (2013, p. 1) and they also cite the need for increased fusion center engagement with the private sector, since most of the nation's critical infrastructure is held privately.

In order for fusion centers to remain viable for the future, they will need to provide timely, valuable, accurate, actionable, and standardized intelligence that is reflective of uniform professional standards regarding tradecraft. This intelligence must be rigorous in a strict adherence to civil rights and civil liberties protections contained in the Constitution and the Bill of Rights. Finally, intelligence products prepared in fusion centers must posit information on criminal activity that has demonstrable value and clearly apparent, as well as verifiably positive results and outcomes. Absent of these criteria, fusion centers may not successfully confront strident calls for their dissolution.

NOTES

1 This chapter was adapted with the permission of Cambridge University Press from *The Cambridge Handbook of Surveillance Law* (David Gray & Stephen Henderson, eds., 2017).

2 The Gadsden Flag is a symbol of the American Revolution dating to 1775 depicting a coiled rattlesnake and the words "Don't tread on me."

REFERENCES

American Civil Liberties Union. (2014, July 11). Gill v. DOJ–Challenge to government's suspicious activity reporting program. *ACLU*. Retrieved from: www.aclu.org/cases/gill-v-doj-challenge-governments-suspicious-activity-reporting-program?redirect=national-security/gill-v-doj-challenge-governments-suspicious-activity-reporting-program.

Barnosky, J. (2015). Fusion centers: What's working and what isn't. *Brookings Institution*. Retrieved from: www.brookings.edu/blogs/fixgov/posts/2015/03/17-fusion-centers-barnosky.

Carter, D. L. (2002). *Law Enforcement Intelligence Operations.* 8th ed. Tallahassee, Florida: SMC Sciences, Inc.

Carter, D. L. (2009). *Law Enforcement Intelligence: A Guide for State, Local, and Tribal Law Enforcement Agencies.* 2nd ed. Washington D.C.: COPS.

Council on American-Islamic Relations. (2015). Brief on Countering Violent Extremism (CVE). *CAIR*. Retrieved from: www.cair.com/government-affairs/13063-brief-on-countering-violent-extremism-cve.html.

Department of Homeland Security. (2006). *DHS strengthens intel sharing at State and Local Fusion Centers.* Retrieved from www.hsdl.org/?view&did=476394.

Department of Homeland Security. (2009a). *Leftwing extremists likely to increase use of cyber attacks over the coming decade.* Retrieved from: http://fas.org/irp/eprint/leftwing.pdf.

Department of Homeland Security. (2009b). *Rightwing extremism: Current economic and political climate fueling resurgence in radicalization and recruitment.* Retrieved from: http://fas.org/irp/eprint/rightwing.pdf.

Department of Homeland Security. (2012a). *Handbook for Safeguarding Sensitive Personally Identifiable Information.* Retrieved from: www.dhs.gov/sites/default/files/publications/Handbook%20for%20Safeguarding%20Sensitive%20PII_0.pdf.

Department of Homeland Security. (2012b). *The Role of Fusion Centers in Countering Violent Extremism Overview.* Retrieved from: www.it.ojp.gov/documents/roleoffusioncentersincounteringviolentextremism_compliant.pdf.

Department of Homeland Security. (2015a). *2014 National Network of Fusion Centers Final Report.* Retrieved from: www.archives.gov/isoo/oversight-groups/sltps-pac/national-network-of-fusion-centers-2014.pdf.

Department of Homeland Security. (2015b). *Department of Homeland Security Federal Information Sharing Environment Privacy and Civil Liberties Policy.* Retrieved from: www.dhs.gov/publication/department-homeland-security-federal-information-sharing-environment-privacy-and-civil.

Department of Homeland Security. (2016). *Fusion Center Locations and Contact Information.* Retrieved from www.dhs.gov/fusion-center-locations-and-contact-information.

Department of Homeland Security. (2018). *System of Records Notices.* Retrieved from: www.dhs.gov/system-records-notices-sorns.

Electronic Privacy Information Center. (2008). EPIC v. Virginia Department of State Police: Fusion center secrecy bill. *EPIC.* Retrieved from: https://epic.org/privacy/fusion/.

German, M. (2015, February 6). The U.S. intelligence community is bigger than ever, but is it worth it? *Brennan Center for Justice.* Retrieved from: www.brennancenter.org/analysis/does-1-trillion-national-security-enterprise-actually-make-us-safer.

Harumi Mass, J., & Handeyside, H. (2015, February 25). This secret domestic surveillance program is about to get pulled out of the shadows. *ACLU.* Retrieved from: www.aclu.org/blog/speakeasy/secret-domestic-surveillance-program-about-get-pulled-out-shadows.

Institute for Intergovernmental Research. (2016). Criminal intelligence systems operating policies (28 CFR Part 23). *IIR.* Retrieved from: www.iir.com/28CFR_Program/28CFR_Resources/Executive_Order/.

Memorandum of understanding between the Federal Bureau of Investigation and the Virginia Fusion Center. (2008). *EPIC.* Retrieved from: https://epic.org/privacy/virginia_fusion/MOU.pdf.

Monahan, T., & Palmer, N. (2009, December). The emerging politics of DHS fusion centers. *Security Dialogue, 40,* pp. 617–636.

Moynihan, C. (2014, May 22). Officials cast wide net in monitoring Occupy protests. *The New York Times,* p. A12.

National Counterterrorism Center. (2014, May). Countering violent extremism: A guide for practitioners and analysts. *NCTC.* Retrieved from: www.documentcloud.org/documents/1657824-cve-guide.html.

Nelson, R., & Wise, R. (2013). Homeland Security at a crossroads: Evolving DHS to meet the next generation of threats. *Center for Strategic & International Studies.* Retrieved from: http://csis.org/publication/homeland-security-crossroads-evolving-dhs-meet-next-generation-threats.

Nixon, J. W., Britt, J. M., Keathley, J. F., & Godsey, V. (2009). The modern militia movement. *Missouri Information Analysis Center.* Retrieved from: www.constitution.org/abus/le/miac-strategic-report.pdf.

Office of Justice Programs. (1998). 1998 Policy clarification. *IIR.* Retrieved from: www.iir.com/Documents/28CFR/1998PolicyClarification_28CFRPart23.pdf.

Price, M. (2013, December 10). National security and local police. *Brennan Center for Justice.* Retrieved from: www.brennancenter.org/publication/national-security-local-police.

Regan, P., & Monahan, T. (2014). Fusion center accountability and intergovernmental information sharing. *Publius 44,* pp. 475–498.

Regan, P., Monahan, T., & Craven, K. (2015, August). Constructing the suspicious: data production, circulation, and interpretation by DHS fusion centers. *Administration & Society, 47,* pp. 740–762.

Sanchez, J. (2014, May 23). Your Homeland Security dollars at work: Tracking "Occupy." *Cato Institute.* Retrieved from: www.downsizinggovernment.org/our-homeland-security-dollars-work-tracking-occupy.

United States Congress. (2002). *An Act to Establish the Department of Homeland Security, and for Other Purposes, PUBLIC LAW 107-296—NOV. 25, 2002.* Retrieved from: www.dhs.gov/xlibrary/assets/hr_5005_enr.pdf.

United States Congress. (2007). *H.R.1—Implementing Recommendations of the 9/11 Commission Act of 2007.* Retrieved from: www.congress.gov/bill/110th-congress/house-bill/1.

United States General Accounting Office. (2010). *Federal Agencies Are Helping Fusion Centers Build and Sustain Capabilities and Protect Privacy, But Could Better Measure Results.* Retrieved from: www.gao.gov/assets/320/310268.pdf.

United States General Accounting Office. (2014). *DHS is Assessing Fusion Center Capabilities and Results, But Needs to More Accurately Account for Federal Funding Provided to Centers.* Retrieved from: http://eds.a.

ebscohost.com.proxy3.noblenet.org/eds/pdfviewer/pdfviewer?vid=7&sid=391955c8-3b95-4c2c-a2c2-759c1d764 ebf@sessionmgr4002&hid=4202.

United States Government Printing Office. (2009). *Privacy Act of 1974, 5 U.S.C. § 552a*. Retrieved from: www.gpo. gov/fdsys/pkg/USCODE-2012-title5/pdf/USCODE-2012-title5-partI-chap5-subchapII-sec552a.pdf.

United States Intelligence Community. (2016). *Seventeen Separate Organizations Unite to Form the Intelligence Community (IC)*. Retrieved from: www.intelligencecareers.gov/icmembers.html.

United States Senate. (2012a). *Permanent Subcommittee on Investigations. Investigative Report Criticizes Counterterrorism Reporting, Waste at State & Local Intelligence Fusion Centers*. Retrieved from: www.hsgac. senate.gov/subcommittees/investigations/media/investigative-report-criticizes-counterterrorism-reporting-waste-at-state-and-local-intelligence-fusion-centers.

United States Senate. (2012b). *Federal Support for and Involvement in State and Local Fusion Centers, Majority and Minority Staff Report, Permanent Subcommittee on Investigations*. Retrieved from: www.hsgac.senate. gov/subcommittees/investigations/media/investigative-report-criticizes-counterterrorism-reporting-waste-at-state-and-local-intelligence-fusion-centers.

Utah Statewide Information and Analysis Center. (2016). Situation report (SITREP). Funeral for LaVoy Finicum. *SIAC*. Retrieved from: https://d1ai9qtk9p41kl.cloudfront.net/assets/db/14546824645342.pdf.

Virginia Fusion Center. (2009). 2009 Virginia terrorism threat assessment. *VFC*. Retrieved from: www.infowars. com/media/vafusioncenterterrorassessment.pdf.

Chapter 10

Perilous Policing

"That's the Signpost Up Ahead"

Perilous Communities

Policing is nothing if not an undertaking that is fraught with the potential for peril for all of those implicated in its enactment: the police themselves, victims of crime, those who witness acts of violence and criminality, and those who interact with the police as a matter of course. As has been articulated throughout these chapters, this is particularly true for residents of communities of color in cities across the United States, too many of whom see contact with law enforcement as often potentially perilous.

Peril in this sense is often incomprehensible to those of us who are white, working or middle class, and almost certainly men, who embrace values that privilege education, determination, conformance to laws, religious beliefs, and civic engagement, as pathways to career, financial, and social success. Cast aside in this worldview is the foreclosure of such opportunities to many women and to members of racial and ethnic origin groups who are just as determined, educated, law-abiding, and engaged with their communities as are their white male counterparts. Often overlooked is that opportunities for the fortunate are enacted and enabled as much by race, gender, social class, political and legacy connections, and other affinity groups as they are by education and determination.

Thomas Cottle (2001), in writing about the perils afflicting our cities, describes this duality: "We are in many respects a culture reeling out of control partly because of the irreconcilable nature of excesses on one end of the social spectrum and deprivation at the other" (p. 6). This is no more obviously in evidence than in our system of criminal justice, and particularly in law enforcement policies and practices that perpetuate a de facto system of racial oppression and discrimination—a system that continues, despite protestations to the contrary, to place many people of color in peril.

For those in the dominant group, the police are seen as kindred spirits, the "thin blue line" between order and anarchy, the standard bearers of a shared legacy, one in which order, the rule of law, conformance to expectations, and behavioral norms are validated and maintained. But for those who do not share in the benefits of membership in the dominant group, the police are often seen as threatening, menacing, dangerous, and encounters with them are hazardous, potentially perilous, and even fatal. And those in the dominant group are often reluctant to criticize the police and hesitant to second-guess the decisions made by and the policies that govern the police practice. Cottle's observation regarding the hidebound and rules-focused orientations of bureaucracies could easily apply to the police: "We react to the bureaucratic neutrality foisted on us by institutions that cannot rise above an almost childlike obsession to mindless rules…" as we too often fail to realize that "in the eyes of imperiled people most affected by these institutions, sometimes (the police) actually appear to revel in dehumanizing processes and policies" (2001, p. 6).

Interactions and encounters with the police are, for the poor, disenfranchised, LGBTQ individuals, and people of color, scripted and choreographed reenactments of roles performed, staged, and long characterized by deference, submission, subservience, and obsequiousness on the one hand, and dominance, aggression, authoritarianism, and control on the other. When these long-prescribed roles are challenged by non-dominant group members, the results are often calamitous and perilous for those who fail to adhere to their designated script and part.

As Cottle has observed, "our mental representations of ourselves and of the world are profoundly affected by still unresolved matters of racism, sexism, poverty, even colonialism…" (2001, p. 6). Colonialism that for many in cities, and specifically communities of color, is a legacy that remains from an earlier era, one that continues to be enabled and perpetuated by contemporary law enforcement actors.

Perilous Pursuits

On July 28, 2018, police in the small Cape Cod, Massachusetts, town of Mashpee initiated a high-speed pursuit of a vehicle whose driver had been speeding and failed to stop for a stop sign. He had also, according to the pursuing officer, committed "marked-lane violations." These are all civil, non-criminal, non-arrestable violations in Massachusetts (although failing to stop for the police is a criminal offense). The vehicle's license plate was plainly visible to the pursuing officer who was able to check the plate via computer and determine the owner's name and address, an address that the pursuing officer stated via radio transmission was the direction in which the vehicle was headed. At some point during the chase the vehicle being pursued, a 2000 Toyota Sedan, being driven by a 22-year-old man with a 24-year-old woman passenger, left the roadway and crashed, killing both the driver and the passenger.

According to *The Boston Globe*,

The car (being pursued by police) collided head-on with an SUV driven by Kevin P. Quinn, a new father on his way home from a hospital visit with his wife and newborn daughter. The 32-year-old Mashpee man had survived two combat tours in Afghanistan as a Marine.

(Hilliard et al., 2018)

Quinn was extricated from his vehicle by rescue workers using a Jaws of Life device but later died at a hospital. Three people had been killed during an unnecessary and extremely dangerous police pursuit of a motorist who could easily have been sent a civil citation in the mail. Perilous policing indeed.

And so, the perils and risks that the police often pose to the communities that they police are in no way limited to the oppressive and violent tactics inflicted upon African Americans and other marginalized groups. The routine, mundane, and too often unquestioned practices engaged in by officers on the lowest level of the police organizational hierarchy pose risks that are often dangerous and even fatal to those who are innocent bystanders or low-level (even non-criminal) offenders. The consequences to these violent, often deadly, outcomes are most often inconsequential, administrative penalties imposed by the police department itself: retraining, punishment duty, reprimand, perhaps a suspension in the most egregious instances of officer excess. Rarely are officers terminated for engaging in imprudent and perilous activities on the street.

On April 3, 2018, police in Indianapolis engaged in a high-speed pursuit of a pickup truck with four occupants that ended in a crash and the death of one of the passengers and the injury of five others, including the driver of the vehicle being pursued. According to police, the vehicle had been speeding and engaging in "unsafe lane movement" (Associated Press, 2018).

On September 11, 2016, police in Washington, D.C. shot and killed an unarmed 31-year-old African American man named Terrence Sterling after Sterling ran a red light while driving his Kawasaki motorcycle. D.C. police officer Brian Trainer opened fire after he and his partner, Jordan Palmer, engaged in an unauthorized pursuit of the motorcycle at speeds up to 100 miles per hour over 30 city blocks in the district. According to *The Washington Post*, "the city settled for $3.5 million a wrongful-death lawsuit filed by Sterling's family. Prosecutors reviewed the shooting but did not file charges." The department's internal affairs division "declared the shooting unjustified, and officials recommended that Trainer be fired" (Hermann, 2018).

Fred Rivara and C. D. Mack's 2004 study, one of the most recent available on the topic, examined the number of deaths related to police pursuits and crashes between 1994 and 2002 and found that many of the deaths related to crashes involving police pursuits were innocent victims. The authors reported that

> There were 2654 fatal crashes involving 3965 vehicles and 3146 fatalities during the nine-year study period. Of these, 1088 were to people not in the fleeing vehicle. These crashes often occurred at high speed, in the night, on local roads. Most of the pursued drivers had prior motor vehicle related convictions.
>
> (Rivara & Mack, 2004, p. 93)

In 2017 a civil grand jury in Los Angeles examined police pursuits and police pursuit policies in the Los Angeles Police Department (LAPD) as well as the Los Angeles Sheriff's Department. Among its findings were that "police pursuits are causing unnecessary bystander injuries and deaths. Most vehicle pursuits are not provoked by serious crimes. Vehicle pursuits are not assured of satisfying police goals—for example: arrests, reducing dangers to the public, issuing citations" (Los Angeles County Civil Grand Jury, 2017, pp. 149–150). The *Los Angeles Times* reported that LAPD officers "are allowed to chase motorists suspected of felonies or misdemeanors," and that "the LAPD also chases suspected drunk and reckless drivers more frequently than other departments in the state" in a practice where the decision to initiate a high-speed pursuit is often left to the discretion of the individual officer (Queally, 2017).

According to a 2017 report compiled by the Bureau of Justice Statistics (BJS), "state and local law enforcement agencies conducted an average of 186 vehicle pursuits per day in 2012," or approximately 68,000 pursuits over the course of the year. "Nearly one person a day was killed in a pursuit-related crash in 2012 for a total of 351 deaths," according to the BJS (2017). The report cited figures from the National Highway Traffic Safety Administration's Fatality Analysis Reporting System, which found that "there were more than 6,000 fatal pursuit-related crashes from 1996 to 2015. More than 7,000 persons died during this period for an average of 355 per year (about 1 per day)" (Bureau of Justice Statistics, 2017). And while nearly two-thirds of the persons killed were occupants of the vehicle being pursued, "a third of those killed were occupants of a vehicle not involved in the pursuit (29%) or bystanders not in a vehicle (4%). Slightly more than 1% of the fatalities were occupants of the pursuing police vehicle" (Bureau of Justice Statistics, 2017).

And so, the potential for a perilous outcome to a police vehicle pursuit exists as well for the officers who are themselves involved in the pursuit, for either the officer initiating the pursuit or for other officers who engage in the pursuit in a support capacity. According to the Federal Bureau of Investigation (FBI), of the 47 officers killed accidentally in the performance of their duties in 2017, "35 died as a result of motor vehicle crashes … 4 were engaging in vehicle pursuits" (Federal Bureau of Investigation, Uniform Crime Reports, 2018). As of the end of July 2018, 21 police officers had been killed in motor vehicle crashes, three of those killed while pursuing another vehicle (Federal Bureau of Investigation, Uniform Crime Reports, 2018). Interestingly, it wasn't until 2017 that the Law Enforcement Officers Killed and Assaulted report that is compiled annually by the FBI in its Uniform Crime Report even began to record statistics on the number of police officers killed while engaging in vehicle pursuits.

The BJS reported that "the majority of local police departments (71%), sheriffs' offices (63%), and state law enforcement agencies (53%) had a policy that restricted pursuits based on specific criteria, such as speed, type of offense, and surrounding conditions," but that "many departments allowed officers to use their own discretion in deciding to initiate a vehicle pursuit" (as was apparently the case cited earlier in Mashpee, Massachusetts).

> Agencies with a discretionary policy had the highest vehicle pursuit rate (17 pursuits per 100 officers), and agencies that discouraged or prohibited pursuits had the lowest pursuit rate (2 per 100). Agencies with a restrictive policy conducted 8 per 100.
>
> (Bureau of Justice Statistics, 2017)

So the need for strict policies that impose clear governance over the circumstances in which vehicle pursuits will be permitted is of paramount importance. It is clear that allowing the unfettered discretion of individual officers in initiating high-speed pursuits has perilous consequences for communities.

Dangerous high-speed pursuits by police are but one of the means through which police practice as enacted in the contemporary criminal justice milieu places individuals, communities, and even the police themselves at peril. Police militarization, police involvement in immigration enforcement, their use of technology to potentially skirt Fourth Amendment protections, their advancing of a false narrative regarding a "war on cops," their use of force and particularly deadly force against unarmed men and women of color, and their ongoing collaboration with federal and state law enforcement agencies in the establishment and perpetuation of what can only be seen as a police "juggernaut," all contribute to an overarching and pervasive sense of excess and apprehension for those who are most profoundly and intimately affected by this emergence of what can be accurately described as a monolithic law enforcement enterprise.

Perilous Policing: The Abolition of the Police

At a time when what appears to be for many an onslaught of law enforcement excess in the form of racist, oppressive, and discriminatory policing that continues unabated and without any form of meaningful oversight or accountability, there are those who advocate for the abolition of the policing function as it has evolved over its successive iterations that began in earnest in the middle of the nineteenth century. Some observers and activists have argued that policing has strayed so far from its original (and often ill-defined and poorly understood) mission of upholding the Constitution, ensuring respect for individual and group civil rights and civil liberties, and maintaining community safety, that a reimagining, even revocation of the authority and power granted to law enforcement agencies is overdue and primed for reconsideration.

Alex Vitale, the author of *The End of Policing* (2017) has argued that

> When we apply policing as the primary solution to a set of problems that are really driven by histories of economic exclusion and racialized oppression, then we produce outcomes that are racially skewed regardless of the attitudes or biases of individual officers.
>
> (Vitale as quoted in Feliciano & Green, 2018)

Vitale (2017) also argues that "the answer is to quit using police to solve every social problem under the sun" and he has called for the use of "non-coercive and non-punitive alternatives" to addressing the types of problems that we have come to rely on the police for more frequently, particularly in the last several decades. These are societal and behavioral problems, such as operating in the gray-market economy, homelessness, and mental health concerns that the police are ill-equipped to deal with and are often criticized for when they handle them with an outsized and excessive response.

Vitale (2017) has cited the response of the police following the scrutiny and objection of affected communities to unwarranted police violence over the last several years as evidence that the police are finally instituting necessary reforms to professionalize their practices and policies. But, he contended,

> even if we reduce the most egregious use of force we're not really addressing the tens of thousands of non-violent punitive interactions between police and the public that produce the resentment and the escalation of tensions between police and the public.
>
> (Vitale as quoted in Feliciano & Green, 2018)

He cites the example of the Eric Garner case in New York City as evidence of these types of interactions, encounters that are daily, ongoing, and normative occurrences for many who have witnessed and experienced police excess and violence as an integral part of their day-to-day lives.

In 2016 the activist organization "Movement for Black Lives" launched a protest in an area of City Hall Park in New York City that they reclaimed and called "Abolition Square" (Norton, 2016). Calling themselves police "abolitionists" and not "reformers," the protestors distributed a "Shut Down City Hall NYC" orientation guide (Millions March NYC, 2016), and made three demands of the police in New York City: "First is an end to 'Broken Windows' policing"; they then called for reparations to be paid to victims of police brutality. "Third of the demands is the defunding of the NYPD's $5.5 billion annual budget and the reinvestment of tax dollars in Black, Brown and working-class communities"; this is an emerging plea from activists seeking to disband and abolish the police through the revocation of funding for police budgets and the redistribution of those resources to communities that have historically borne the brunt of discriminatory and racist police practices. "The protesters say the NYPD is an undemocratic and racist institution. They say they want community-based forms of policing in its place that are accountable to residents" (Millions March NYC, 2016).

Ben Norton, reporting in *Salon*, wrote that while "Movement for Black Lives" activists were setting up "Abolition Square" in New York City, in Los Angeles "Black Lives Matter activists created a similar encampment, in an action called Decolonize LA City Hall," while "in Chicago, activists occupied a public space that they dubbed 'Freedom Square' in a show of solidarity with other police abolitionists" (Norton, 2016).

Matt Taibbi, writing in *Rolling Stone*, suggested that in the aftermath of the 2014 shooting death of Michael Brown by police in Ferguson, Missouri, the police have a "legitimacy" problem in the eyes of many. He argued that "law-enforcement resources are now distributed so unevenly, and justice is being administered with such brazen inconsistency, that people everywhere are going to start questioning the basic political authority of law enforcement" (2014). People have an absolute right to question the legitimacy of the police he writes, and that "when they do, it's going to create problems that will make the post-Ferguson unrest seem minor" (Taibbi, 2014).

Taibbi derides reporters and commentators whose refrain in the aftermath of these deadly force incidents is to cite the crimes committed or the lack of compliance with police on the part of the victims as somehow justifying their deaths at the hands of officers (Eric Garner was selling untaxed, loose cigarettes; Freddy Gray was carrying a folding pocket knife; Michael Brown had marijuana in his system and "failed to comply" with a police command). Echoing Vitale's comments, Taibbi argues that "the real issue is almost always the hundreds of police interactions that take place before that single spotlight moment, the countless aggravations large and small that pump up the rage gland over time" (2014).

Far too many people have long lived with an awareness that there are two systems of law enforcement and two sets of laws in cities like New York: one for middle-class and affluent whites (like Taibbi), and another for the poor and people of color: "We flood poor minority neighborhoods with police and tell unwitting officers to aggressively pursue an interventionist strategy that sounds like good solid policing in a vacuum" (Taibbi, 2014). That may account for why six police officers surrounded, attacked, and killed Eric Garner—"Broken Windows" indeed. Of the legitimacy of the police Taibbi declared:

You can't send hundreds of thousands of people to court every year on broken-taillight-type misdemeanors and expect people to sit still while yet another coroner-declared homicide (Eric Garner's) goes unindicted. It just won't hold. If the law isn't the same everywhere, it's not legitimate.

(2014)

James Baldwin, writing in *The Nation* in 1966, believed that the police "are the hired enemies" of the "Negro population" of American cities.

They are present to keep the Negro in his place and to protect white business interests, and they have no other function. They are, moreover—even in a country which makes the very grave error of equating ignorance with simplicity—quite stunningly ignorant; and, since they know that they are hated, they are always afraid. One cannot possibly arrive at a more surefire formula for cruelty.

(Baldwin, 1966)

Almost 50 years later, Mychal Denzel Smith, also writing in *The Nation*, seeing that little if any change had taken place in policing America's cities since Baldwin's time, asked the question: "What do you do with an institution whose core function is the control and elimination of black people specifically, and people of color and the poor more broadly?" His answer: "You abolish it" (Smith, 2015). For too many residents of color in America's cities, the police are not seen as protectors or those who will keep people safe and communities secure; rather they are often seen as an existential threat and a looming danger, something to be avoided in all circumstances. When asked what he envisioned for a world without police, Smith admitted that he didn't know what such a world would look like, but "I only know there will be less dead black people. I know that a world without police is a world with one less institution dedicated to the maintenance of white supremacy and inequality" (Smith, 2015).

Meghan McDowell and Luis Fernandez (2018), considering the issue of the abolition of the police, contend that only in disempowering, disarming, and ultimately disbanding the police can we "dismantle the racial capitalist order" (p. 373). The authors see the role of the police in contemporary society as replicating and perpetuating their historic role and what many see as the raison d'être for the existence of the police: the maintenance of a racial social order that privileges white supremacy. They argue "that by attacking the police as an institution, by challenging its very right to exist, the contemporary abolitionist movement contains the potential to radically transform society" (p. 373). Citing the annual number of deadly force incidents involving the police that consistently exceed 1000, "disproportionately Native American and Black men in the prime of their lives," using not only firearms, but electronic control devices (Tasers), "rubber bullets, asphyxiation, and assault," McDowell and Fernandez argue that "the call to disarm law enforcement seems not only intuitive, but also justifiable given the rate at which police officers use deadly force in a manner that is perceived as illegitimate by growing numbers of the public" (p. 381).

Of "disempowering" the police, the authors suggest that tactics such as eviscerating the tools that undergird the power of the police, such as court orders, warrants, laws, and ordinances, would serve to delegitimize the means through which the police exercise their authority:

Disempowerment uses a diverse and often mutually reinforcing set of tactics to confront and erode police power, catalyze (or deepen) a legitimacy crisis for the police, and build a world where the function of policing itself has been rendered obsolete.

(McDowell & Fernandez, 2018, p. 383)

McDowell and Fernandez (2018) cite the example of activists in Oakland, California, who successfully fought the police use of so-called "gang injunctions" to target young men of color for police intervention, arrest, and prosecution as a means of disempowering the police.

Divestment campaigns that seek to reduce and eliminate funding for the police (as the Movement for Black Lives advocated in New York City), see such defunding "as an immediate act of harm reduction" in communities most affected by police overreach: "Divestment ideally deflects funding away from law enforcement and toward other, more life-giving priorities" (McDowell & Fernandez, 2018, p. 385). The fourth approach advanced by McDowell and Fernandez in this article involves establishing alternatives to the traditional law enforcement model and keeping communities safe through means other than law enforcement: "Building alternatives to the police is about changing how we respond to harm, replacing banishment, policing, and criminalization with healing, transformative justice, and new understandings of safety" (p. 385). Police abolition is for these authors "full of potential. It is a struggle to build new modes of sociality, 'insurgent forms of safety' and to develop more complete forms of freedom and justice" (p. 387).

I first learned about the movement to abolish the police when I spoke at an event hosted by the American Constitution Society in Washington, D.C. in March 2017, called the "National Symposium on Policing in a New Political Era." Following the symposium, I was asked for some written comments on the movement. I noted then that the role of the police has evolved into one where they are expected to provide responses to situations involving medical emergencies, mental health crises, and to provide counseling, social work, and legal services (as well as an ever-evolving host of other services), that they are neither trained nor qualified to provide. In so doing, we have "overprescribed" the police and caused them to stray markedly from their intended functions. I wrote that:

We do not need state, county and local law enforcement agencies to enforce immigration laws; to provide mental health care or medical services; to engage in social work; to teach in schools; to extract revenue from the poor; to engage in domestic warfare, or to spy on us. When we authorize and empower the police to act in these wildly divergent roles we grant them a broad authority to direct, to control and to regulate our society in ways that could hardly have been envisioned at the dawn of policing in the mid-nineteenth century. The juggernaut that policing has become in the second decade of the twenty-first century needs to be corralled, reined in, and re-envisioned. Failing that, calls for the abolition of the police will no doubt become more strident.

(Nolan, 2017)

The police are experiencing a crisis in their perceived "legitimacy," and it is this interrogation of the legitimacy of the police by those who most frequently interact (or avoid interaction) with law enforcement that drives calls for defunding and the abolition of the police. It is clear that in order to abate this crisis that reform must be undertaken and enacted.

Discussion post *

Tracey Meares (2017) examines the issue of "legal cynicism," whereby "people would decline to call the police to report crime after a serious incident of police brutality." "Police cynicism," according to Meares "means that some people are making decisions not to call on public servants who have sworn to protect and help them even after they have been seriously victimized" (p. 1359). This legal cynicism is widespread in communities of color in cities across the United States and is a precursor to communities questioning the legitimacy of the police and ultimately in calling for their abolition.

In their interactions with authorities, Meares argues that how people are treated, fairly and respectfully, is more determinative of their perception of a successful outcome with police than whether or not an arrest was made or some other official action taken. She calls this "procedural justice": "Procedural justice turns out to be the key in determining whether the public will conclude that legal authorities behave fairly" (2017, p. 1362).

Meares believes that there are four factors that determine whether or not procedural justice has been achieved. The police would do well to be mindful of the factors implicated in enacting procedural justice amid challenges to their legitimacy and calls for their abolition.

> First, participation and voice are critical. People report higher levels of satisfaction in encounters with authorities when they have an opportunity to explain their situation and perspective on that situation. Even when people are aware that their participation will not impact the outcome, they nonetheless want to be taken seriously and listened to. Second, people care a great deal about the fairness of decision making by authorities…. Third, people care a great deal about how they are treated by legal authorities such as police officers…. Fourth, in their interactions with authorities, people want to believe that authorities are acting out of a sense of benevolence toward them.
>
> (2017, pp. 1362–1363)

M.C. Question.

Is Reform Imperiled?

There can be no doubt that the many issues raised thus far in this writing are a clarion call for a re-examination of the role that the police should occupy in the twenty-first century polity. Their functions and the inexorable and too often inflexible grip that the police have arrogated to themselves vis-à-vis the regulation and oversight of public and often private behavior are being interrupted and questioned. The calls for a reimagining of this ubiquitous and monolithic footprint are becoming more vocal in the aftermath of the many publicly reported instances of police wrongdoing amid widely circulated recordings, videos, documents, and other often incendiary attestations of the police conducting themselves and their affairs in ways that were historically unavailable and unimaginable.

Perhaps the most confounding and seemingly insurmountable obstacles to what I would contend are the comprehensive reconfigurations necessary for policing to regain and sustain its legitimacy are the existential threats to any changes to policing policies and practices posed by police unions. These associations, originally established to collectively bargain with government representatives over wages, hours, and working conditions, have posed and will continue to pose the bulwark to meaningful changes in the ways that the police operate in our communities.

In full disclosure: during most of my 27-year career as a police officer, I was an elected representative and active participant in the two unions in which I held membership (this was mentioned earlier in this volume). I was actively involved in the union that represented uniformed superior officers (one that was separate from the union representing superior officer detectives), and I was for a period of time its elected vice president. I was also chair of the union's "grievance committee," and in this capacity I initiated the many grievances that were filed alleging violations of the collective bargaining agreement purportedly committed by police management (that the union's members were almost wholly constitutive of the police department's management is an irony certainly not lost on me). I would then shepherd the many grievances through the established grievance process, which could often result in a hearing before an outside arbitrator or even, in extreme situations, a hearing or a trial before a judge in a court, occasionally the federal court.

Police unions have evolved over the decades since their original establishment beginning in the 1960s into powerful and influential political organizations. Many observers, for example, credit the political endorsement of George H. W. Bush by the Boston Police Patrolmen's Association in the 1988 presidential election as pivotal in Bush's victory over Massachusetts Governor Michael Dukakis (Boston police union breaks, 2004). By the time of my tenure in the late 1990s and early aughts, the union position that I held was a full-time position based in the union's offices; I was paid a union salary in addition to my police lieutenant salary, yet performed no police duties. Police department administrators were prohibited by federal and state law from even enquiring as to what I did while engaging in protected union activities. This relatively small union (fewer than 300 members) was very well funded through union dues and other sources of financing. The union owns an expensive commercial property and is represented by one of the most formidable labor-law firms in the area. This is far from being exceptional.

Wesley Skogan (2008) has examined the issue of police unions and their resistance to reform and cites the variance in the abilities of police unions to affect proposed reforms, depending largely on the various state laws governing public employee unions. According to Skogan, "in many big cities they are a force to be reckoned with" (p. 28). In seeking to implement reforms,

> a crucial issue can be the match between the demands of a new program and rules stipulated in the contract between the union and the city. These contracts bind the parties to work rules, performance standards, and personnel policies that can run counter to organizational change.
>
> (Skogan, 2008, p. 28)

This severely restricts the ability of police administrators and managers to implement even the slightest and most incremental changes. Many cities require that their employees, including police officers, reside in the city, thus establishing an influential base of city residents and an established voting bloc. Skogan (2008) observed that "along with their many friends and family members, organized police groups can also be a formidable force in local electoral politics. This inhibits politicians from pushing them too hard in directions they do not choose to go" (p. 28).

According to *The New Yorker*,

for the past fifty years, police unions have done their best to block policing reforms of all kinds. In the seventies, they opposed officers' having to wear name tags. More recently, they've opposed the use of body cameras and have protested proposals to document racial profiling and to track excessive-force complaints.

(Surowiecki, 2016)

Unlike other public-sector workers, police officers are, in the words of Egon Bittner, "the bearers of non-negotiable force" (Cohen and Feldberg, 1991, p. 50), including deadly force. "Union control over police working conditions necessarily entails less control for the public" (Surowiecki, 2016), and inhibits necessary reform efforts.

While police unions have posed, and will no doubt continue to pose, formidable challenges to police reform, the unions are hardly the only barrier that those who advocate progressive police reforms will confront. Barbara Armacost (2016), writing in the *Harvard Business Review*, argued that it is the police organization itself that is resistant to reform and that the police culture exists in opposition to meaningful change, a culture that perpetuates and condones police excess and violence. Police misconduct is not, contrary to the argument of many police administrators, the result of a "few bad apples" or "rogue cops." Of the so-called bad apples who are in fact the subjects of the majority of excessive force complaints in most police departments, "those officers tend to repeat their abusive behavior with impunity. Repeated brutality that is not addressed by higher-ups is a systemic problem, not a problem of rogue individuals" (Armacost, 2016).

Armacost believed that

no police leader would instruct his or her officers to brutalize suspects. But certain features of police culture reward aggressive behavior or send a subliminal message that a certain amount of brutality is permitted or even necessary. Sometimes this starts at the police academy, where cops are taught that "complacency kills."

(2016)

This refers to training at the academy intake level that emphasizes immediate and decisive action as key to officer safety and survival, as opposed to hesitancy, considered assessment, or reflection before taking action that can have undesirable (weak) outcomes. Of police leaders who commend and endorse such forceful decisiveness, she argued that "by rewarding aggressive actions—which may even be dubbed heroic—this system undergirds a style of policing that can escalate police citizen confrontations" (Armacost, 2016).

Another barrier to the organizational change that consistently demands attention and focus is the systemic and institutional racism that is a feature (not an aberration) of many of the police departments that have been plagued by repeated instances of officer misconduct: Ferguson, Baltimore, New York City, Chicago, Oakland, Albuquerque, Los Angeles, North Charleston, St. Louis, and Baton Rouge among them. Armacost reiterates what has been a theme in this volume: that "African Americans are more likely to be stopped, frisked, and arrested, and are two-and-one-half times more likely to be shot by police than whites," and that "while some part of this disparity may result from intentional discrimination, it also results from deeply entrenched, unconscious racism affecting the way police officers perceive potentially dangerous circumstances" (2016).

Samuel Walker (2013) has written of the long and troubled history of police reforms that have been undertaken with much fanfare and that too often "just fade away." The continuity of accountability-related police reforms, Walker argued, has been hobbled in its inability to sustain long-term and meaningful change in street-level officer conduct. He believes that "the major limitation of the administrative rulemaking approach to reform relates directly to the issue of the organizational culture of a police department, which is at the heart of the problem of making reforms endure" (p. 66). Administrative rulemaking that attempts to reform officers' use of force for example, "will have no meaningful impact on police conduct if it is not properly enforced through a reporting requirement, thorough investigations, and the imposition of appropriate discipline where it is warranted," (p. 67).

Walker (2013) observed however, that the police organizational subculture is not a stagnant, immutable, unchanging phenomenon that is uniformly embedded and entrenched in police departments across the country. Citing the increase in the diversity and demographic characteristics of police officers that has evolved over the last several decades, where African Americans, women, immigrants, and LGBTQ persons have assumed significant roles in police organizations nationwide, Walker sees cause for cautious optimism regarding police reform, for "if the officer subculture is not as monolithic as traditionally portrayed, there are potential sources of support for innovation and accountability-related reform within police departments" (p. 71). He does acknowledge the role of police unions in potentially confounding progressive reforms, particularly in their ability to influence local elections and the appointment of police chiefs and commissioners, leaders who may be sympathetic to union positions.

Walker's model for instituting accountability-related police reform emphasizes the importance of training, both at the intake level as well as field training, and ongoing in-service training. The training that the officers receive "should cover the nature of the specific reform or reforms, the underlying values, and the potential benefits to the department, individual officers, and the community." He stressed that "the potential benefits of accountability-related reforms are arguably the most neglected aspect of the reform process" (2013, p. 82). Walker goes on to argue that the "accountability-related reforms should also be reinforced by including them in performance evaluations and the promotional process" (2013, p. 83), and that the reforms should be monitored on a continuous basis by outside auditors to ensure that they remain in full force and effect so that they do not "fade away," as has been the history of so many past police reform initiatives.

Ronald Weitzer (2015), writing in *The Criminologist*, expressed two initial reservations that the events that began in Ferguson in the summer of 2014 would lead to significant police reform: the first in "not (being) sure how many police chiefs are learning lessons from the cities where police are now embroiled in controversy," and second, echoing Walker's sentiment regarding the "fade away," that "even when reforms are initiated, criminologists know just how hard it is to make them 'stick'–becoming institutionalized in rewards and punishments and embraced in the police subculture."

Weitzer did express cautious optimism regarding the potential for meaningful reform post-Ferguson in "that the mass media are now raising the issue of reform" in ways that are without historical precedent. Post-Ferguson "countless news reports and talk shows have discussed body cameras, community policing, racial diversification, demilitarization, new accountability mechanisms, and abandoning zero-tolerance and stop-and-frisk policies" (2015). Weitzer did, however, lament the lack of inclusion of scholarly and academic voices in this "new-found" clarion call for police reform, and the fact that "each of the above 'remedies' has been advocated for *decades*" by scholars and other advocates (2015).

But are the police in fact resistant to change and is there uniformity among all (or even most) police in their sentiment and perspective regarding the need for organizational reform? A study completed for the National Police Research Platform, a project funded by the National Institute of Justice, measured police officer receptivity to change and to innovation. The researchers, Stephen Mastrofski and Dennis Rosenbaum (2011), examined two large police departments that had a reputation for adopting large-scale organizational change and for fostering innovations in police practices. They asked officers of all ranks about their department's environment for fostering innovation. They solicited three types of officer evaluations: "(a) the general environment for innovation and change, (b) the need to adopt administrative innovations, and (c) the department's approach to adopting specific innovations that have achieved or are achieving visibility."

Mastrofski and Rosenbaum found that "in general, striking differences surfaced between agencies in the levels of approval expressed for almost all innovations" (2011, p. 6). This would indicate that there is no one consistent mind set and attitude regarding change and innovation across the spectrum of police agencies and that officers are not uniformly inflexible and resistant to innovation and reform. The innovations that the officers were asked about were hardly ground-breaking, novel approaches to the police practice; most had been around for decades. The officers in the study were asked about: respectful policing initiatives, "hot-spot" policing, crime analysis, "broken-windows" policing, intelligence-led policing, victim assistance programs, problem-oriented policing, affirmative action, early-warning disciplinary systems, "CompStat," and in-car cameras.

These authors found that "the two most powerful predictors of a positive organizational environment for innovation were the department's identity and the effectiveness of the organization's internal communications system and practices" (Mastrofski and Rosenbaum, 2011, p. 7). They also found that officer age was a positive predictor of receptivity to innovation, with older officers being less receptive to change than younger officers. Also of interest: the researchers found that officer level of education had no effect on their perception of their department's approach to innovation.

Mastrofski and Ronsenbaum believed that "the most important implication of this research is that those who want to implement innovation must first take care to consider carefully the organizational environment into which it is to be introduced" (2011, p. 8). They argue that an organizational environment that "nurture(s) a culture of innovation" (p. 9) will have more success in implementing change and adopting innovation and, on the other hand, officers will report that higher levels of dissatisfaction are more likely than "when the innovation focuses on directing, controlling, or correcting discretion and practice" (p. 5). So, whether the officers believed that there would be an incentive for a positive outcome in the implementation of the reform on the one hand, or a "punitive bureaucratic" response for an unsuccessful result on the other hand, served to figure prominently in whether or not officers looked favorably upon the particular reform or innovation being adopted and promoted.

Renascence

Tracey Meares (2017) advocated a new metric for the mission of the police, one that could prove invaluable in re-establishing police legitimacy, particularly in communities of color:

> Rather than crime reduction at all costs, the goal of policing should reflect the public's expectation that those responsible for protecting us from one another should understand that their first mission is to protect the sanctity of life—all life, equally.
>
> (p. 1368)

The historical emphasis on crime fighting, crime rates, and crime reduction—regardless of the means used to achieve these—has led to police aggression and violence. Broken windows policing has meant "broken kneecaps" policing for too many who have borne the brunt of such "zero tolerance" and "quality of life initiatives."

Meares argued that

> to undertake this work, retraining of police officers and leaders is necessary. It is a point of first order to teach police that a commitment to enhancing their own public legitimacy is at least as, if not more, important than the technology of crime reduction.
>
> (2017, p. 1368)

Barry Friedman (2017) has advocated for an active public role in police reform in what he calls "democratic policing": "Democratic policing is the idea that people should take responsibility for policing, as they do for the rest of their government, and that police agencies should be responsive to the people's will" (p. 27). He cites the many constitutionally troublesome practices that the police have engaged in and continue to employ in their ongoing wars: on drugs, on terror, and in some troubling forms, immigration.

Friedman (2017) observed that police searches without warrants, without probable cause, discriminatory searches, policing in secret, as well as the increased use of surveillance technology, the cloud, and shared databases are all practices and policies that the police have employed in the furtherance of what they believe (rightly or wrongly) is their mandate and within the scope of their authority; he believes that these practices need to be revisited and re-examined with the active participation and approval of the public, in accordance with democratic principles.

Toward that end, I would propose that "democratic policing" include a revisiting, re-evaluation, and a reimagining of the issues, practices, and policies that follow. Although not intended to be prescriptive, the currency and immediacy of these topics demand an open and public examination and legitimate, thoughtful, and earnest consideration. This is in no way offered as an exhaustive and comprehensive list, but rather as a plea to commence the dialogue. In initiating this discussion, be mindful that the police are *our* police; we are not their subjects.

Community Oversight of the Police

That the police have unilaterally appropriated to themselves the presumptive authority to investigate internal complaints of officer wrongdoing and misconduct, as well as their use of force and compliance with the criminal laws and agency rules and procedures, should not itself serve to challenge the public's demonstrable interest in having these types of inquiries and complaints handled by investigators who are not themselves members of the affected law enforcement agency. This is the standard practice in virtually all realms of professional endeavor: medical, legal, aviation, transportation, social work, and education (among others).

That the police conduct their own internal investigations of all instances alleging misdeeds at the hands of their colleagues, most often in secret, is inimical to the fairness, impartiality, and probity that such investigations demand. This is particularly true when the allegations involve excessive force and specifically deadly force. Having been part of the internal investigative apparatus for a significant part of my career in law enforcement, I can attest to the subcultural demands and the tacit understandings that guide and inform internal police investigations, and that these often do not privilege the truth, justice, or fairness. Rather, the maintenance of the status quo, reputation, career, the image of the agency, the family of the officer, as well as the career of the internal investigator, all figure prominently, often given pre-eminence over the legitimacy of the allegations. Overzealous internal investigators learn quickly to temper their zeal, lest they suffer consequences to their career or even to their safety.

In 2017 the city of Chicago established the Civilian Office of Police Accountability (COPA), an agency consisting of 150 unarmed civilian investigators who look into all allegations of wrongdoing against Chicago police officers, including the use of force. COPA is also the primary agency that investigates shootings and deadly force incidents involving Chicago police officers. This is the most comprehensive model of civilian oversight of the police in the United States as of this writing, but similar models of civilian oversight of the police exist in New York City, Washington, D.C., Seattle, New Orleans, Cleveland, Atlanta, and Oakland.

Civilian Oversight of the Police, Surveillance, and Technology

The rapid and accelerated acquisition of surveillance technology by local law enforcement is without precedent in the law enforcement practice. The public has certainly long recognized that federal agencies concerned with defense, national security, and complex national and international criminal investigations have utilized sophisticated and most often secret technology in conducting complicated confidential investigations.

More recent developments have seen local police departments, in cities, counties, suburbs, and even college campus agencies, acquiring sophisticated technologies that have enabled surveillance, data mining, and warrantless searches of devices in common and everyday use by anyone equipped with any number of internet-connected devices. The use of so-called

Discussion post

"Stingray" and "dirtbox" technologies, as well as facial recognition and face scanning, license plate readers, GPS and location data, drones, and social media monitoring software by local police, are raising concerns about law enforcement overreach and "mission creep." That these devices and technologies were acquired by local police without public input, review, approval, or even awareness, and that they have been used to conduct warrantless and suspicionless surveillance of unknowing individuals and groups in practices that may be violative of Fourth Amendment protections, are of particular concern to civil rights and civil liberties advocates.

These devices and technologies should not be adopted for use by local law enforcement agencies without strict oversight and approval by affected community members, outside legal representatives such as the American Civil Liberties Union, and those constituencies who are concerned with civil rights and civil liberties issues. Without divulging the specifics of what may be sensitive criminal investigations, law enforcement should nonetheless be required to submit to a civilian oversight and approval process that describes the need for the acquisition of the technology, the justification for the expenditure of tax dollars for this purpose, as well as the legal basis, justification, and authority for the use of invasive technology to monitor what many believe to be behavior and activity governed by privacy protections.

There can be little doubt that the vast majority of police officers, administrators, and policy makers are motivated by and committed to the public interest. Their practice is characterized, for the large part, by fairness, respect, compassion, and a dedication to social justice. The inclusion of members of their constituent communities in any consideration of the many needed reforms, particularly by those communities most directly affected by the police imprint, is essential for the police to reconnect to the communities where they are most needed. The rupture in the goodwill and trust between certain of the police and those whom they are duty-bound to protect needs to be re-established, and the collaboration that is essential to community well-being renewed and restored.

This can help build *police legitamacy.*

Conclusion

While much if not most of what the police enact in our communities is undertaken with noble intentions and is successful on many levels in keeping communities safe and ensuring that policies and practices that the police engage in embrace principles of fairness, equal treatment, and social justice, the reality is that for many residents of marginalized communities the police are seen as imperiling community health and safety, and their mission as inimical to community well-being. The reform of the police will necessarily entail a manifest subcultural paradigm shift, and this has proven and will continue to prove a most vexing challenge.

In the absence of a significant, ongoing, and a very public shift to policies, practices, and strategies that privilege and endorse consequential input, counsel, guidance, and approval from those in communities that have been historically marginalized by criminal justice policies that have been de facto oppressive, racist, discriminatory, and often violent, crucial reform will remain elusive. Status quo policing has proven too often perilous for those who are often most in need of the very services that have proven nocuous and ultimately deleterious to community health and safety.

REFERENCES

Armacost, B. (2016, August 19). The organizational reasons police departments don't change. *Harvard Business Review*. Retrieved from: https://hbr.org/2016/08/the-organizational-reasons-police-departments-dont-change.

Associated Press. (2018, April 5). Police: Man in deadly pursuit crash was under surveillance. *US News*. Retrieved from: www.usnews.com/news/best-states/indiana/articles/2018-04-05/police-man-in-deadly-pursuit-crash-was-under-surveillance.

Baldwin, J. (1966, July 11). A report from occupied territory. *The Nation*. Retrieved from: www.thenation.com/article/report-occupied-territory/.

Boston police union breaks with tradition, endorses Kerry. (2004, October 20). *PoliceOne.com*. Retrieved from: www.policeone.com/archive/articles/92949-Boston-Police-Union-Breaks-With-Tradition-Endorses-Kerry/.

Bureau of Justice Statistics. (2017). *Police Vehicle Pursuits, 2012–2013*. Retrieved from: www.bjs.gov/content/pub/pdf/pvp1213_sum.pdf.

Cohen, H., & Feldberg, M. (1991). *Power and Restraint: The Moral Dimension of Police Work*. Westport, CT: Praeger Publishing.

Cottle, T. (2001). *At Peril: Stories of Injustice*. Amherst, MA, United States: University of Massachusetts Press.

Federal Bureau of Investigation, Uniform Crime Reports. (2018). *Law Enforcement Officers Killed & Assaulted, 2017*. Retrieved from: https://ucr.fbi.gov/leoka/2017.

Feliciano, I., & Green, Z. (2018, May 26). Has policing in America gone too far? *PBS, News Hour Productions*. Retrieved from: www.pbs.org/newshour/show/has-policing-in-america-gone-too-far.

Friedman, B. (2017). *Unwarranted: Policing Without Permission*. New York: Farrar, Straus and Giroux.

Hermann, P. (2018, April 19). City attorney: Police chase began with D.C. officers angry over a red-light runner and ended in a fatal shooting. *The Washington Post*. Retrieved from: www.washingtonpost.com/local/public-safety/city-attorney-police-chase-began-with-dc-officers-angry-over-a-red-light-runner-and-ended-in-a-fatal-shooting/2018/04/19/307826b4-3fcb-11e8-a7d1-e4efec6389f0_story.html?utm_term=.f931d732c3ee.

Hilliard, J., Oide, T., & Fox, J. (2018, July 29). A new father, killed on his way home from the hospital: Tragedy strikes in Cotuit. *The Boston Globe*. Retrieved from: www.bostonglobe.com/metro/2018/07/29/police-chase-ends-with-two-deaths-cotuit/3zrezIEvVo2JYNLOS7jEsL/story.html.

Los Angeles County Civil Grand Jury. (2017). Final report. *County of Los Angeles*. Retrieved from: http://grandjury.co.la.ca.us/pdf/LOSANGELESCOUNTY2016-2017CIVILGRANDJURYFINALREPORT.pdf.

Mastrofski, S., & Rosenbaum, D. (2011, January). Receptivity to police innovation: A tale of two cities. *National Institute of Justice, National Police Research Platform*. Retrieved from: http://static1.1.sqspcdn.com/static/f/733761/10444481/1296183364910/Receptivity+to+Police+Innovation+A+Tale+of+Two+Cities++FINAL.pdf?token=IWHw3ZRWurozm%2Fta%2BolITEUJHrw%3D.

McDowell, M., & Fernandez, L. (2018). "Disband, disempower, and disarm": Amplifying the theory and practice of police abolition. *Critical Criminology*, 26 (3), pp. 373–391.

Meares, T. (2017). The path forward: Improving the dynamics of community-police relationships to achieve effective law enforcement policies. *Columbia Law Review*, 117 (5), pp. 1355–1368.

Millions March NYC. (2016, August). Orientation guide. *MillionsMarch.org*. Retrieved from: http://media.wix.com/ugd/881d51_12abc618efc746b0bc72a4fe47b6c90e.pdf.

Nolan, T. (2017, March 15). Is it time to abolish the police? American Constitution Society. *ACS Blog*. Retrieved from: www.acslaw.org/acsblog/is-it-time-to-abolish-the-police/.

Norton, B. (2016, August 5). Black Lives Matter activists launch Abolition Square encampment, demanding reparations, end to Broken Windows policing. *Salon*. Retrieved from: www.salon.com/2016/08/05/black-lives-matter-activists-launch-abolition-square-encampment-demanding-reparations-end-to-broken-windows-policing/.

Queally, J. (2017, July 12). Police pursuits cause unnecessary deaths and injuries, L.A. County grand jury says. *Los Angeles Times*. Retrieved from: www.latimes.com/local/lanow/la-me-ln-police-pursuits-dangers-20170711-story.html#.

Rivara, F. P., & Mack C. D. (2004). Motor vehicle crash deaths related to police pursuits in the United States. *Injury Prevention*, 10, pp. 93–95.

Skogan, W. (2008). Why reforms fail. *Policing & Society*, 18 (1), pp. 25–34.

Smith, M. D. (2015, April 9). Abolish the police. Instead let's have full social, economic, and political equality. *The Nation*. Retrieved from: www.thenation.com/article/abolish-police-instead-lets-have-full-social-economic-and-political-equality/.

Surowiecki, J. (2016, September 19). Why are police unions blocking reform? *The New Yorker*. Retrieved from: www.newyorker.com/magazine/2016/09/19/why-are-police-unions-blocking-reform.

Taibbi, M. (2014, December 5). The police in America are becoming illegitimate. *Rolling Stone*. Retrieved from: www.rollingstone.com/politics/politics-news/the-police-in-america-are-becoming-illegitimate-76132/.

Vitale, A. (2017). *The End of Policing*. London: Verso Books.

Walker, S. (2013). Institutionalizing police accountability reforms: The problem of making police reforms endure. *Saint Louis University Public Law Review*, XXXII (57).

Weitzer, R. (2015). Is American policing at a crossroads? *The Criminologist*, 40, 4.

Index

Printed in Canada